104

INLAND REVENUE

Rm 816, Mel Hse

Library Ref :-

SERIAL 54152

U.D.C. 662.336.200

UK Oil
Taxation

UK Oil
Taxation

by

David Bland, BA (Oxon)
Principal, Arthur Young

Longman

© 1988
David Bland

ISBN 0 85121 420 7

Conditions of Sale
All rights reserved. No part of this publication may be reproduced, stored in a retrieval system, or transmitted, in any form or by any means, electronic, mechanical, photocopying, recording or otherwise, without the prior written permission of the publishers.

No responsibility for loss occasioned to any person acting or refraining from action as a result of the material in this publication can be accepted by the author or publishers.

The views expressed in this book are those of the author and not necessarily those of Arthur Young.

Printed and bound in Great Britain by Biddles of Guildford Ltd.

Contents

Table of cases xi
Table of statutes xv
References and Abbreviations xxi

Chapter 1	**Introduction**	1
Chapter 2	**Development of UK Oil Taxation**	
2.1	Main Changes Since 1975...	3
2.2	Rates of Tax and Relief for Expenditure	10
Chapter 3	**Administration**	
3.1	Introduction	13
3.2	Department of Energy	14
3.3	Inland Revenue	15
Chapter 4	**Petroleum Licensing**	
4.1	Introduction	17
4.2	Model clauses	18
4.3	Licences in issue	19
4.4	Licence payments	20
4.5	Abandonment of offshore installations	21
4.6	Participation	22
Chapter 5	**Royalties**	
5.1	Introduction	24
5.2	Exemption of New Fields	24
5.3	Rates of Royalty..	25
5.4	Payment of Royalty...	26
5.4.1	Repayment of Royalty	26
5.5	Calculation of Royalty Payable	27
5.5.1	Quantity and value..	27
5.5.2	Royalty in kind...	29
5.5.3	Conveying and treating costs	29
5.5.4	Prior years adjustments..	34
5.5.5	Report of independent accountant........................	34
Chapter 6	**Petroleum Revenue Tax**	
6.1	The Nature of PRT	35
6.2	What is chargeable	36

6.3	Who is chargeable	37
6.4	Determination of a field	39
6.5	Chargeable periods	41
6.6	The PRT computation	41
6.6.1	Chargeable period 1 July 1987–31 December 1987	42
6.7	Production Income	42
6.7.1	Sales at arm's length	43
6.7.2	Market value	45
6.7.3	The nomination scheme	49
6.7.4	Valuation of gas	57
6.7.5	Valuation of ethane used for petrochemical purposes	58
6.7.6	Alternative valuation of light gases	59
6.7.7	CIF gas sales	60
6.7.8	Oil stocks	61
6.7.9	Take or pay contracts and capacity payments	62
6.7.10	Blended oil	62
6.8	PRT exemptions	63
6.8.1	Gas sold to British Gas Corporation under pre-July 1975 contracts	63
6.8.2	Oil used for production purposes	64
6.8.3	Oil in transit	64
6.8.4	Royalty in kind	65
6.9	Gas banking	65
6.10	Tariff and disposal receipts	66
6.10.1	General	66
6.10.2	Qualifying assets	67
6.10.3	Tariff receipts	68
6.10.4	Purchase of oil at place of extraction	69
6.10.5	Tariff receipts allowance	69
6.10.6	Disposal receipts	72
6.10.7	Particular disposals	73
6.10.8	Non arm's length receipts	74
6.10.9	Anti-avoidance provisions	74
6.11	Receipts from foreign field assets	77
6.11.1	Outline and definitions	77
6.11.2	The charge to tax	78
6.11.3	Double taxation relief	79
6.12	Chargeable sums: conveying and treating contributions	79
6.13	Relief for royalty payments	80
6.14	Relief for expenditure: general	81
6.14.1	Outline	81
6.14.2	Expenditure incurred	82
6.14.3	Capital or revenue	82
6.15	Field expenditure	83
6.15.1	Claim periods	83
6.15.2	The responsible person	84
6.15.3	The purpose test	84
6.15.4	Indirect expenditure	85

Contents vii

6.15.5	Expenditure not allowable	86
6.15.6	Allowable field expenditure	89
6.16	Expenditure on assets: the background	95
6.16.1	The old rules: expenditure incurred before 1 July 1982	96
6.17	Expenditure on assets – the new rules	97
6.17.1	Non-mobile assets and mobile assets dedicated to a field	97
6.17.2	Non-dedicated mobile assets	103
6.18	Transitional provisions	104
6.19	Supplement	105
6.19.1	Bringing about commencement of production or transportation	105
6.19.2	Appraisal	106
6.19.3	Improving the rate of production: preventing or reducing a decline in that rate	107
6.19.4	Providing for initial treatment or initial treatment storage	108
6.19.5	Assets giving rise to tariff receipts	109
6.19.6	Hiring	109
6.19.7	Asset disposals: restriction of supplement	109
6.19.8	Rates of supplement	110
6.19.9	Cut-off of supplement: payback	111
6.19.10	Contractor financing	113
6.20	Exploration and appraisal expenditure	114
6.20.1	Restriction of relief: interests acquired in mature fields	118
6.21	Abortive exploration expenditure	119
6.22	Research expenditure	119
6.23	Cross-field allowances	121
6.24	Provisional expenditure allowance	123
6.24.1	Reversal of provisional allowance	124
6.25	Spreading of expenditure relief	125
6.26	Transactions not at arm's length	126
6.27	Contributions to expenditure	126
6.27.1	Regional development grants	127
6.28	Oil allowance	127
6.28.1	Increased oil allowance for certain new fields	130
6.28.2	Reduced oil allowance for certain new fields	131
6.28.3	Interaction of oil allowance and expenditure relief	131
6.29	Loss relief	133
6.29.1	Unrelievable field loss	134
6.30	Safeguard	135
6.30.1	Safeguard Calculation	136
6.30.2	Interaction of safeguard and other reliefs	137
6.31	Returns	138
6.31.1	Return by responsible person	139
6.31.2	Return by participator	139
6.31.3	Additional return by participator	141
6.32	Claims by responsible person	141
6.32.1	Decisions on claims	142

6.32.2	Appeals against decisions	144
6.32.3	Variations of decisions on claims	146
6.33	Claims for field expenditure by participators	146
6.34	Claims for exploration and appraisal expenditure	147
6.34.1	Claims for abortive exploration expenditure	148
6.34.2	Claims for research expenditure	148
6.34.3	Elections for cross-field allowance	148
6.35	PRT assessment	148
6.35.1	Payment of assessment PRT	149
6.35.2	Interest on assessed PRT	150
6.35.3	Interest on PRT repayments	150
6.35.4	Appeals against PRT assessments	150
6.36	Advance petroleum revenue tax	151
6.36.1	Credit of APRT against PRT	151
6.36.2	Repayment of APRT	152
6.37	Schedule of payments of APRT and PRT	152
6.37.1	Instalment payments	153
6.37.2	Payment on account	154
6.37.3	Interest on unpaid APRT and PRT	155
6.37.4	Schedule of payments	156
6.38	Double taxation relief for PRT	157
6.39	Supplementary petroleum duty	158
6.40	Obsolete payment provisions	158
Chapter 7	**Corporation tax**	
7.1	Introduction	160
7.2	Scope of CT charge	161
7.2.1	Companies resident in the UK	161
7.2.2	Companies not resident in the UK	163
7.2.3	UK oil extraction activities	164
7.2.4	Contractors not resident in the UK	165
7.3	The ring fence	167
7.4	CT profits	168
7.4.1	CT computation	169
7.4.2	Payment of tax	169
7.5	Trading	170
7.6	Trade profit or loss	172
7.6.1	General rules	172
7.6.2	Ring fence profits	172
7.7	Oil trading income	173
7.7.1	Sales at arm's length	173
7.7.2	Sales not at arm's length	174
7.7.3	Appropriation of oil	174
7.7.4	Oil stocks	175
7.7.5	Underlifting and overlifting	176
7.7.6	Ballast recovery oil	176
7.8	Tariff etc receipts	177
7.9	Income from oil rights	177

7.10	Interest Income	178
7.11	Expenditure	178
7.11.1	Capital or revenue	178
7.11.2	Distribution of profit	179
7.11.3	Annual payments	180
7.11.4	Pre-trading expenditure	181
7.11.5	Financing costs	181
7.11.6	Royalties and other licence payments	186
7.11.7	Currency exchange gains and losses	186
7.11.8	Deduction for PRT	187
7.11.9	Abandonment costs	188
7.12	Relief for exploration and development expenditure	189
7.13	Scientific research	190
7.13.1	Disposal of scientific research assets	192
7.14	Mineral extraction allowances	194
7.14.1	General	194
7.14.2	Qualifying expenditure	195
7.14.3	Pre-trading expenditure	195
7.14.4	Restoration expenditure	196
7.14.5	Land	197
7.14.6	Second-hand acquisitions	197
7.14.7	Balancing adjustments	199
7.14.8	Disposal receipts	200
7.14.9	Mines and oil wells allowances	201
7.14.10	Inter-action between mineral extraction and mines and oil wells allowances	201
7.15	Development drilling	203
7.16	Plant and machinery	204
7.17	Industrial buildings and structures	205
7.18	Capital contributions and grants	206
7.19	Know-how	206
7.20	Capital allowances: the ring fence	207
7.21	Relief for losses	207
7.22	Restriction of pre 1973 losses	208
7.23	Ring fence restrictions on losses	209
7.24	Advance corporation tax (ACT)	209
7.24.1	Credit for ACT	210
7.24.2	Ring fence restriction of ACT credit	211
7.24.3	Carryback of surrendered ACT	212
7.24.4	Surrender of ACT by consortium companies	212
7.24.5	ACT and double taxation agreements	213
7.25	Transactions between associated companies	214
7.25.1	Petroleum companies	214
7.26	Capital gains	216
7.26.1	Gains of companies not resident in the UK	217
7.26.2	Gains on disposal of licence interests	218

Chapter 8 Changes in UK licence interests
8.1	Introduction	220
8.2	Farm-ins	221
8.3	Tax consequences: general	223
8.4	Reimbursement of expenditure	224
8.5	Drilling costs	226
8.6	Royalty and other subordinated interests	227
8.7	Development carry	228
8.8	Transfer of a field interest	230
8.8.1	PRT effects	230
8.8.2	CT effects	235
8.9	Capital gains on transfers of licence interests	236
8.9.1	Disposal of an asset	237
8.9.2	Work obligation farm-ins	237
8.9.3	Licence exchanges: undeveloped areas	239
8.9.4	Other licence disposals	240
8.9.5	Allowable costs	241
8.9.6	Part disposals	242
8.9.7	Rollover relief	243
8.10	Acquisition of licence interest by share purchase	243
8.10.1	Share acquisition: producing field	244
8.11	Illustrative agreements	246
8.12	Unitisation	249

Appendix 1	Offshore licences	256
Appendix 2	Examples of calculation of cash equivalent of tariff receipts allowance (TRA)-s9 and Sched 3, OTA 1983	258
Appendix 3	Joint revenue and UKOITC memorandum expenditure on exploration for and development of oil and national gas resources	261

Index 265

Table of Cases

	Para.
Amoco UK Exploration Company *v* IRC [1983] STC 634	6.28.3
Bentley *v* Pike 53 TC 590	7.2.6
Birmingham and District Cattle By-Products Company Limited *v* CIR (1919) 12 TC 92	7.5
Bullock *v* Unit Construction Company (1959) 38 TC 712	7.2.1
Chevron Petroleum (UK) Ltd and Others *v* BP Petroleum Development Ltd and Others [1981] STC 689	8.12
De Beers Consolidated Mines *v* Howe (1906) 5 TC 198	7.2.1
Gaspet Ltd *v* Elliss [1987] STC 362	7.13, 8.11
Mobil North Sea Ltd *v* CJR [1987] STC 458	6.19.9
Ostime *v* Duple Motor Bodies Ltd (1961) 39 TC 537	7.7.4
Pattison *v* Marine Midland Ltd [1984] AC 362; [1984] 2 WLR [1984] STC 10	7.11.7
Queen *v* Attorney-General, *ex parte* Imperial Chemical Industries plc [1987] 1 CMLR 72	6.7.5
RTZ Oil and Gas Ltd *v* Elliss [1987] STC 512	7.11.9

Table of Statutory Instruments

	Para
Petroleum (Production) Regulations 1976 (SI No 1129)	4.2
Oil Taxation (Gas Banking Scheme) Regulations 1982 (SI No 92)	6.9
Petroleum Production Regulations 1982 (SI No 1000)	4.1, 4.2
Sched 5	4.2
Cl 39	4.1
Petroleum Revenue Tax (Nomination Scheme for Disposals an Appropriations) Regulations (SI No 1338) — para 3–7, 11–17, 19, 20	6.7.3

Table of Statutes

Petroleum (Production) Act 1934	4.1, 6.2
Continental Shelf Act 1964	4.1, 4.3
Petroleum (Production) Act (Northern Ireland) 1964	6.2
s1	6.2
Capital Allowances Act 1968—	
Pt I	7.12
Chapter III	7.14.10
ss2, 3	7.17
s4	7.11.9, 7.17
ss5–7	7.17
Pt II	7.12
s77	8.8.2
ss84, 85	8.11
s91	8.11
(2)	7.13
s92	7.13, 7.13.1, 8.5
s93	7.13
s94	7.13, 8.4
s95	7.13
(6)	8.4
Sched 7, paras 2, 4	7.14.6
Income and Corporation Taxes Act 1970—	
s134	7.14.5
ss273, 278	8.10.1
s412(2)	6.15.6
Taxes Management Act 1970—	
s34	6.35
Finance Act 1971—	
Pt III	7.12
s44	7.14.8
Sched 8, para 14	7.11.9
Industry Act 1972—	
Pt I	6.27.1
Finance Act 1973—	
s38	7.2.4, 7.26.1
(1), (3), (4)	7.2.3
(5)	8.11
Sched 15	7.2.4
Finance Act 1975—	7.7.2
s17	
Oil Taxation Act 1975	1, 2.1, 6.2, 6.9, 6.10.1, 6.12, 7.1
s2(4)	8.8.1
(5)	6.7
(*d*)	6.7
(8)(*b*)	6.24.1
(9)(*a*)	6.24
(10)	6.24.1
(11)	6.24

xvi UK Oil Taxation

Oil Taxation Act 1975—*cont*
- s3(1) 6.15.2, 6.15.3, 6.15.6
  - (*a*) 6.15.5, 6.15.6, 6.19.2
  - (*b*) 6.15.3, 6.15.5, 6.15.6
  - (*c*) 6.15.5, 6.15.6, 6.19.2
  - (*d*)–(*h*) 6.15.6
  - (*i*) 6.15.5
  - (2) 6.15.6
  - (3) 6.15.5, 6.20
  - (4)(*a*)–(*c*) 6.15.5
    - (*d*) 6.15.5, 8.6
    - (*e*) 6.15.5, 8.4, 8.5
    - (*f*) 6.15.5
  - (5) 6.19, 6.19.6
    - (*a*) 6.19.1
    - (*b*) 6.19.2
    - (*c*) 6.14.3, 6.19.3
    - (*d*) 6.19.4
  - (5A) 6.19.5
  - (6) 6.15.3, 6.15.4
  - (7) 6.15.3, 6.17.1
- s4 .... 6.16.1
  - (10) 6.15.5
- s5 .... 6.21
  - (2) 6.20
- s5A 6.20, 6.7.7, 8.5
- 5B(*c*) 8.4
- s6(22) 6.29.1
- s7(1)–(3) 6.29
- s8 .... 6.28
  - (4) 6.28
- s9 .... 6.30
- s10 .... 6.8.1
  - (1)(*b*) 6.8.1, 8.8.1
  - (2) 6.15.5
  - (3)(*a*) 6.15.5
    - (*b*) 6.15.5
- s12 .... 6.3, 6.7.4, 6.8.2, 6.13, 6.15.6, 8.11
  - (2) 6.15.3, 6.17.1
  - (3) 6.4
- s13 .... 7.6.2, 7.22
- s14 .... 7.6.2, 8.6
  - (4A) 7.7.3
- ss15, 16 .... 7.6.2
- s17 .... 7.6.2
  - (3) 7.24.1
- s18 .... 7.6.2
- s19 .... 7.6.2
- Sched 1 .... 6.4, 6.15.6, 8.8
- Sched 2 para 2 .... 6.31.2
  - paras 3, 4 .... 6.31.2
  - paras 5, 6 .... 6.31.1
  - paras 7–9 .... 6.31.1, 6.31.2
  - paras 10, 11 .... 6.35
  - para 12 .... 6.35
  - para 13 .... 6.35.1
  - para 14 .... 6.35.4
  - para 15 .... 6.35.3

Oil Taxation Act 1975—*cont*
   Sched 3 para 1 .... 6.7.1, 6.15.1
         para 2 .... 6.7.2, 6.7.5
         para 2A 6.7.2
             (2); (3) 6.7.4
         para 2D 6.7.2
         para 4 .... 6.8.4
         para 5 .... 6.3, 8.11
         para 6 .... 6.3, 8.6, 8.7
         para 8 .... 6.8.3, 6.12, 6.27
         paras 9, 10 .... 6.25
         para 11 .... 6.28.3
   Sched 4 para 1 .... 6.17.1, 8.12
         para 2 .... 6.26
         para 4 .... 6.16.1
         para 5 .... 6.2
   Sched 5 .... 6.32, 6.32.3
         paras 1, 2 .... 6.15.1
         para 3 .... 6.32, 6.32.2
         para 5 .... 6.15.1, 6.32.2
         paras 6–8 .... 6.32.2
   Sched 6 .... 6.33
   Sched 7 .... 6.34, 6.34.1
   Sched 8 .... 6.29.1
   Sched 9 .... 6.32.3
Petroleum and Submarine Pipe-line Act 1975 .... 4.2
   s4(3) 6.13
   s19 .... 3.2, 5.5.1
   s41(3) 5.4, 6.12, 7.11.6
Capital Gains Tax 1979 .... 7.2.3
   s12 .... 7.26.1
   s20 .... 8.9.1
   s29A 8.9.5
   s85 .... 8.10.1
   ss115–119 .... 8.9.6
Finance (No2) Act 1979—
   s19 .... 6.19.8
   s22 .... 6.3
Finance Act 1980 .... 6.7.3
   s107 .... 6.2, 8.12
   s108 .... 6.9
   s109 .... 6.15.6
   Sched 17 .... 8.8, 8.11
        para 1 .... 8.12
Petroleum Revenue Tax Act 1980 .... 6.37.2
Finance Act 1981—
   s111 .... 6.19.9
      (6) 6.32
      (7) 6.19.9
   s112 .... 8.8.1
   s113 .... 6.19.9
   s114 .... 6.30
   s115 .... 6.19.10
   s118 .... 6.12
   ss122–8 .... 6.39
   Sched 16 .... 6.39
Finance Act 1982—
   s39(14) 6.35.4

Finance Act 1982—*cont*

s60	7.11.3
s133	6.7.5
s134	6.7.5
s135 (1)(2)	6.4
s137	6.27.1, 7.18
s138	7.18
s142	6.36.1
Sched 18	6.7.5
Sched 19	6.3.6
para 2	6.37.1
para 10	6.37.3
paras 11–13	6.40

Industrial Development Act 1982

Part II	6.27.1

Oil and Gas (Enterprise) Act 1982 .... 6.8.1

Finance Act 1983 .... 6.10.1, 6.36

s36	5.2, 6.28.1

Oil Taxation Act 1983 .... 6.3, 6.11.1, 6.15.6, 6.19, 6.32.1

s1	6.17.2
s2	6.17.1
s3(2)	6.16
(6)	6.15.5
s4	6.17.1
(1)	6.15.5
s5(4)	6.17.1, 8.11
s6	6.10.3
s7	6.19.7
(3)	8.12
(4)	6.10.7
s8	6.10.2, 7.8
s9	6.10.5
s11	7.8
s13	6.18
s35	6.25
Sched 1 paras 1–3	6.17.1
para 5(1), (3)	6.17.1
paras 6–9	6.17.1
Sched 2	6.3
para 2	6.10.9
para 5	6.10.8
para 6	8.8.1
paras 9, 10	6.10.7
para 11	6.10.9
para 12	6.10.4
Sched 3	6.10.5
Sched 5	6.18
para 5	6.18
para 7	6.18

Petroleum Royalties (Relief) Act 1983 .... 5.2

Finance Act 1984 .... 7.1, 7.12

s78	8.8.2
s79	7.26.2
s80	7.26.2, 8.9.7
s81	7.2.3
s113	6.20, 6.29.1
s114	6.7.9
s115	6.7.1, 6.31.3, 7.7.2

Finance Act 1984—*cont*
  s124 .... 7.2.4
Finance Act 1985—
  s56 .... 6.14.2
  s57 .... 7.16
  s90 .... 6.20
  s91 .... 6.19.9, 6.30
Finance Act 1986—
  s55 .... 7.14.1, 7.14.3
  s108 .... 6.20
  s109 .... 6.7.7
  Sched 13 .... 7.12
    paras 5, 6 .... 7.14.3
    para 8 .... 7.14.4
    para 10 .... 7.14.8
    paras 11, 12 .... 7.14.7
    para 13 .... 7.14.4
    para 14 .... 7.9.12
    paras 16–18 .... 7.14.5
    paras 19–22, 26 .... 7.14.6
  Sched 14 paras (5)–(8) 7.14.10
  Sched 21 .... 6.7.7
Finance Act 1987 .... 6.7.3
  s61(2), (8) 6.7.3
  s62 .... 6.7.2, 6.31.3
  s63 .... 6.7.10
  s65 .... 6.23
  s66 .... 6.28
  s67 .... 6.32.3
  Sched 10, paras 2, 8–12 .... 6.7.3
  Sched 12 .... 6.7.10
  Sched 13 .... 6.22, 7.14.1
    paras 4, 7 .... 7.14.2
  Sched 14 .... 6.23, 7.14.1
    para 2 .... 7.14.10
Finance (No 2) Act 1987 .... 6.7.3, 7.4
  s74 .... 7.26
  s80 .... 7.26.2
  Sched 8, para 5 .... 6.7.3
Petroleum Act 1987 .... 4.5, 5.5.1, 5.5.3, 7.11.9
Finance Act 1988 .... 2.1, 8.9.4, 8.9.5
  s62 .... 8.9.2, 8.9.4
  s63 .... 8.4, 8.9.5
  s66 .... 7.2.1
  s91 .... 7.26
  s138 .... 6.28.1
  Sched 7 .... 7.26
Income and Corporation Taxes Act 1988—
  s6 .... 7.4
  s11 .... 7.2.2
  s57 .... 7.11.5
  s74 .... 7.11.1, 7.11.5
  ss77, 124 .... 7.11.5
  s125 .... 7.11.3, 8.6
  s209 .... 7.11.3
  s237 .... 7.11.5
  ss239–40 .... 7.24.1
  ss242–3 .... 7.24

Income and Corporation Taxes Act 1988—*cont*

s247	7.24
s249	7.11.5
ss338–40	7.11.5
s343	8.10.1
ss393, 394	7.21
s401	7.11.4
s416	7.3
ss420–423	7.2.1
s492	7.3, 7.2.3
s493	7.7.2, 7.7.3
s494	7.11.3, 7.11.5
s497	7.24.2
s498	7.24.3
s499	7.24.4
s500	7.11.8
s502	7.3, 7.7
ss530–33	7.19
ss747–56	7.2.2
s768	8.10.1
s770	7.25
s771	7.25, 7.25.1
ss772, 773	7.25
s839	6.10.9
Sched 4	7.11.5
Sched 17	7.2.1
Scheds 24–26	7.2.2
Sched 30	7.22

References and Abbreviations

Statutory references are to the Oil Taxation Act 1975 unless otherwise stated.

APRT	Advance Petroleum Revenue Tax
BGC	British Gas Corporation
The Board	The Board of Inland Revenue
BNOC	The British National Oil Corporation
CT	Corporation Tax
CAA	Capital Allowances Act
DoE	Department of Energy
FA	Finance Act
FNo2A	Finance (Number 2) Act
ICTA	Income and Corporation Taxes Act
LPG	Liquid Petroleum Gas
NGL	Natural gas liquids
OTA	Oil Taxation Act
OTO	Oil Taxation Office
OPA	Oil and Pipelines Agency
PA	Petroleum Act
P(P)R	Petroleum (Production) Regulations
PRT	Petroleum Revenue Tax
PSPA	Petroleum and Submarine Pipeline Act
SI	Statutory Instrument
SOV	Statement of Value
SPD	Supplementary Petroleum Duty
STC	Simons Tax Cases
TC	Tax Cases
UK	United Kingdom
UKOOA	United Kingdom Offshore Operators Association
UKOITC	United Kingdom Oil Taxation Committee
UKCS	United Kingdom Sector of the Continental Shelf

Chapter 1
Introduction

The story to date of the development of the United Kingdom's oil resources is one of remarkable success. In the space of a decade, the UK emerged as one of the world's major oil producing nations. The discovery of the Groningen gas field in Holland in the 1950s had suggested the possibility that the North Sea might also be rich in hydrocarbons, but it was not until ratification of the Geneva Convention on the Continental Shelf in 1964 that exploration of the UK sector began in earnest. A number of gas discoveries were made in the 1960s in the Southern Basin of the North Sea, followed by discovery of the small Montrose oil field in December 1969 and the giant Forties field a year later. By 1980, the UK had reached self sufficiency in oil and had become a net oil exporter. Although the level of production is now in decline, an unexpectedly high rate of discovery of new, albeit smaller, fields has extended the likely period of self sufficiency well into the 1990s.

The history of oil taxation is not quite so illustrious. The fabric of the system is a patchwork of separate taxes, each amended and adjusted in response to changing circumstances and forming less than a cohesive whole. The state secures its share of the economic rent from its indigenous oil by charging a royalty on oil produced and taxes on oil production and related profits. It has also exacted auction or premium payments for the award of certain oil licences. The royalty and tax receipts, including corporation tax, reached a peak in 1985/6 of about £11.5 billion, a level then expected to be maintained for the remainder of the 1980s. The collapse in oil prices in 1986 altered the expectations quite dramatically, reducing the expected yield for 1986/7 to about £6 billion. Nevertheless, oil revenues play a vital role in the Government's current financing and medium term economic strategy. By the same token, taxation removes a considerable slice of the producers' profits. Oil taxation issues, then, continue to be of great interest both to Government and to the oil companies.

UK oil taxation has three tiers. Firstly, a 12 ½% royalty is charged on production from fields for which development consent was given before April 1982; secondly, a field – based petroleum revenue tax (PRT) is charged, currently at 75%, on production and related profits net of royalty payments; and thirdly, company-based corporation tax is

UK Oil Taxation

charged on production and related profits net of both royalty and PRT payments. Royalty was adopted from earlier onshore licence conditions, but the other main features of the structure were purpose built to cope with the expected boom in offshore production. The Oil Taxation Act 1975 introduced PRT and erected a corporation tax ring fence around UK oil production operations. Notwithstanding the description of the Oil Taxation Bill by a member of the then Conservative opposition in 1974 as a 'horrid, mis-shapen beast', the framework of the system remains more or less intact, although there have been many alterations in detail.

The UK oil industry and the tax system, like the author, are showing signs of middle age. There is increasing preoccupation with the commercial and fiscal implications of abandonment of oil fields, and with the after-life of continued use of field facilities for the purposes of other fields. As the large first generation fields decline, to be replaced by new generations of much smaller fields, the impact of PRT also declines. Increasing debate may be expected about possible radical alterations to the tax structure, ranging from removal of the field basis to abolition of PRT. In the meantime, the tax system will continue to be used as an instrument of economic policy and, in the broadest sense, of depletion policy. The importance of taxation, in the eyes of Government and taxpayers, does not diminish in proportion to the tax base.

The law cited in this book is that in force at August 1988. References to oil include natural gas unless the context requires otherwise.

Chapter 2
Development of UK Oil Taxation

2.1 Main Changes Since 1975

The main scheme of UK oil taxation dates from 1975. There already existed some revenue-raising instruments designed specifically for UK oil production and related profits: onshore licences carrying a liability to royalties on production had been issued since the 1930s and the first offshore production licences were issued in 1964; and in 1973 the UK taxing jurisdiction was extended so that persons not resident in the UK who derived profits from operations in connection with UK reserves on the UKCS came within its scope. But the introduction of PRT and the CT ring fence in 1975 represented an entirely new approach by government to the taxation of oil profits. It signalled recognition not simply that the existing tax system required reinforcement but that taxation would be used to secure a full share for the Exchequer of the enormous economic rent expected to be derived from UK oil production.

The stimulus for change found expression in a Report from the House of Commons Committee of Public Accounts, published in February 1973. The Committee found that 'under the present arrangements the UK will not obtain either for the Exchequer or the balance of payments anything like the share of the "take" of oil operations on the Continental Shelf that other countries are obtaining for oil within their territories'. There were two main reasons for this shortfall. Oil companies had accumulated massive tax losses as a result of the artificially high posted price at which Middle East crude was transferred between group companies, and those losses were available to offset UK production profits. Secondly, losses within a group of companies, generated perhaps by high capital allowances on a tanker fleet, could also be used under the group relief provisions to offset production profits. The Committee recommended that 'the Government should take action substantially to improve the effective tax yield from operations on the continental shelf'. It was also critical of the terms on which offshore licences had been awarded in the four Rounds to date, questioning whether bigger returns to the Exchequer could not have been obtained from the auctioning of licence blocks.

Given the high rate of tax which the Government was now contemplating, it was not feasible to adapt the CT system with its then 52% rate

2.1 UK Oil Taxation

in order to achieve it. The two alternative instruments were either some form of excess profits tax using the CT base or a new and separate tax; the Government decided on the second of these. PRT was introduced as, and remains essentially, a field-based tax on production profits, though its scope was extended in 1983 to include tariff and other receipts. It is the second of the three tiers of oil taxation: royalties are deducted in arriving at PRT profit and both royalties and PRT paid are allowed in arriving at CT profit. The PRT rate was 45% up to 31 December 1978.

The Oil Taxation Act 1975 also superimposed on the CT system the ring fence concept. A company's UK oil exploration and production activities were segregated from its other activities: losses arising outside the ring fence could no longer be used to relieve UK oil production profits, and restrictions were placed on the amount of interest payments which could be allowed against those profits. As a complementary measure, relief for the tax losses which oil companies had accumulated largely as a result of the posted price system was severely restricted. No such losses incurred before 1973 could be allowed against UK production profits, and the amount allowable against other profits of a company was restricted to £50m.

The years since 1975 have seen a bewildering number of changes in UK oil taxation. They have affected particularly the PRT provisions which, after a quiescent bedding-down period of four years from 1975, were substantially amended in each of the years 1979 to 1983 and again in 1987 and 1988. The main changes are summarised in the following analysis.

1976

Royalties on production under licences issued before 20 August 1976 are calculated effectively on the well-head value. Under later licences the basis is the UK landed value.

1979

Because of the very heavy front-end reliefs, the first payment of PRT was not made until 1978. In July of that year, the Labour Government, having become increasingly concerned that at a time of falling real oil prices PRT as the special oil tax was not producing the intended yield, issued a Green Paper outlining proposed changes in PRT. The changes were enacted in 1979 by the then Conservative Government. Coincidentally, oil prices had begun a series of leaps and bounds which took the price per barrel from about $15 in early 1979 to $35 by mid 1980.

The PRT rate was increased from 45% to 60% from 1 January 1979. Supplement, the additional allowance on certain expenditure, was reduced from 75% to 35% for expenditure incurred under contracts made after 31 December 1978. Expenditure incurred after 1 January 1979 under contracts made before that date continued to attract supplement at 75%, except that, under a transitional provision, such expenditure which was attributable to 'change orders' qualified at a rate of 66 ⅔%. The amount of the oil allowance, which exempts an amount of production from PRT, was halved to 250,000 tonnes per chargeable period and to 5 million tonnes per field from 1 January 1979.

The British National Oil Corporation (BNOC) had been exempt from PRT. That exemption was removed with effect from the chargeable period beginning 1 July 1979. Since the after-tax surplus of the Corporation was paid to the National Oil Account, the change had no real effect on total Exchequer benefit from UK oil production.

1980

The Oil Taxation Act 1975 required payment of PRT, at the earliest, four months after the end of a six month chargeable period. Although this time lag was substantially shorter than that for CT (usually nine months), the Government initiated a series of changes designed to speed up the flow of oil taxation to the Exchequer. The first of these changes was the introduction of a form of self assessment for PRT, which requires participators to calculate their liability for a chargeable period and to make a payment on account in accordance with that calculation within two months of the end of the period. The normal due date for accounting for PRT was therefore advanced by two months: any tax unpaid which is ultimately shown to be payable on formal assessment for the period carries interest from two months after the end of the period. These provisions apply to the chargeable period ended 31 December 1979 and later periods.

The second acceleration device was advance payment of PRT. For the chargeable periods for which the provisions remained in force, from 1 January 1981 to 30 June 1983, a participator was required to make an advance payment at the time when the payment on account for the previous period was due, that is, two months after the end of that period. The amount of the advance was 15% of the greater of that payment on account and the tax assessed for the last but one chargeable period.

For periods ending after 31 December 1979, the rate of PRT was increased from 60% to 70%.

There were also important amendments in 1980 in the PRT rules relating to taxation of gas, ensuring that the added value attributable to fractionation was included within the charge: and provision was made enabling a transferee to inherit unused PRT expenditure and losses on transfer of an interest in a field.

2.1 UK Oil Taxation

1981

Government concern about some features of the oil taxation regime was reflected in 1981 legislation. PRT was seen to be insufficiently sensitive and responsive to increases in oil price, and at the same time the generous front-end reliefs delayed tax liabilities. The 1980 acceleration measures provided only a partial solution, and a production levy was therefore introduced.

Supplementary petroleum duty (SPD) was charged at 20% on gross production less an exempt allowance equivalent to about 20,000 barrels per day, and was deductible in calculating profits for PRT and CT purposes; and, as a further aid to advancement and 'smoothing' of government revenues, a system of advance payment of SPD was introduced. SPD was much disliked by the oil industry. It represented a fourth tier of oil taxation, in addition to royalty, PRT and CT, and since it was not profit based it did not discriminate between profitable fields which had 'paid out' and those which were just commencing production; and it had a substantial impact on company cashflows. It was imposed initially for three periods only beginning with the chargeable period ended 30 June 1981; in the event it ran for a fourth period before repeal and replacement by advance petroleum revenue tax (APRT).

The Government had also been concerned for some time about the possibilities of 'wasteful expenditure', that is, the scope to spend money in particular forms and at particular times in such a way as to achieve more in terms of tax relief than the amount of expenditure itself. Supplement, the proxy relief for interest, was in any case conferring benefits in circumstances in which no real interest cost arose. The increases in PRT rate to 70% would have had the effect in most fields of bringing into play the safeguard limitation, a relief which had been intended as a safety net for unprofitable fields. The availability of supplement was therefore terminated for expenditure incurred after payback, and the number of periods for which safeguard is available was restricted to one and a half times the number between the first chargeable period and the payback period inclusive.

1982

There began in late 1981 a period of intensive lobbying and representation by the oil industry aimed at persuading the Government that the fiscal regime should be relaxed and particularly that SPD should be discontinued. For example, the Institute for Fiscal Studies produced a report which criticised the complexity and lack of sensitivity to profit of the existing system and recommended its complete replacement by a single tax levied at varying rates according to profitability. Partly because the report appeared somewhat late in the course of the process of consultation between the industry and government and partly because the industry did not feel able to support a major upheaval in the tax system and its attendant transitional problems, it was not received with enthusiasm. In the event, however, the general pressure for change bore some fruit. As the means of raising government revenue on early production, SPD was replaced by APRT, to apply from the chargeable period ending 30 June 1983 but for not more than ten chargeable periods for each field. Like SPD, it was charged at 20% on gross production less an exempt allowance equivalent to about 20,000 barrels per day; but unlike SPD it was an advance of PRT and allowable as a credit against PRT. The industry was mollified but far from satisfied. The change actually left some companies worse off because, whereas SPD was deductible for CT purposes, an amount paid as APRT did not become so deductible until it was credited against PRT liability.

The 'smoothing' of tax payments which had been a feature of the SPD mechanism was extended to encompass both APRT and PRT liabilities. Six monthly instalments were required beginning two months into a chargeable period, the amounts so paid being utilised against APRT and PRT liabilities due two months after the end of the period. In order to compensate for the reduction in tax take resulting from the changeover to APRT, the rate of PRT was increased to 75% with effect from 1 January 1983. An alternative formula was introduced for the valuation of ethane destined for use in the petrochemical industry.

1983

The process of tightening of the fiscal regime applying to UK oil production had continued uninterrupted since 1975. In 1983 the industry saw, if not the beginning of a reversal of the trend, at least a significant relaxation, chiefly intended to encourage exploration and appraisal of UK resources and development of new fields.

APRT was phased out, ceasing to apply to any field after 31 December 1986. The PRT oil allowance was doubled for new fields, excluding those onshore or in the southern basin of the North Sea. The increased allowance exempts from PRT the approximate equivalent of 20,000 barrels per day for ten years. Relief for exploration and appraisal expenditure is now allowed to be taken against any field without the need to demonstrate that the expenditure is abortive. Those new fields which qualify for the increased oil allowance were exempted from royalty. All of these changes provided a substantial boost to drilling activity.

In May 1982 the Government had issued a Consultative Document

2.1 UK Oil Taxation

dealing with two related PRT problem areas. It was becoming apparent that the system of allowance for expenditure on field assets was under strain as more fields came into production and the sharing of transportation and related systems became commonplace. At the same time, allowances for payment of the substantial tariffs and other consideration arising from these developments was not fully balanced by tax on the recipients; the Document described this asymmetry as 'PRT leakage'. The remedies, outlined in the Document but reflecting in part industry representations, were to confirm front-end relief for expenditure whether or not the asset is likely to be used also by other participators, and to bring into the PRT charge tariff and disposal receipts. This extension of the charge also brings within the scope of PRT receipts derived by participators in foreign fields from use of their assets situated in the UK or the UKCS.

1984

In a well publicised sale in November 1983, BP disposed of about 10% of its interest in the Forties field, a sale which owed its success partly to the prospect of tax relief for exploration and appraisal expenditure to be incurred by the purchasers. Following the announcement of the tender for sale, the Government acted to prevent the PRT offset of past costs of a purchaser against an interest acquired in a mature field. Capital gains realised in disposing of field interests and field assets were brought within the CT ring fence, so that they cannot be relieved by losses outside the oil production sphere.

The 1984 changes of widest significance were the general CT amendments. The 100% first year allowance for plant was phased out, and the rate of CT was reduced successively from 52% to 35%.

1985

The Government concluded that the regime applying to onshore developments was sufficiently benign without the encouragement of immediate relief for expenditure on exploration or appraisal, usually taken against offshore field profits. With effect from 1 April 1986, the exploration and appraisal relief introduced in 1983 was withdrawn for expenditure in relation to UK onshore areas: no PRT relief is now available for such expenditure unless it is incurred for the purpose of an onshore field. The increasing incidence of production tests highlighted the risk that, under existing legislation, oil won from areas which might not be included within a determined field would escape the PRT charge: the relative income in such cases is now offset against expenditure otherwise qualifying for exploration and appraisal relief. Technical amendments prevented artificial elongation of the safeguard period on

Development of UK Oil Taxation 2.1

the one hand and the premature triggering of the payback limitation to supplement on the other.

1986

Areas of land around the UK, between the high water line and the land-ward boundary of the territorial sea, which are part of the UK in general law, are now treated as though they formed part of the territorial sea so that, in particular, they are not caught by the 1985 withdrawal of exploration and appraisal relief. An alternative formula was introduced for the valuation of certain methane or ethane, similar to the 1982 rules relating to ethane used for petrochemical purposes.

1987

The rules for measuring, for PRT purposes, income derived from crude oil production, which had remained virtually unchanged since 1975, were now subjected to radical revision. The Government announced its intention in November 1986 to counteract 'spinning' and related practices which were thought to be causing substantial loss of tax. The proposals for legislation, which were aimed specifically at Brent blend crude, were abandoned in the course of consultation with the oil industry in favour of the nomination scheme, which was enacted in the first 1987 Finance Act and supplemented by Inland Revenue Regulations published in July 1987. Arm's length sales of equity crude would, apart from the scheme, be taxed by reference to the selling price: now, such sales which are not made in pursuance of a contract which has been nominated may be charged effectively at the higher of 'market value' and actual selling price. The Government also introduced in the second 1987 Finance Act reserve powers to bring in sanctions aimed at other perceived abuses, particularly the late switching between arm's length and non arm's length outlets for equity production.

Other major changes were made in the rules for establishing the market value of oil which is not sold at arm's length. The deals which are taken into account in the comparative data base are now defined, though the Revenue has discretion to adopt other standards if application of the primary base to particular crudes is deemed inappropriate. A new PRT relief was introduced for research expenditure not related to a field; and allowance for up to 10% of certain expenditure on new fields may now be claimed against another field.

Capital gains of companies are now charged at the same rate of CT as income, subject to offset of ACT. In partial alleviation of the difficulties of ring fence companies in utilising ACT, a limited right was introduced to carry back ACT surrendered to them; and ring fence consortium

2.1 UK Oil Taxation

companies owned in equal shares by two companies may now accept surrender of ACT paid by the shareholders. A loophole in the ring fence relating to ACT on preference share dividends was closed. Restrictions were imposed on the utilisation of loss and other reliefs of certain dual resident companies.

1988

Two of the oil industry's main submissions leading up to the 1988 Budget were requests for easement of the burden of royalties and removal of the fiscal handicaps which had been imposed in 1983 on Southern Basin developments in comparison with other offshore fields. The Government announced abolition of royalties for both Southern Basin and onshore fields which received development consent after March 1982. The oil allowance for those fields, however, was reduced to 125,000 tonnes per chargeable period and to 2.5 million tonnes overall. The vehemence of the industry's reaction in 1987 to the retrospective denial of rollover relief for capital gains on disposals of interests in oil licences had persuaded the government to authorise a re-appraisal of the capital gains regime in this area. The 1988 Finance Act gave tax-free treatment to certain work obligation farm-outs and licence exchanges.

2.2 Rates of Tax and Relief for Expenditure

The three tiers of Government take which apply to UK oil production are:

    Royalty —12½% maximum. Fields receiving development consent after 31 March 1982 are exempt;

    PRT — 75%. If the safeguard limitation applies, the average rate is less than 75% and the marginal rate is 80%;

    CT — 35% from 1 April 1986.

Royalty is allowed as a deduction in calculating both PRT and CT: PRT is allowed as a deduction for CT.

The marginal rate of tax applying while the PRT rate remained at 45% was 76.9%. With the introduction of SPD (in force from 1 January 1981 to 31 December 1982) and increase in the PRT rate to 70%, the marginal rate rose to 89.3%; and, following repeal of SPD and increase in the PRT rate from 75%, to 89.5%. Given a CT rate of 35% from 1 April 1986, the marginal rate is 85.78% or, for those fields exempt from royalties, 83.75%. The 85.78% rate is calculated as follows:

Development of UK Oil Taxation 2.2

Profit	100	
Royalty 12½%	12.5	12.5
	87.5	
PRT 75% (a)	65.62	65.62
	21.88	
CT 35%	7.66	7.66
Company retains	14.22%	
Government takes		85.78%

(a) Safeguard assumed not to apply.

Rates of relief for expenditure

Under licences issued before 20 August 1976, expenditure incurred in conveying and treating oil is allowable in calculating royalty liability.

Leaving aside royalty relief, the rate of relief for expenditure depends on whether it qualifies for PRT supplement and whether the PRT liability is limited by safeguard. If the expenditure does not qualify for supplement and PRT is payable at the 75% rate not limited by safeguard, the maximum relief, assuming a CT rate of 35%, is 83.75%. For expenditure qualifying for supplement (broadly, most capital expenditure incurred before payback), the relief is:

Expenditure	100
Supplement 35%	35
	135
PRT saving 75%	101.25
Less: Additional CT 35% × 1.25	0.44
Total relief	100.81%

The incidence of safeguard may increase the effective relief, as the following example shows:

> Company D takes eight chargeable periods to reach payback: PRT payable for the next four periods is limited by safeguard. D incurs before payback 100 expenditure qualifying for supplement.

Relief ignoring safeguard		100.81
Safeguard 'base' increased by 100:		
PRT additional saving for each safeguard period is:		
80% × (100 × 15%)	12	
Less: additional CT 35% × 12	4.2	
	7.8	
Four periods × 7.8		31.2
Total relief		132.01%

11

2.2 UK Oil Taxation

It will be apparent that both the timing and form of expenditure can affect significantly the amount of effective tax relief. At the same time, it should be borne in mind that the actual interest cost attaching to the expenditure in question is not allowable as a PRT expense, so that relief on that cost will be restricted to the CT rate 35%. It is likely that, in the case of a field potentially liable to PRT, a company will generally aim to incur pre-payback expenditure in a form which qualifies for supplement. Nevertheless, there may in some circumstances be overall commercial advantage in pursuing a different course. For example, it may suit a company to lease a production asset even though the lease payments are unlikely to qualify for supplement and the corresponding accretion to the safeguard capital base. An increasing number of new fields are likely to be comparatively small, yielding profits which are largely sheltered from PRT liability by oil allowance.

Chapter 3
Administration

3.1 Introduction

The taxation and royalty systems relating to UK oil operations are administered by two Government Departments, the Inland Revenue and the Department of Energy. Other Departments also have interests in the fiscal regime: for example, the Department of Industry is concerned in the inter-relation between the methods and costs of abandoning oil fields and the relative tax reliefs, the Foreign and Commonwealth Office in the incidence of UK tax on residents of other countries and, perhaps most significantly, the Treasury in the present and future contribution to the Exchequer of oil exploration and production. Officials of the Treasury, the Department of Energy and the Inland Revenue monitor the performance of the tax system and its impact on the level of commitment to UK exploration and on the economics of particular fields, especially those of 'marginal' profitability. The manner in which the two main responsible Departments administer the tax and royalty provisions is subject to scrutiny by the Comptroller and Auditor General, and his reports are periodically reviewed and examined by the Public Accounts Committee of the House of Commons.

Given the very high rates of tax applying to profits on UK oil production and the substantial contribution which the oil industry makes to the UK economy, there is an obvious need for dialogue between the industry and Government. Although the industry cannot always speak with a single voice, its representative bodies are able to act as a conduit for the collective views of members. The United Kingdom Offshore Operators Association (UKOOA) is the main channel for consideration of general matters of policy including the level of taxation, the nature of the instrument used to collect it and the distribution of the burden. It made forceful representations, for example, on the need, recognised by the Government in 1983, for a relaxation of the regime in order to encourage further exploration. UKOOA also keeps a watching brief on licensing policies and provides the industry voice in matters related to the administration of royalties. The United Kingdom Oil Industry Taxation Committee (UKOITC), a sister organisation of UKOOA, is a forum for consideration of the

3.1 UK Oil Taxation

many and varied technical issues which emerge in the operation of the PRT and CT systems and in proposed new legislation. It holds regular joint meetings with the Inland Revenue. The Association of British Independent Oil Exploration Companies (BRINDEX) represents the British independent companies which hold interests in licence consortia but which may not be operators for the licence.

The aims which Government sets in establishing and adjusting the North Sea fiscal regime were published by the Inland Revenue in 1982 and remain in force. They are:

Maximum Government take consistent with incentive to develop;

Timing: reasonably early Government take consistent with quick cost recovery;

Flexibility to respond to major changes in oil field economics;

Avoiding distortions, for example incentives to bad oil field practice, over- or under-incentives to incremental investment etc;

Manageable administratively.

3.2 Department of Energy

The Department of Energy (DOE) is the agent of the Secretary of State for Energy, who is responsible for licensing and for supervision of operations under licences. The DOE issues the guidelines to be taken into account in the consideration of licence applications, vets the suitability of applicants and ensures that licensees fulfil their responsibilities. All changes or assignments of licence interests and changes of control of licensees require the consent of the Secretary of State, and the DOE deals with the day to day business of examination and negotiation of such applications.

The Oil Division of the DOE administers the royalty provisions. Assessment teams examine the Statements of Value (SOV) submitted by licensees for each chargeable period. Much of the work concerns examination of the accounting systems of the licence operator and translation of the operator's accounting data into the 'joint costs' to be allowed to the holders of the licence in respect of conveying and treating oil produced under the licence. From time to time, proposals have been made that the base for royalty allowances should be the expenditure allowed by the Inland Revenue for PRT purposes, or alternatively that the royalty and PRT administrations should be amalgamated, but the difficulties have prevented progress towards these ends. The DOE also undertakes the considerable responsibilities of administering the abandonment procedures, including the approval of programmes and their execution and of the financial arrangements made by licensees to meet the costs.

Although the DOE and the Inland Revenue are entirely independent, they are authorised to exchange information.

> Any information which the Commissioners of Inland Revenue possess in connection with petroleum won by virtue of a licence granted under the Petroleum (Production) Act 1934 . . . may be disclosed by the Commissioners to the Secretary of State, or to an officer of his who is authorised by him to receive such information, in connection with the provisions of the licence relating to royalty payments [PSPA 1975, s19].

The values of production for royalty purposes are the values agreed for PRT purposes (or, in the case of gas exempt from PRT, for CT purposes), and those values are notified to the DOE by the Inland Revenue. It is likely that information will also be exchanged concerning proposed assignments of licence interests including the making or cancellation of an Illustrative Agreement under which licence rights and obligations are assumed by an associated company (see 8.11).

3.3 Inland Revenue

In 1975 the Inland Revenue set up the Oil Taxation Office (OTO) to administer the newly enacted PRT and to take over from local Tax Districts the responsibility for CT applying to companies carrying on UK oil exploration and production activities. The OTO works closely with the Inland Revenue Policy Division which oversees the manner in which the legislation is interpreted and implemented and keeps Ministers informed of the possible need for changes.

The OTO has four main operational responsibilities:
(1) It assesses PRT liabilities of companies which are participators in fields. It examines the returns by participators of oil production and establishes the values taken into account for both PRT and royalty assessment, and deals with claims for expenditure allowances.
(2) It receives and examines the accounts and computations of CT liabilities of those companies which derive profits from UK oil extraction activities and oil rights, that is, profits within the 'ring fence'.
(3) It performs a similar function in relation to CT liabilities of companies which are engaged in oil-related business outside the ring fence, particularly the worldwide activities of UK based groups and the UK refining, marketing, shipping and service

3.3 UK Oil Taxation

operations of foreign-owned companies: in this area intra-group transfer prices receive particular attention.

(4) The OTO assesses the CT liabilities of companies not resident in the UK which provide services to exploration and production companies in connection with UKCS operations. Other offices, particularly Special Office (Edinburgh) and Centre One, have responsibility for establishment of the liabilities of those companies to account for employee's tax.

The OTO is normally prepared to consider in advance proposed transactions in connection with UK exploration and production and to give an opinion on the company's understanding of the tax consequences. The evolution of this practice reflected the Government's wish to assist in the development of the UK's oil resources. Apart from the very limited circumstances in which the legislation provides a formal clearance procedure, the opinions given by the OTO do not have statutory force and are not comparable with formal clearances issued by the Internal Revenue Service in the USA.

CT computations are generally based on and reconciled to audited accounts. Because of the shorter timeframe within which the PRT machinery operates, PRT expenditure claims are often made before the relative statements have been audited. In examining claims, particularly the first claim for a particular field, the OTO aims to achieve an understanding of the claimant's accounting systems and provision of the data which underlie the claims. As part of the process, it may examine in depth one or more blocks of expenditure or sections of the claim, following the 'audit trail' of constituent elements of expenditure making up the whole.

Even so, the OTO may not regard claims as finally approved until they have been reconciled with the relative accounts and CT computations. The Public Accounts Committee has attached some importance to the completion of such reconciliations. The expected format varies from case to case, but in general the OTO requires a reconciliation of the bulk of field development expenditure up to first production, and periodic, though not necessarily annual, reconciliations for later periods.

Chapter 4
Petroleum Licensing

4.1 Introduction

Exploration for and production of oil in the UK and the UKCS is conducted under the terms of licences issued by the Secretary of State for Energy. The licence serves to establish the rights of the licensee in substances produced from the licensed area and to regulate the manner in which operations under the licence are conducted. It also provides an instrument of government for direction of exploration effort into particular areas and for control of the rate of depletion of resources. Title to oil in place in the UK and the UKCS vests in the Crown (Petroleum (Production) Act 1934 and Continental Shelf Act 1964); but under the terms of a licence oil which the licensee wins belongs to the licensee. Onshore, or landward, licences have a considerably longer history than offshore, or seaward, licences, which were first issued in 1964.

Licences are issued under Regulations which the Secretary of State is empowered to make by virtue of the Petroleum (Production) Act 1934. The Regulations currently relevant to issue of new offshore production licences are the Petroleum (Production) Regulations 1982 (SI 1982 No 1000). The Regulations lay down conditions for application for licences, while the criteria which the Secretary of State adopts in considering applications are published in a London Gazette Notice. Recent such Notices have indicated that the Secretary of State will have regard, *inter alia*, to:

technical competence;

financial viability;

the applicant's previous history as a licensee in prosecuting licence interests including the contribution made to the UK economy and interests;

whether the applicant subscribes to the policy of full and fair opportunity to UK industry, and its previous history in this respect;

4.1 UK Oil Taxation

if the applicant is incorporated outside the UK, whether its home state is likely to provide equitable treatment to a UK applicant.

In awarding offshore licences in the ninth and tenth Rounds in 1985 and 1987, the Secretary of State also had regard to the applicants' commitment to encourage the development of UK technology. The form of application in outline is set out in the Petroleum (Production) Regulations 1982, though more detailed guidance is available from the Department of Energy.

A company was required under Rounds one to four of offshore licensing to be a UK incorporated company. This is no longer a precondition, but it is a *de facto* requirement that the central management and control of the company be situated in the UK: failure to maintain such status may lead to revocation of the licence (for example, Petroleum (Production) Regulations 1982 Sched 5 cl 39). Subject to transitional rules, a company incorporated in the UK is now resident in the UK for tax purposes, regardless of the site of management and control. It is likely that the Department of Energy will continue to require licensees to have a substantial management presence in the UK.

For onshore licences issued after 18 December 1984, the relevant regulations are the Petroleum (Production) (Landward Areas) Regulations 1984. Separate provisions apply to Northern Ireland licences.

4.2 Model Clauses

The Regulations also include Model Clauses, which are incorporated in and form part of a licence. For production licences issued up to 1976, including offshore licences issued under the first to fourth licensing Rounds, the Model Clauses in operation are those derived from the Petroleum and Submarine Pipelines Act 1975. Later production licences adopt the clauses contained in the Petroleum (Production) Regulations 1976 (SI 1976 No 1129); and from August 1982 the applicable clauses are derived from the Petroleum (Production) Regulations 1982. The Model Clauses for offshore, or seaward, licences are contained in Petroleum (Production) Regulations 1982 Sched 5. In outline, the clauses deal with the following main subjects:

1–6 right of licensee to search, and bore for, and get petroleum in the seabed and seaward area (the extent of the area being defined in a schedule to the licence): the term of the licence and provision for surrender;

Petroleum Licensing 4.3

7–10 payments under the licence including royalty, and royalty in kind;

11–12 measurement of production and the keeping of accounts;

13–37 work obligations, and the conduct of operations under the licence, including undertaking to deliver petroleum to the UK;

38 restrictions on assignment of licence rights;

39 powers of revocation;

40 arbitration.

4.3 Licences in Issue

Onshore licences
Large areas of England are now under licence, chiefly in the South East and South West, East Midlands, North East and North West. Smaller areas in Scotland and Wales are also licensed.

The system of onshore licensing was revised in 1984. Instead of the former exploration and production licences, there are three new types:

EXL — exploration licence valid for six years, permitting seismic surveys, exploration drilling and short term testing;

AL — appraisal licence valid for five years, permitting appraisal drilling and extended testing: this licence will only be awarded following a discovery on an EXL;

DL — development licence valid for 20 years, extendable at the discretion of the Secretary of State, permitting production of oil or gas.

EXL licences are issued in Rounds. The first such licences were awarded in 1986, and provision was also made for conversion of existing exploration licences to EXLs. Second Round licences were awarded in 1988.

Offshore licences
The 1958 Geneva Convention authorised coastal states to exercise certain powers in their sectors of the continental shelf, including jurisdiction over mineral exploration and extraction. The Convention was ratified by the UK in 1964. Those parts of the UK sector in which that jurisdiction is exercised are the Designated Areas, the designation being made by Order in Council authorised by the Continental Shelf Act 1964. For the purpose of licensing, each quadrant is divided into 30

4.3 UK Oil Taxation

blocks of about 250 sq km. A single licence frequently covers more than one block, and those blocks may be in different and widely separated quadrants. A part block may be included in a licence, usually where that part has been surrendered under the terms of an earlier licence.

There are two types of offshore licence. An exploration licence lasts for three years with an option to extend for a further three years and permits only initial exploratory work such as seismic survey and very shallow drilling. Production licences are much more significant, entitling the holder to 'search and bore for and get petroleum . . .', and lasting for a substantially longer period. In the eighth Round, for example, although one half of the licensed area has to be surrendered after six years, the remainder may be retained for a further 30 years.

Offshore licences have been issued in ten Rounds between 1964 and 1987, and eleventh Round awards will be made in 1989. Details of the awards are given in Appendix I. Under the first three Rounds, licences were awarded solely at the discretion of the Secretary of State, with the intention of directing exploration effort into particular areas and so opening up the UKCS, bringing in a large number of licensees of which a fair proportion would be British owned. There was a good deal of concern after the small third Round issue that the UK was not moving quickly enough nor securing the best return to the Exchequer from UK resources: in late 1970 OPEC countries had begun to increase oil prices, and companies involved in the UKCS were being constrained by the limited amount of acreage under licence. The fourth Round in 1971/72 was very much larger than the third. It was decided to continue with the discretionary system, but as an experiment 15 blocks were auctioned for a total price of £37 million. The fifth, sixth and seventh Rounds were again made under the discretionary system, though in the case of the seventh Round a number of blocks were awarded on payment of a premium of £5 million. The eighth and ninth Rounds, like the fourth, combined discretionary awards with the auction of a small number of designated blocks, realising £33 million and £121 million respectively. The tenth Round, announced after the collapse in oil prices early in 1986, was a discretionary issue.

4.4 Licence Payments

Exploration licences are subject to a small annual payment. Production licences, other than in respect of those areas awarded for a premium or at auction, require an initial payment. They also require periodic payments, or annual rentals, the scale of which increases, in the case of offshore licences, with the length of time since the licence was issued. Royalties payable on production under a licence are expressed as consideration for the award of the licence.

4.5 Abandonment of Offshore Installations

As a condition of the Government's consent to installation of offshore platforms and other facilities, operators assume an obligation in the event of abandonment to clear the site in a manner satisfactory to the Government. The standard and extent of removal of offshore installations, however, depends on international law or, more precisely, on the manner in which the Government gives effect to international law. The 1958 Geneva Convention on the Continental Shelf states the principle that exploitation of the natural resources of the Continental Shelf must not result in any unjustifiable interference with navigation, fishing or conservation of the living resources of the sea; and it requires that installations which are abandoned or disused must be entirely removed. The 1982 United Nations Convention on the Law of the Sea also adopts the principle that there should be no unjustifiable interference with other users of the sea. Although it requires removal of abandoned or disused installations as a general principle, it envisages that some installations may not be totally removed. The UK is not, at the time of writing, a signatory of the Convention, but it may in practice subscribe to the provisions relating to abandonment. In any event, the Government acknowledges that the International Maritime Organisation is the competent international organisation which the Convention relies on to produce international standards of abandonment. The Organisation has not yet established those standards, but it seems likely that some installations will have to be totally removed while others, because of deeper water or other reasons, may be partially removed or remain in place. The treatment of marine pipelines also remains to be clarified.

The Model Clauses in licences make little direct reference to abandonment. They provide that a licensee must have the consent of the Secretary of State for the abandonment of a well. Operators of installations and submarine pipelines are normally obliged to clear the site or otherwise remove hazards to navigation and shipping. Much of the machinery which establishes liability for abandonment and security for the costs is now found in the Petroleum Act 1987. The Secretary of State is empowered to require the submission of a programme of abandonment, including an estimate of the costs and provision for continuing maintenance of facilities which are not completely removed, and the carrying out of the approved programme. These responsibilities may be attached not only to operators, licensees and other persons having an interest in the installations, but also to any companies associated with those parties. Formal steps to join associated compa-

4.5 UK Oil Taxation

nies in the liability will not be taken if the licensees themselves make satisfactory arrangements for abandonment and for the provision of resources to meet the costs. If those charged with the duty to carry out abandonment fail to do so, the Secretary of State may undertake some or all of the work and seek to recover the costs from the defaulters. There are rights of appeal to the High Court against actions of the Secretary of State in pursuance of these powers.

The Petroleum Act does not specify the extent or nature of the abandonment works which will be required in particular cases. Instead, the Secretary of State has power to make regulations to:

(*a*) Prescribe standards and safety requirements in respect of the dismantling, removal and disposal of installations and pipelines;
(*b*) Prescribe standards and safety requirements in respect of anything left in the water in cases where an installation or pipeline is not wholly removed;
(*c*) Make provision for the prevention of pollution;
(*d*) Make provision for inspection, including provision to meet the costs (PA 1987).

Licensee groups need to make arrangements to ensure that each member of the group is capable of meeting its share of abandonment costs. One of the possible security arrangements may be a form of trust to which the licensees contribute funds sufficient to meet estimated abandonment liabilities: adoption of such arrangements may depend on suitable taxation treatment and approval of the Secretary of State.

4.6 Participation

The nature of state participation in UK oil and gas production has undergone a number of changes, ranging from mandatory intervention to the present residue of reserve powers held by the Oil and Pipelines Agency and the Secretary of State's exercise of rights to take royalty in kind. The National Coal Board and the British Gas Corporation held quite extensive equity interests in offshore licences issued in early Rounds, but use of state organisations to safeguard the nation's interest in its offshore natural resources first emerged as an instrument of policy with the establishment of the British National Oil Corporation (BNOC) in 1975. BNOC took over the licence interests formerly held by the National Coal Board. Under first to fourth Rounds, BNOC negotiated with licensees participation rights which entitled it to purchase at arm's length prices up to 51% of production from a field in the licensed area. In most cases, the licensee had an option to buy back at the same price some or all of the 51% participation production, leaving the licensee neither better nor worse off. Under 5th and 6th Round licences state interests, whether BNOC or BGC, held a direct equity interest in at least 51% of the petroleum won. In later licensing rounds, the nature of participation is akin to that applying in Rounds 1 to 4, the licensee being obliged, if required to do so, to sell at market prices up to 51% of production to the state body (now the Oil and Pipelines Agency (OPA)).

Much of the panoply of participation was effectively dismantled from 1982 onwards. The exploration and production interests of BNOC were transferred in 1982 to Britoil Plc, the shares in which were then sold to the public in tranches in 1982 and 1985: Britoil was taken over by BP in 1988. Similarly, the oil interests of BGC were transferred to Enterprise Oil Plc in 1984, followed by privatisation of the shares in that company. The Government retained in both Britoil and Enterprise a 'golden share', the rights of which might be used to prevent an unwelcome change of control of the company. The Enterprise 'share' expires in 1988. The Government's former majority stake in British Petroleum has also been sold to the public in tranches, concluding in 1987.

After a period in which the activities of BNOC in taking and disposing of participation crude generated substantial losses funded by the Government, the decision was taken in March 1985 to abolish the Corporation. On the winding up on 30 November 1985, some of its functions were taken over by the newly formed Oil and Pipelines Agency. The Agency is responsible for selling oil which the Secretary of State takes as royalty in kind, and for maintaining all existing participation agreements and negotiating such new agreements required by the Secretary of State.

In June 1988, the Government announced its intention to wind up OPA. Royalties will not be taken in kind after the end of 1988, and participation agreements will be terminated.

Chapter 5
Royalties

5.1 Introduction

All UK petroleum production licences, other than those relating to certain new fields (see 5.2), carry a liability to pay a royalty to the Secretary of State. The liability is established in the Model Clauses which are incorporated in the licence, and is expressed as consideration for the grant of the licence. The amount of royalty payable is a percentage of the value of production. Under licences issued before 20 August 1976, royalties are based effectively on well-head values, calculated as UK landed values less the costs of conveying and treatment. Under later licences, including offshore licences issued in the fifth and later Rounds, royalties are calculated on UK landed values without deduction for conveying and treatment costs.

5.2 Exemption of New Fields

Under the Petroleum Royalties (Relief) Act 1983, production from certain new fields is exempt from royalties. Those same fields also qualify for increased PRT oil allowance. A 'relevant new field' is a field:
(*a*) no part of which lies in a landward area or in an area to the East of the UK and between latitudes 52° and 55° North; and
(*b*) for no part of which consent for development was granted by the Secretary of State before 1 April 1982; and
(*c*) for no part of which a programme of development had been served on the licensee or approved by the Secretary of State before that date (FA 1983 s36).

The Chancellor of the Exchequer indicated in his Budget speech on 13 March 1984 that the Government had considered whether the 1983 reliefs for new fields should be extended to fields in the southern basin of the North Sea, but had concluded that because those fields were generally less costly to develop, such extension was not warranted.

However, following renewed representations by the industry that the fiscal regime discriminated unfairly against southern basin fields, the Chancellor announced in his 1988 Budget that all southern basin and 'onshore' fields for which development consent was given after 31

Royalties 5.3

March 1982 would be exempt from royalty with effect from 1 July 1988. The necessary legislation is not expected to be enacted until 1989. For this purpose, it is assumed that the fields affected will be identified by the reverse of the definition of relevant new fields adopted in the 1983 Petroleum Royalties (Relief) Act referred to above. The southern basin and 'onshore' fields to be covered by the new exemption qualify for oil allowance only at the reduced rate of 125,000 tonnes per chargeable period and a cumulative limit of 2.5 million tonnes.

The effect of these changes is that royalty is abolished for all fields for which development consent is given after 31 March 1982.

5.3 Rates of Royalty

Different rates of royalty apply to onshore (landward) and to offshore (seaward) licences:

Royalty percentage (of annual production in tonnes)		*Basis and deductions*
Onshore licences		
Licences issued up to 19 August 1976		
First 100,000	5%	Arm's length sales value less conveying and treatment costs. Periodic payments are deducted from royalty due.
Next 50,000	7½%	
Next 50,000	10%	
Over 200,000	12½%	
Licences issued 20 August 1976– 31 January 1983		
As above		Arm's length sales value
Licences issued after 31 January 1983		
All production	12½%	Arm's length sales value
Offshore Licences		
Licences issued in Rounds 1–4		
	12½%	Arm's length sales value less conveying and treatment costs. Periodic payments are deducted from royalty due
Licences issued in Rounds 5–10		
	12½%	Arm's length sales value

5.4   UK Oil Taxation

5.4 Payment of Royalty

Royalties are calculated by reference to chargeable periods of six months ending 30 June and 31 December. A return, known as a Statement of Value (SOV), is required two months after the end of each period. In some circumstances a provisional return may be made by the due date provided that a complete SOV is submitted within the next month. Since royalties are levied by reference to a licence and are not field-based like PRT, the production derived from a licensed area may relate to more than one field: in that case, some parts of the SOV are required to show separately details for each field. In practice, no SOV is required before production begins.

Royalty liabilities indicated by the SOV are required to be paid when the return is due, that is, two months after the end of each chargeable period. When the actual liability is agreed, any balance of royalty becomes payable, and carries interest from two months after the end of the period: if the amount already paid is excessive, repayment is made with interest.

The Secretary of State has the option to require some royalty liabilities to be satisfied in kind. Otherwise, royalties are payable in cash, either in satisfaction of the full liability or in discharging the balance of liability where the value of oil delivered to the Secretary of State as royalty in kind falls short of the full liability. The Government announced in June 1988 that royalties would cease to be taken in kind after the end of 1988.

The Model Clauses provide an appeals procedure enabling a licensee to refer to an arbitrator a dispute about the amount of royalty determined by the Secretary of State.

5.4.1 Repayment of Royalty

Cash royalty overpaid is repayable with interest: the interest is normally calculated from two months after the end of the chargeable period, but to the extent that the repayment relates to allowance of costs incurred after the end of the period, particularly abandonment costs, interest does not run until two months after the period in which the costs were incurred. The repayment is chargeable to PRT, by adjustment of the licence debit or credit (see 6.13), and to CT: the interest addition is chargeable to CT but not to PRT.

Royalties 5.5.1

The Secretary of State has discretion to refund the whole or part of royalty already paid, in order to encourage or facilitate continued production from a particular field. He has not yet exercised that discretion, nor defined the parameters within which it would be appropriate to do so. Refunds under this provision are exempt from charge to PRT and CT (PSPA 1975 s41 (3)).

5.5 Calculation of Royalty

The Model Clauses indicate how royalty liabilities are to be calculated. The Secretary of State is empowered to determine the mode or method of calculation, including the deductions for conveying and treatment costs. He issues Modes and Notes which explain in detail the deductions available and the manner in which returns are to be completed. The Modes and Notes are in Series, each of which applies to different categories of licence.

The Series are:
 (1) Offshore – Rounds 1-4 southern North Sea areas
 (2) Offshore – Rounds 1-4 other than Series 1
 (3) Onshore – licences issued prior to 20 August 1976
 (4) Offshore – the Rough field (a gas storage field)
 (5) Offshore – Rounds 5-8 other than the Rough field
 (6) Onshore – licences issued between 20 August 1976 and 31 January 1983
 (7) Onshore – licences issued after 31 January 1983.

The bulk of royalty liabilities arise under licences to which Series 2 relates, and that Series is used as the basis for discussion of calculation of royalties in the remainder of this chapter.

The SOV for each chargeable period calls for completion of six sections:
 (1) general information and declaration
 (2) report by independent accountant
 (3) calculation of royalty and remittance
 (4) quantity and value of petroleum
 (5) costs of conveying and treating
 (6) adjustment to prior chargeable periods.

5.5.1 Quantity and Value

The value of oil for royalty purposes is the value, as determined for PRT, of the aggregate of:

 disposals in sales at arm's length;

5.5.1 UK Oil Taxation

disposals otherwise than in sales at arm's length; appropriations;

and closing stocks (the full value not, as for PRT, one half of the value);

less opening stocks (the full value not, as for PRT, one half of the value).

The royalty values adopted are those ultimately agreed for PRT purposes and notified by the Revenue, under the terms of exchange of information powers provided for in PSPA 1975 s19. As for PRT, oil used for production purposes is not chargeable, nor is oil in transit to the UK. If the oil is exempt from PRT either as sold to British Gas under pre-July 1975 contracts or under the *de minimis* rule covering other oil from an exempt gas field (see 6.8.1), the value to be included is the value 'as determined for the purposes of income tax or the charge of corporation tax on income' of production disposed of or relevantly appropriated in the period. In this case, stocks of oil are left out of the royalty calculation.

If oil has been taken by the Secretary of State as royalty in kind, that quantity is brought into the calculation of total royalty value for the period, in order to ascertain the extent to which the royalty in kind liftings have satisfied the liability for the period. Residual cash royalty is calculated by attributing a deemed value to the royalty in kind liftings, a value ascertained by reference to the average arm's length value of other liftings and stock movements in the period. In a simple example:

	£m
Value of liftings by licensee, 500,000 tonnes × £80	40.0
Deemed value of royalty liftings, 55,000 × £80	4.4
	44.4
Less total conveying and treating costs	8.0
Chargeable to royalty	36.4
Royalty at 12½%	4.55
Taken as royalty in kind	4.4
Cash royalty	0.15

A somewhat more complex alternative method of calculating the residual cash royalty, known as the MC 9(3) method, was abandoned when the relative model clause was repealed (PA 1987).

5.5.2 Royalty in Kind

If the Secretary of State exercises his option to take oil as royalty in kind, he is entitled to take up to 12½% of volume of the licensee's share of production for the chargeable period. The option has been exercised in respect of most offshore oil fields, but not in respect of any gas field or any onshore field. Royalty will cease to be taken in kind after 1988. The OPA acts as the agent of the Secretary of State in selling royalty in kind oil. Delivery of the oil is made at a point at which the licensee would normally deliver oil in a sale at arm's length. Since the value of royalty taken in kind almost inevitably departs from a precise 12½% of the gross value of production, cash adjustments are required. If the deliveries to the Secretary of State prove to be less than 12½% of the gross value, the licensee is required to make a balancing cash payment. Less commonly, the deliveries to the Secretary of State prove to exceed the Minister's entitlement; in that case, the excess is deemed to have been sold by the licensee to the Secretary of State and a cash settlement is made which is chargeable to PRT and CT in the normal way.

In calculating royalty liabilities under licences issued before 20 August 1976 including Rounds one to four offshore licences, deductions are due for the costs of conveying and treating the oil. Royalty in kind deliveries which are made up of amounts up to 12½% of production volumes before taking account of the conveying and treating costs are therefore likely to exceed the final royalty liability. In these circumstances, the Secretary of State pays to the licensee amounts representing the costs of conveying and treating the oil which is delivered to him. Payments are normally made on account during the period and final settlement is made some time after the end of the period. These receipts are charged to PRT (see 6.12) and to CT.

5.5.3 Conveying and Treating Costs

Under licences issued before 20 August 1976 deductions are available in calculating the royalty liability for the costs of conveying and treating the oil. This applies most significantly to offshore fields under the first to fourth licensing Rounds but also to onshore fields under licences issued before the material date. The Mode for ascertaining the allowable costs referred to in this paragraph is that established in Series 2 relating to offshore fields, excluding those in the southern basin of the North Sea. A revised Series 2 Mode was issued in July 1983 having effect from 1 January 1983, and there have been subsequent amendments to some of its provisions. Claims for allowances are required to distinguish between joint costs, incurred by the operator on behalf of

5.5.3 UK Oil Taxation

licensees, and own costs. A somewhat similar distinction applies in PRT procedures, though for PRT purposes the joint costs are claimed by the responsible person on behalf of participators rather than by each participator separately. The quantum of joint costs to be claimed is derived from the records of expenditure incurred by the operator, not from the recording of the licensee's share of the expenditure in its own books.

Expenditure is allowable if it is incurred in connection with conveying, treating and initial storage of petroleum falling to be valued for royalty purposes, insofar as it is incurred, or relates to assets situated, between the well-head and the point at which the petroleum is valued. That point is the place at which the oil is treated as being delivered for the purposes of determining the value taken into account for PRT purposes or, in the case of exempt gas, CT purposes.

The definition of initial treatment reflects almost exactly the definition used for PRT purposes (see 6.15.6). It covers, broadly, the cost of stabilisation and fractionation but excludes deballasting and activities associated with refining. The definition of initial storage also mirrors the PRT provision (see 6.15.6). For royalty purposes, however, the ten days' capacity limitation may be lifted if the excess over that amount is essential for continuous production from the field.

The cost of transporting oil from an offshore field to the UK is normally allowable. If the oil is exported by tanker from an offshore field without first having been landed in the UK, the transport costs are allowed if the delivery port is within a permitted distance (broadly, north west Europe and Scandinavia); if the port is not within that area, the allowance is limited to the notional costs of transport to the nearest reasonable UK port.

If the total of conveying and treating costs exceeds the value of production in a chargeable period, the excess is carried forward for relief in later periods.

Depreciation allowance for assets

Expenditure on assets used for conveying or treating purposes qualifies for depreciation allowance. The qualifying cost is the net capitalised cost falling on the company, after deduction of government grants, including attributions of overheads provided that they are also capitalised. The qualifying cost is allowed by straight-line write-off over eight years, or over the life of the field if shorter. Assets which are provided by a licensee solely for use by other fields in different ownership in consideration for tariffs do not qualify. Tariffs derived from such assets do not reduce the licensee's qualifying conveying and treating costs. The costs relating to qualifying assets which are shared by fields in the same ownership are apportioned between the fields on the basis of throughput of oil.

If an asset on which allowance has been given is disposed of or written off, the profit or loss determined by reference to the royalty written down value of the asset is deducted from or added to, as appropriate, the total allowance for conveying and treating costs. Transfer of an asset from one field to another in the same ownership takes place at written down value.

Interest on capital employed
For the chargeable period in which the conveying of oil commences and for each subsequent period, an allowance is made for interest on capital. The rate of interest is an average of the six month sterling London Interbank Offered Rates (LIBOR) for the period. The capital base is the average of the written down values at the beginning and end of the period of the fixed assets employed in conveying and treating, whether or not the assets are in use at the beginning and end of the period. For periods ending after 31 December 1982, working capital is not included in this calculation. There is no allowance for actual interest payments.

Pre-conveying costs
Costs incurred to the period in which conveying commences which can be demonstrated to relate to conveying and treating are allowable. Those costs also attract an allowance for interest on capital employed for each relevant pre-conveying period, and the aggregate pre-conveying allowances are carried forward for relief in the period in which conveying begins.

The provisions applying to periods up to 31 December 1982 were more restrictive, defining the categories of cost which qualified and requiring that those costs should be capitalised in the books of the licensee.

Insurance
Allowance is given for reasonable insurance premiums relating to conveying and treating risks. Insurance recoveries are set against allowable costs to the extent that the relative premiums are allowed. If loss or damage is not insured, the royalty written down value of the asset or the cost of repairs as appropriate is allowed.

The provisions relating to periods up to 31 December 1982 were considerably more complex and provided an option to claim the notional cost of providing insurance where risks were not insured.

Licensees' own costs
The bulk of expenditure on conveying and treating is incurred by the

5.5.3 UK Oil Taxation

operator on behalf of the licensees, and amounts allowable are notified by the operator for inclusion in SOVs. Costs which a licensee meets directly, rather than through the joint venture account, which relate to provision or insurance of physical assets used for conveying and treating may also be claimed by the licensee on its own account.

This facility does not extend to indirect costs, including head office or other overhead and currency exchange differences arising on translation of joint venture costs. Instead, for each chargeable period licensees may claim an allowance of the greater of £50,000 or 3% of their share of eligible joint direct or indirect costs excluding depreciation and interest, subject to a maximum of £250,000 in the case of operators.

Abandonment costs

Expenditure on abandoning assets which have been used for conveying and treating purposes is allowable 'but only if, and to the extent that, the expenditure is incurred in complying with a statutory requirement, the terms of a petroleum licence or a term of, or a condition attached to, any government approval, authorisation, consent or permission' (Series 2 Mode). Because much of the abandonment cost will be incurred after production from the licenced area has ceased, effective relief will be obtained only by carrying back allowance to earlier periods of liability. The Secretary of State has power to provide for inclusion in the conveying and treating allowance costs incurred in relation to assets which are no longer in use and costs incurred after the end of the chargeable period for which the SOV is made. The precise mechanics of relief for abandonment costs remains to be settled, but it is envisaged that allowable costs, after setting off tariffs and other receipts in the period between cessation of production and abandonment, will be taken into account in a recalculation of the liability for the final period of production, and that any resulting excess of costs will be carried back to earlier periods. This does not mean that relief can be anticipated before the abandonment expenditure is actually met. Royalty paid which proves to be in excess of the revised liability is repayable. Parallel provisions will enable costs to be carried back in calculating amounts payable by the Secretary of State in respect of conveying and treating costs relating to oil which he has taken as royalty in kind (Model Clauses as amended by PA 1987).

Apportionment of costs

Much of the plant and structure related to an oil field is not specifically dedicated either to a conveying or treating function or to a production or other function. Rules are provided for apportioning costs which are common to both conveying and treating and to other functions: the eligible percentages (Series 2) are summarised as follows:

Royalties 5.5.3

Cost category	Capital Costs Eligibility	Operating Costs Eligibility
Offshore production platform Floor area used for C&T functions –		
More than 92½%	100%	100%
Between 7½% and 92½%	70%	60%
Less than 7½%	0%	0%
Pipelines, offshore loading systems and remote flares Used for conveying petroleum to point of valuation or flaring petroleum with no value	100%	100%
Otherwise	Same eligibility as operating costs of using facility.	
Crude oil terminal	95%	95%
Gas terminal	100%	100%
Vessels	According to utilisation	
Sub-sea completions Production of petroleum	60%	In accordance with eligibility of operating costs of platform to which petroleum flows
Water or gas injection	0%	

Receipts in respect of conveying and treating assets
Sums receivable from third parties for the use of conveying and treating assets are to be deducted from conveying and treating allowances. Such sums may include tariff receipts in respect of the sharing of the field pipeline system by licensees in other fields and receipts from ship owners or charterers for use of tanker berths and loading facilities. Income which derives from assets which are dedicated to tariffing, the costs of which do not qualify for relief, is left out of account.

5.5.4   UK Oil Taxation

5.5.4 Prior Years Adjustments

Details of adjustments to the values or costs relating to earlier chargeable periods, other than normal accounting corrections of estimates such as accruals, are to be reported on the SOV, and the independent accountant is required to comment on them. The effect on the royalty liability is calculated separately for each period to which the adjustments relate, and the aggregate increase or decrease in liability is then added to or deducted from the amount of royalty to be remitted for the period for which the SOV is being submitted.

5.5.5 Report of Independent Accountant

Each SOV has to be accompanied by a report by an independent accountant who is qualified under the terms of the Companies Acts to act as auditor of the licensee company. Most such reports are in fact made by the person or firm then acting as the company's auditor. The required format is set out in Section two of the Mode and Notes (Series 2). The accountant is asked to confirm that, subject to any reservations he may have, the quantities and values of production and the amounts of conveying and treating costs claimed in his opinion fairly represent the quantities values and amounts relative to the chargeable period, and accord with the terms of the licence and Notes, and that the royalty payable is correctly calculated. All of this requires of the accountant detailed knowledge of the company's relevant transactions.

The DOE relies on the report for confirmation that receipts and costs reflected in the SOV derive from the accounts of the licensee, and that the accounts are prepared in accordance with standard accounting practice; that relevant transactions can fairly be described as being on arm's length terms; and that proper allocations of costs have been made where appropriate. The accountant is also asked to comment on the treatment of particular items which are not dealt with specifically in the Mode.

Chapter 6
Petroleum Revenue Tax

6.1 The Nature of PRT

PRT is essentially a tax on production, though its scope was substantially enlarged in 1983 to encompass tariff and other receipts derived from oil field assets. It has its own unique rules. The PRT profit or loss is not based on the accounting profit or loss and bears no direct relationship to the profit or loss for CT purposes. Instead, it emerges as the difference between two sums representing, broadly, income and expenditure, each of which is arrived at by precisely defined steps. The measurement of production income is taken at the point at which, in general terms, the production is sold or appropriated to refining. Expenditure is allowable only if it is incurred for certain specified purposes. No distinction is made between revenue and capital expenditure, but expenditure incurred on long term assets is subject to particular rules. One of the distinguishing features of PRT is front-end relief for expenditure, that is, full allowance for expenditure by reference to the period in which it is incurred. Some categories of expenditure do not qualify for PRT relief: most significantly, no relief is available for interest payments, but instead a supplement, now 35%, is given on certain qualifying expenditure, chiefly development capital outlays. The impact of PRT is intended to be discriminatory applying less harshly to less profitable fields. Two reliefs in particular were designed to achieve this:
(1) An oil allowance exempts from charge an amount of production from each field. For those fields for which development consent was given before 1 April 1982, the allowance per chargeable period is 250,000 tonnes, subject to an overall limit of 5 million tonnes; for later offshore fields outside the southern basin of the North Sea, the allowance is 500,000 tonnes and the overall limit 10 million tonnes; and for later fields in the southern basin or onshore, the allowance is 125,000 tonnes and the overall limit 2.5 million tonnes.
(2) The amount of tax payable is limited for a number of periods by a relief known as safeguard.

Safeguard was conceived as a mechanism which would provide that no PRT was payable until a minimum return on capital invested in a field was achieved and that a marginal relief would apply thereafter.

6.1 UK Oil Taxation

The expectation was that it would benefit fields of low profitability in the later years of field life. The character of safeguard has been substantially altered by subsequent developments: it now gives a very significant measure of relief, but that relief falls in the early years of field PRT liability after which, following changes made in 1981, it ceases to be available.

PRT is charged by reference to oil fields as they are determined by the Secretary of State for Energy. It is field-based, that is, the profit from each field is charged in isolation from any profit or loss arising in relation to other areas. There are important exceptions to this rule. Any balance of loss remaining unrelieved at the end of the life of a field may be utilised against profits from other fields; expenditure incurred on exploration or appraisal in any UK offshore area and expenditure on research may be relieved against field profits; and a cross-field allowance permits a percentage of certain pre-payback expenditure incurred in one field to be relieved in another.

The charge to PRT encompasses both oil and natural gas. Gas sold to the British Gas Corporation (now called British Gas) under a contract made before July 1975, however, is exempt, and expenditure relating to production of such gas is not normally allowable. Although at the time of the passing of the 1975 Oil Taxation Act virtually all relevant UK production was of gas, the first offshore oil field not commencing production until June 1975, the Act was unclear in its application to gas fractions (methane, ethane, propane, butane and condensates). The doubts were resolved by amendments in 1980 which required each fraction or stream to be considered separately.

In computing profit or loss for PRT purposes, a deduction is allowed for royalties payable. PRT paid is itself allowed as a deduction in arriving at CT profit or loss.

6.2 What is Chargeable

PRT is charged

> in respect of profits from oil won under the authority of a licence granted under the Petroleum (Production) Act 1934 or the Petroleum (Production) Act (Northern Ireland) 1964: and in this Part of this Act 'oil' means any substance so won or capable of being so won other than methane gas won in the course of operations for making and keeping mines safe (s1).

The oil may be produced from licensed areas onshore in the UK, in the UK territorial sea or in designated areas of the UKCS. It may also come from a field through which runs the transmedian line dividing the Continental Shelf between the UK sector and a foreign sector: the chargeable oil is deemed to be the participator's share won from the field as a whole (FA 1980 s107). Oil includes natural gas, and references to oil in this chapter, as elsewhere in the book, include gas unless the context requires otherwise. The definition is wide enough to include water and other elements having no value; their inclusion can depress the value of the oil allowance (see 6.28).

Certain categories of oil are excluded from the PRT charge (see 6.8). In addition, oil products such as naphtha and ethylene are implicitly outside its scope, since PRT is charged on disposals, appropriations or stocks of oil either crude or having undergone only 'initial treatment'. Oil recovered in the course of deballasting of tankers is not charged.

Apart from production of oil, the charge under the 1975 Act effectively included certain receipts from hire of field assets (Sched 4 para 5). In 1983, it was fundamentally extended to encompass tariffs and other receipts for use or disposal of field assets, including receipts accruing to participators in overseas oil fields for use of assets in the UK or the UKCS (see 6.10-6.11).

6.3 Who is Chargeable

PRT is charged on a participator in an oil field. A participator to all intents and purposes is a person who is, or was at some earlier relevant time, a licensee as that term is defined (s 12). A licensee for this purpose is

    (*a*) a person entitled to the benefit of a licence or, where two or more persons are entitled to the benefit of a licence, to a share of the benefit; and

    (*b*) a person who has rights under an agreement approved by the Board of Inland Revenue and is certified by the Secretary of State to confer on that person rights which are the same as, or similar to, those conferred by a licence.

Questions may arise as to the meaning of 'the benefit of a licence'. In the normal course, a licensee for PRT purposes is a person who holds a legal interest in a licence which confers directly on him the rights and obligations, or a share of those rights and obligations, under the licence. Arguably, less direct interests in oil won from a field established by a variety of royalty and other arrangements entitle the holder to the benefit of a licence. This proposition, however, seems to be denied when the whole of the definition of licensee is read as a unity.

6.3 UK Oil Taxation

Since the arrangements contemplated by part (*b*) of the definition are only those which 'confer on that person rights which are the same as, or similar to, those conferred by a licence', it is reasonable to assume that part (*a*) contemplates only direct legal interests in a licence. Part (*b*) of the definition may encompass a sub-licensee under arrangements having the necessary approval which achieve a full pass-through of rights or obligations under the licence.

A holder of an indirect interest is not normally chargeable. If such a person, who is not himself a participator, is entitled to a proportion of a participator's share of oil won and saved (as distinct from a specific quantity of oil comprised in that share), the participator and not the owner of the oil is chargeable in respect of that oil. This may apply, for example, in the case of an oil royalty interest held by a financial institution. However, if the person in question were to own a specific quantity of oil rather than a proportionate part, the position would be less clear. The participator from whose share the interest is carved out seems not to be chargeable in respect of that part, since he does not own it or does not deliver it. In these circumstances, the owner may be chargeable as a person having rights under an agreement approved by the Secretary of State which are similar to rights conferred by a licence (Sched 3(6)). Payments of royalty or similar interests out of oil owned by a participator may be disallowed in calculating the participator's liability (see 6.15.5).

Participation rights granted to BNOC entitled it to acquire up to 51% of oil won under certain licences. Where the rights were exercised, the licensee which ceded part of its share to BNOC, remaining responsible for all of the licence obligations relating to it, continued to be chargeable on the full share. The participation rights were transferred to OPA on the demise of BNOC (Sched 3(6A)). BNOC was exempted from PRT when it was established in 1975. The exemption was withdrawn with effect from 1 July 1979 (F(No 2A) 1979 s22).

Under an arrangement usually known as an Illustrative Agreement, requiring the approval of the Secretary of State, a company may agree with an associated licensee company to undertake and to finance the licence obligations in return for the benefit of the licensee company's share of any oil won under the licence (see 8.11). The company acquiring that benefit does not thereby become a licensee for PRT purposes. It is, however, treated as a participator, chargeable on its share of oil accruing under the agreement and entitled to appropriate reliefs and allowances (Sched 3(5)).

The Oil Taxation Act 1983 for the first time brought within the scope of PRT persons who are not participators in UK oil fields. The charge now extends to a 'participator' in a 'foreign field', that is, a person who is a licensee or has rights, interests or obligations of a licensee in an area outside UK jurisdiction which is specified by the Secretary of State for the purposes of the Act as a foreign field. Such a participator may be chargeable on receipts derived from assets of his field which are situated in the UK or the UKCS and are used in connection with UK activities (see 6.11).

The Oil Taxation Act 1983 also imposes a charge in respect of certain consideration receivable by persons who are not themselves participators but who are connected with or associated with a participator. In those cases, however, the charge is on the actual participator, to whom the consideration is attributed (OTA 1983 Sched 2).

All participators presently liable to PRT are thought to be companies. The legislation does not preclude the possibility that a licensee for these purposes may be either an individual or a partnership, but the obtaining of the Secretary of State's consent and other constraints are inhibiting factors. If an English partnership were to obtain a licence interest, it is likely that the partners rather than the partnership would be regarded for PRT purposes as the licensees and therefore participators, since such a partnership is not a legal entity in English law.

6.4 Determination of a Field

Each participator is charged separately in respect of its interest in an oil field. If it has an interest in more than one field, a separate charge is raised in respect of each of those fields.

An oil field is a licensed area which the Secretary of State for Energy, or the Department of Commerce for Northern Ireland if appropriate, 'may determine to be an oil field'. A notice of proposed determination allows 60 days for representation by affected licensees, after which the determination is confirmed or modified as appropriate. Determinations are made on the basis of geological criteria, so that the field boundaries, which are normally drawn by reference to degrees and seconds of longitude and latitude, should follow as nearly as possible the best assessment of the outline of the oil-bearing structure or structures representing the oil field (Sched 1).

It has sometimes happened that production of oil has commenced from an area before it has been determined as a field. In these circumstances, if a determination is subsequently made there is deemed to have been a determination of the field immediately before the winning of oil began, so that in particular the income derived from production prior to actual determination of the field does not escape the

6.4 UK Oil Taxation

PRT net. This provision may also apply where a production test prior to determination of a field gives rise to income (FA 1982 s135 (1)).

A field may be redetermined in the light of improved knowledge to include an area previously outside the boundary. Oil won from that area, whether before or after the redetermination, is oil won from the field and chargeable to PRT accordingly. A variation of a determination might take other forms, to exclude an area presently within the field or to hive off an area which becomes part of another field or a new field in its own right. These would raise questions which the legislation does not adequately answer (FA 1982 s135 (2)).

Expenditure which would otherwise qualify for relief as field expenditure is not precluded simply because it is incurred before the determination of the field which includes the area to which the expenditure relates. The expenditure is treated as incurred in connection with the area of the field as subsequently determined (s12(3)): and under the general expenditure rules, the first claim period includes an unlimited time prior to actual determination of the field.

The manner in which fields are determined can have a very material effect on PRT liability. An oil allowance attaches to each field, exempting from charge production of 5 million tonnes or, in the case of certain fields receiving development consent after 31 March 1982, 10 million tonnes and of other such fields in the Southern Basin and onshore, 2 million tonnes. Because of the oil allowance, determination of an area as a separate field rather than as part of a larger field will usually benefit the licensees. There may on the other hand be cases in which separate field status would not be beneficial, particularly where the cost of phased or satellite developments within one field can be fully offset and matched against income from the field. The timing of a determination is also important. Once an area is determined as part of a field, expenditure incurred in relation to that area can no longer qualify for exploration and appraisal relief or research relief. On the other hand, cross-field allowance does not begin to run until the area in relation to which the expenditure is incurred is determined as a field. These considerations explain the concern of licensees that determination policy should permit some practical flexibility. The complexities of petroleum geology provide a good deal of scope for differing interpretations. For example, two oil-bearing structures which overlap may require determination as two separate fields if those structures are indeed unconnected.

There is no necessity that the production systems of a field should be self-contained and self-sufficient. A number of fields are developed by the use of facilities such as subsea wells and manifolds tied into the transportation and treatment systems of neighbouring fields.

6.5 Chargeable Periods

PRT is charged by reference to chargeable periods of six months duration ending 30 June and 31 December. The first chargeable period for a field, however, is the period ending with the end of the 'critical half year' and including an unlimited time prior to the beginning of that half year. The critical half year is the half year ending 30 June or 31 December at the end of which the total of oil ever won and saved from the field exceeds 1,000 tonnes, taking 1,100 cubic metres of gas at 15° centigrade and pressure of one atmosphere as equivalent to one tonne.

The first chargeable period for a field, established by reference to the total of oil ever won and saved from the field by all parties having an interest in it, is the first chargeable period for all of the participators, whether or not they happen to have chargeable income in that period. The point is of some consequence, because the duration of the term for which safeguard may apply is governed by the number of chargeable periods from the first to that period which is the participator's net profit period (see 6.30).

Chargeable periods succeed each other without break. The permanent cessation of the winning of oil from the field does not end the sequence. Participators may be liable in respect of tariff or disposal receipts falling into chargeable periods after production of oil from the field has ceased. However, expiry, revocation or termination of the production licence for the field area would seem to bring the field to an end.

In determining whether production from the field has reached 1,000 tonnes, all oil 'won and saved' from the field is to be taken into account. Although offshore oil in transit to the place of first landing in the UK is excluded from the PRT charge, it is nevertheless oil won and saved. Similarly, oil appropriated and used for field production purposes is specifically excluded from the charge, but is part of the total of oil won and saved. On the other hand, oil or gas which is flared at an offshore field probably cannot be said to be oil which is saved.

6.6 The PRT Computation

In simple terms, the PRT profit or loss for a chargeable period is the difference between two sums, the positive amounts (income) and the negative amounts (expenditure). From any resulting profit is deducted allowable losses and the participator's share of oil allowance; and any remaining profit is charged at the PRT rate of 75% but subject to limitation under the safeguard rules. An example of a computation is given at 6.6.1.

6.6.1 UK Oil Taxation

6.6.1 Chargeable period 1 July 1987 – 31 December 1987

Paragraph References		£m +	£m –
6.7	Gross profit	100	
6.12	Chargeable sums	2	
6.10.3	Tariff receipts (net of tariff receipts allowance)	8	
6.10.6	Disposal receipts	1	
6.20	Excess allowances	1	
6.13	Licence debit (cash royalties)		2
	Expenditure debit –		
6.24	Provisional allowance	Nil	
6.32	Expenditure and supplement (claims by responsible person)	25	
6.33	Expenditure and supplement (claims by participator)	3	
6.20	Exploration and appraisal expenditure	4	
6.22	Research expenditure	2	
6.23	Cross-field allowance	1	
		35	
6.24.1	Less: reversal of provisional allowance	Nil	35
		112	37
	Assessable profit	75	
6.29	Less: Loss brought forward	10	
		65	
6.28	Less: Oil allowance	15	
	Chargeable at 75%	50	
	Tax	37.5	

6.7 Production Income

The measure of income from production of oil which is taken into account in the PRT computation is, in general terms, selling price in the case of sales at arm's length; market value in the case of sales not at arm's length and appropriations; and one-half of market value in the case of stocks. However, following the introduction of the nomination scheme in 1987, the profit may be increased by the 'excess of the nominated proceeds': that excess may itself be increased by Treasury order.

The gross profit is the aggregate of:
(*a*) the selling price of oil won from the field which:
    (1) was disposed of crude by the participator in sales at arm's length; and
    (2) was delivered by him in the chargeable period;
(*b*) the market value of oil so won which:
    (1) was disposed of by the participator in sales not at arm's length; and
    (2) was delivered by him in the chargeable period;
(*c*) the aggregate market value of oil appropriated by the participator in the period (to refining or to other use apart from field production purposes) without being disposed of;
(*d*) half of the market value of stock which was either:
    (1) not disposed of and not relevantly appropriated; or
    (2) disposed of but not delivered.
(*e*) the excess of the nominated proceeds.
    From the sum of these five amounts is deducted:
(*f*) half of the market value of opening stock, that is, the figure under (*d*) which was taken into account for the previous chargeable period (s 2(4) and (5)).

6.7.1 Sales at Arm's Length

A sale of oil is a sale at arm's length only if it satisfies three conditions:
    (*a*) the contract price is the sole consideration for the sale;
    (*b*) the terms of the sale are not affected by any commercial relationship (other than that created by the contract itself) between the seller or any person connected with the seller and the buyer or any person connected with the buyer;
    (*c*) neither the seller nor any person connected with him has, directly or indirectly, any interest in the subsequent resale or disposal of the oil or any product derived therefrom (Sched 3(1)).

For this purpose, two companies are connected if, broadly, both are under common control or one controls the other either alone or with others.

6.7.1 UK Oil Taxation

The underlying theme is that if the price receivable for oil is to be accepted as an arm's length price, it must be such as would have been agreed by a seller and a buyer unconnected with each other in a contract standing alone. Curiously, a sale between connected persons is not explicitly excluded from sales at arm's length, though it is clear that such a sale is unlikely to satisfy condition (*b*), even if it were to pass the remainder of the test. On the other hand, a sale which is made at market value is not *ipso facto* a sale at arm's length. In practice, the fixing of a price at what appears to be market value may be taken as one of the indicia of an arm's length sale, while the fixing of a price at what appears not to be market value may suggest that the sale is not at arm's length; but in the final analysis the sale stands or falls as an arm's length sale solely by reference to the three conditions.

In regard to condition (*a*), the consideration given by the buyer has to begin and end in the contract price. It is the specific sale in question, of a cargo or other quantity which is disposed of and delivered, which has to be looked at, but the relative contract may extend well beyond that sale. Nevertheless, this does not of itself mean that the consideration for the sale is not encompassed wholly within the contract price. On the face of it, it should be fairly obvious whether a sale does fail to meet this condition. But relationships between large integrated oil groups are often complex and the less obvious reciprocal arrangement, in which part of the consideration for the sale could be said to lie, is no doubt also intended to be caught by this provision.

Condition (*b*) has a potentially wider impact. It appears to mean that whatever may be the consideration for the sale, and while to all appearances it may be at market value, the sale cannot be a sale at arm's length if any other arrangement or relationship between the parties affects the terms of the sale. This is not to suggest that any such arrangement or relationship must of necessity affect the sale, but it is clear that the contract for sale must be quite untainted by relationships between the parties beyond the bounds of the contract. Commonly, arrangements are entered into in association with agreement of a contract for sale of oil which provide for the seller to take delivery of a quantity or value of oil from the buyer or from an associate of the buyer; this may be a direct swap transaction or the matching of the transactions may be more complex and indirect. In either case, the reciprocal acquisition will be seen as affecting the terms of the sale in question. On the other hand, it is quite possible for two companies which have substantial and continuing trading relationships to conclude a contract for sale of oil which is not affected by those relationships. A participator may sell his share of oil won from the field to another participator in the same field in a contract which will be accepted as a sale at arm's length; the fact that the parties are co-participators does not of itself preclude their contracting at arm's length. Similarly, disposal of oil to BNOC or to OPA in pursuance of participation arrangements would normally be accepted as inherently capable of satisfying the arm's length test.

Although oil is not commonly sold for delivery at offshore installations, it is possible to conclude such a sale on terms which satisfy the arm's length test. Similarly, a genuine reduction in a price otherwise to be agreed to take account of handling or other costs to be borne by the purchaser does not normally prejudice the arm's length nature of the sale.

The third condition (c) needs to be applied at the time of sale of the oil in question, even though it makes reference to subsequent events. It may be that the seller or an associate will in the ordinary course of business purchase from the buyer of the oil products refined from the oil, but unless that purchase was contracted for or in contemplation when the oil was sold, it does not seem that the seller of the oil at that time had any interest in re-sale or disposal of products. It is understood that the OTO does not take the view that the fixing of the contract price with some reference to the price to be realised by the buyer in disposals of the oil by him necessarily amounts for this purpose to the seller having an interest in subsequent re-sale or disposal. More clearly, indexation of a price by reference to external data such as Brent published price is a common feature in arm's length sales.

For the purposes of determining whether or not a sale is an arm's length sale or what is the market value of oil, the Board of Inland Revenue has power to require the participator to provide details of any related transaction, to which either the participator or an associated company was a party. The Board may also require any UK resident company which is either the 51% parent or a 51% subsidiary of the participator, or which is with the participator a 51% subsidiary of a third company, to provide any books, accounts, documents or records which relate to transactions relevant to such determination. This power may extend to requiring those companies to give details of transactions by any of their 51% subsidiaries. If the subsidiary in question is not resident in the UK, the company on which the notice is served may apply to have the notice cancelled: if the application is refused, an appeal may be made to the Special Commissioners (FA 1984 s115).

6.7.2 Market Value

The determination of the market value of oil plays a very important part in the calculation of PRT liability. The market value rules apply to oil sold not at arm's length, to oil which is appropriated by the producer

6.7.2 UK Oil Taxation

for refining or other purposes apart from field production, and to stocks in hand at the beginning and end of the chargeable period. The nomination scheme now imports market value in some circumstances into the measurement of income from oil sold at arm's length. In general terms, oil which is charged to PRT at market value also takes that value as income of the CT ring fence trade and as the measure of the consideration provided by the purchaser in the calculation of his CT liability or, in the case of an appropriation, as the price of a deemed purchase outside the ring fence.

As a result largely of much changed market practices, including the disappearance of BNOC and the BNOC 'reference price', and uncertainties in the existing legislation, the Government introduced tighter valuation rules in 1987. They retain the concept of establishing a monthly value by reference to a notional arm's length contract. But the evidential base from which comparable arm's length prices are derived is more clearly defined, as is the timeframe of the deals to be taken into account. They reflect the preponderant influence which spot trading had assumed in the markets, in contrast to the much greater volume of term sales which were common before 1985. The Revenue had already moved to a more spot oriented valuation practice, announcing in June 1985 that in applying the existing rules it would normally have regard only to deals made in the thirty days preceding the mid point of the delivery month. The new rules came into effect from 1 January 1987.

Notional contract

The market value of oil in a month is the price at which 'oil of that kind' might reasonably have been expected to be sold under a notional contract which satisfies the following conditions. In practice, oil of that kind means oil from a particular field or a blended oil such as Brent crude.

(*a*) The contract is for the sale of the oil at arm's length to a willing buyer;
(*b*) It is for the delivery of the oil in the relevant month;
(*c*) It is made within the period beginning on the first day of the month preceding the month of delivery and ending on the middle day of the delivery month: if that month has an even number of days, the middle day is taken as the last day of the first half of the month. The Treasury is empowered to alter the '45 day' period by statutory instrument;
(*d*) It requires the oil to have been subjected to appropriate initial treatment before delivery. What initial treatment is 'appropriate' is not defined but it is probably that which would be necessary to bring the oil to the condition in which in normal commercial practice it would be delivered to a willing buyer at the notional delivery point.

If initial treatment has actually been carried out before the oil is disposed of or relevantly appropriated, appropriate initial treatment includes the whole of that actual treatment;
(*e*) It requires the oil to be delivered:
 (1) in the case of onshore oil, at the place of extraction, or
 (2) in the case of offshore oil, at the place in the UK at which the seller could reasonably be expected to deliver it or, if there is more than one such place, the place nearest to the place of extraction;
(*f*) In the case of stock and certain non arm's length sales and appropriations, the contract is for the sale of the whole quantity of the oil falling to be valued and for no other oil.

The rules provide that 'for the avoidance of doubt' the payment terms to be implied in the contract are to be those which are customarily contained in contracts for sales at arm's length of the kind of oil in question. This is generally taken to mean that the notional contract should incorporate payment terms of 30 days in accordance with the credit period which is commonly found in contracts for sale of North Sea crude. (Sched 3(2)).

Average price for the month
Having set out the terms of the notional arm's length contract, the rules then prescribe the standards for fixing a monthly average arm's length price. Under the main rule, the price is determined by reference to what may be termed the primary evidential base: it is the average of prices achieved under actual contracts for sale of oil of that kind which fulfil these conditions:
(*a*) The sale is by a participator or by a company associated with a participator. For this purpose, two companies are associated if one is under the control of the other or both are under the control of another person or persons;
(*b*) The contract satisfies the conditions prescribed for the notional contract. For this purpose, a 'price formula' contract satisfies the timing test if the price of the oil to be delivered in the month either is determined or subject to review in the '45 day' period relevant to that month, or is determined by reference to other prices which are themselves determined in that period, being prices for oil to be delivered in the month;
(*c*) The terms of payment contain no features not customarily found in contracts for the sale of oil of the kind in question.

The average of the prices is calculated by first determining for each business day in the '45 day' period, or for such other period as may be substituted by Treasury order, an average price for 'oil of that kind', and then taking the arithmetic mean of the daily average prices. The

6.7.2 UK Oil Taxation

monthly average price is not weighted for volume. (Sched 3 (2A)).

The secondary rule provides for valuation by reference to an extended evidential base incorporating deals in other kinds of oil, or by reference to other factors which appear to the Revenue to be appropriate. This standard applies if the Revenue is satisfied that it is impracticable or inappropriate to determine an average monthly price by reference to the primary evidential base alone, whether because of insufficient numbers of deals, the nature of the market for the oil in question or for any other reason. Then, so far as it is practicable and appropriate, the price is to be determined by reference to other contracts in the kind of oil in question or in other oil, whether or not the participator is a party to those transactions, again finding a daily average price from which the monthly average price is derived. Otherwise, the price may be determined 'in such other manner as appears to the Board to be appropriate in the circumstances' (Sched 3(2D)).

Practical application
The application of the valuation rules may vary from field to field. It is likely that only in the case of Brent blend will there be a sufficient number of deals on each day in a month to enable values to be ascertained by reference to the primary evidential base; and even in that case, an insufficiency of daily evidence may render sole reliance on the primary base impracticable for some periods. Brent prices are, nevertheless, derived substantially from Brent deals by participators, although in some instances adjustments may be made to those contract prices, for example, to convert *cif* terms to notional *fob* terms. Prices for days for which inadequate Brent data are available are derived from a combination of Brent price trends and data available to the OTO relating to other deals. The daily price is an average, weighted for volume, of the data prices for the day. The approach to valuation of crudes other than Brent is similar, but the influence of external prices is relatively more important. For those business days for which an average price is not obtained from deals in the oil in question, prices are normally taken as the Brent price for the day adjusted by a differential.

The OTO's approach to the valuation of propane and butane (LPG) is different. It considers reliance on the primary evidential base to be inappropriate: one reason for this is that LPG is normally sold under term contracts at a price prevailing at the time of delivery, so that deliveries in the second half of the month fall outside the valuation reference period which ends on the midday of the month. Instead, the OTO's intention, in relation to 1987 and so long as market conditions remain substantially the same, is to derive values from prices for deliveries under term contracts in the valuation month, adjusted as necessary to *fob* prices. Normally, only so-called Tier I sales will be

Petroleum Revenue Tax 6.7.3

included, excluding those in which the purchaser provides specialised storage, transportation or other services.

The valuation rules afford considerable discretion to the Revenue not only in deciding which of the two valuation standards should be applied but also in determining the scope of the extended evidential base and ultimately in setting a standard of its choosing. The Revenue has indicated that it does not regard participators' rights of appeal to be restricted or prejudiced, and that in its view the Special Commissioners would have both a right and a duty in considering an appeal against an assessment to review the basis of valuation relied on by the Revenue.

Information
The evidential base is built up from information supplied by participators and from other sources. In addition to the details of sales and appropriations which are called for in the PRT return for each chargeable period, a participator is required also to make a supplementary return of other arm's length sales for delivery in the period. The relevant sales are those to which either the participator or a company associated with the participator which is resident in the UK is a party either as seller, buyer or otherwise, excluding sales not exceeding 500 tonnes of oil and sales of gas of which the largest component is methane or ethane or a combination of the two. Two companies are associated for this purpose if one controls the other or both are under common control. Penalties are prescribed for failure to make the return, not exceeding £500 plus a further £100 per day for continued failure; and for incorrect returns, not exceeding £2,500 in the case of negligence and £5,000 in case of fraud (FA 1987 s62).

This further return does not extend to transactions by associated companies not resident in the UK. It is likely that the Revenue will wish in some instances to have knowledge of such transactions, particularly if the primary evidential base is relied on with its apparently mandatory inclusion of all relevant transactions by associated companies whether resident in the UK or not. The Revenue has powers to seek the provision of this information, subject to rights of appeal (see 6.7.1). Some companies agree to supply details of relevant transactions by their overseas associated companies on an informal basis.

6.7.3 The Nomination Scheme

The background
The broad concept of the PRT base is that oil is charged by reference to an arm's length price. The need to determine market values of sales not at arm's length and appropriations means not only that the establish-

6.7.3 UK Oil Taxation

ment of the base is much less rigid and precise than would be the case under a norm price regime, but also that there is at least the possibility that the measure of income in respect of oil sold at arm's length will not be the same as it would be if the same oil were sold not at arm's length or appropriated. The decision by an integrated company, for example, to utilise a cargo of its UK crude for refining purposes rather than sell it at arm's length might have a material effect on the amount chargeable to PRT. This endemic disparity was an accepted feature of the system for some years. However, the developments in market practices from 1985 onwards, particularly the rapid growth of the Brent forward market, caused increasing concern that the tax rules were being manipulated at a substantial cost to the Exchequer. A producer was able, by 'spinning' his equity crude in the market or entering into multiple contracts for sale of that and other crude, to attribute to the equity crude the lowest of the prices under those contracts so fixing the PRT base at that price.

The Government announced its intention in November 1986 to take counter measures. The proposed legislation was to apply in the first instance only to those participators whose equity production comprised or included Brent blend crude. For any month in which the weighted average price of the participators' arm's length sales was lower than the monthly market value emerging from the operation of revised valuation rules, the PRT base for those sales was to be market value and not the price receivable. Alternatively, the participator would be able to elect in some circumstances to be taxed on the average of the prices realised in sales of both equity and other crude.

In the consultation process which followed, the proposals were strongly opposed by sectors of the industry, particularly by those Brent blend producers who were directly affected by them. They were critical both of the inherent discrimination between taxpayers and the departure from the principle of charging arm's length sales by reference to the sales price. In the result, the proposals were withdrawn and replaced by the nomination scheme, published on 9 February 1987 and brought into effect from 1 March 1987. The main framework of the scheme is contained in the two 1987 Finance Acts; but many of the details of the scheme are set out in Inland Revenue regulations which were promulgated in July 1987. The legislation also empowers the Treasury to make regulations affecting important elements of the scheme, particularly in relation to scope and the triggering of surcharge provisions.

The aim of the scheme is to prevent the depression of values of oil production by eliminating or severely restricting the scope for ascribing to arm's length disposals the lowest of the prices under a number of contracts, and the scope for switching between arm's length disposals and non arm's length disposals or appropriations to achieve the lower of market value and selling price as the tax base. The contract for sale of equity crude at arm's length is to be identified, or nominated, well in advance of the date of delivery. Arm's length sales of equity crude which are not covered by nominations may be charged effectively at the higher of market value and actual selling price. Reserve powers are taken to discourage the late switching of equity crude from contracts for sales at arm's length to non arm's length disposals or appropriations, and deliberate failure to proceed with intended refinery movements: in these circumstances, a form of surcharge may be imposed by Treasury order.

The scope of the scheme
The scheme applies to crude oil. It specifically excludes:
(1) 'Oil which is gaseous at a temperature of 15 degrees centigrade and pressure of one atmosphere': this effectively exempts methane, ethane, propane and butane, but not condensates;
(2) 'Oil of a kind which is normally disposed of crude by deliveries in quantities of 25,000 metric tonnes or less': this is a reference to the kind or characteristics of the oil, rather than the circumstances of the participator in question. It is not intended to exempt small participators simply on the grounds that they normally lift oil in quantities below the prescribed limit, but it does have the effect, for example, of excluding oil from most onshore fields and certain categories of condensate which is customarily disposed of in small quantities.

The Revenue has power to add to the exclusions by regulations (FA1987 s61(2) and (8)).

Oil taken by the Secretary of State as royalty in kind, including amounts taken inadvertently in excess of his entitlement, is excluded from the equity production which requires to be reconciled with nominations. So also is oil in stock, that is, oil which has not been delivered or appropriated in the month.

Nominated transactions
A participator may nominate the following categories of proposed transactions:
(a) Arm's length sales of specified quantities of oil for delivery from the field;
(b) Supplies to a company associated with the participator for use in refining either by that company or by another associated company. For this purpose, two companies are associated if one controls the other or both are under common control. All other non arm's length disposals are excluded;

6.7.3 UK Oil Taxation

(c) Appropriations to refining by the participator.
The Revenue has power by regulation to add further categories, and it may also exclude certain types of sale.

A proposed sale may be nominated by reference to the contract for it which is made later: if the contract is not concluded, the nomination lapses. The timing of the nomination may be tied to a date earlier than the contract. The contract must be for a sale by the participator, though that condition is likely to be satisfied if the participator sells through an agent. The inclusion of a right of the seller to assign the contract, however, may invalidate a nomination (FA 1987 Sched 10(2)).

Timing
The time limit for a nomination is set by reference to the 'transaction base date' (TBD); it must be made not later than 5.00 pm on the second business day following that date.
(a) In the case of a proposed sale, the TBD cannot be later than the date on which a price is agreed for sale of the oil for delivery under the contract: this may be earlier than the existence of a binding agreement for the sale. The TBD is the earlier of the date on which a price is agreed for sale of any oil for delivery under the contract and the date on which a price formula is agreed by reference to which the price will be fixed. That rule is qualified in 'price formula' cases, but only if the price formula date precedes the agreed price date and also falls before the first day of the month preceding the delivery month (M minus 1). Then, the TBD is the earliest of:
(1) M minus 1;
(2) the date on which any invariable factor in the formula is itself agreed where that factor is in terms of a per barrel price exceeding $2;
(3) The business day immediately preceding the beginning of a period in which the agreed formula is used in the determination of price;
(4) The date on which the price is agreed.
(b) For proposed supplies to an associated company and proposed appropriations, the TBD is M minus 1.
The facility to nominate movements to refining, either by the participator or through an associated company, is intended to obviate the risk that the oil in question might be charged by reference to a 'realisation' price higher than market value as a result of failure fully to satisfy arm's length sale nominations. The requirement to nominate such movements within the first three days of the month preceding the delivery month, however, renders the facility of little practical use because commercial constraints usually compress decisions on refining intake into a shorter timeframe (SI 1987 No 1338 (7) & (8)).

Period covered

A nomination generally has effect for deliveries and appropriations in one month only. However, 'composite nominations' may be made in the case of certain sales contracts to cover each month in a chargeable period or in two chargeable periods. The relevant contracts are those providing for supplies of oil extending beyond one month, where the terms are the same in so far as they specify the participator, the purchaser, the kind of oil, the price or price formula and the quantity to be supplied. A contract for sale of a participator's entire share of production of crude from a field will normally meet these conditions.

A nomination is required to be made in writing by the participator in question, and can be effected by telex, facsimile transmission, by hand, or by post using the recorded delivery or registered letter service (SI 1987 No 1338 (3) – (6)).

Format of nominations

Nominations must contain the following details:
(*a*) The name of the participator;
(*b*) In the case of a proposed sale, the name of the person to whom the oil is to be sold;
(*c*) The field from which the oil is to be delivered or appropriated;
(*d*) The nominated price of the oil;
(*e*) The nominal volume of the oil;
(*f*) The proposed delivery month;
(*g*) The transaction base date;
(*h*) Such other information as may be prescribed by the Revenue.

The maximum penalty for submission of incorrect information in connection with a nomination is £50,000 in the case of negligence and £100,000 in the case of fraud. The commission of such an offence renders the nomination ineffective.

The 'nominated price' is, in the case of a proposed arm's length sale, the price or price formula provided in the contract, and, in the case of a supply to an associated company or an appropriation, the market value as determined for PRT purposes. The Treasury is empowered to make regulations altering the meaning of nominated price. Rules are provided for translation of foreign currency to sterling.

The 'nominal volume' in relation to a proposed sale means the quantity proposed for delivery under the contract in the month (or months, in the case of a composite nomination). In relation to a proposed supply or appropriation, it is the quantity which the participator proposes to supply or appropriate in the month. The volume may be expressed as a specific quantity plus or minus a percentage tolerance, or the whole or a fraction of equity entitlement for the month (or months) of delivery; or, in the case of an offshore field from which oil is

6.7.3 UK Oil Taxation

transported to the UK by two or more tankers of differing capacities, the participator not knowing at the time of nomination which tanker will be used, the quantity equal to the capacity, or a specified fraction of the capacity, of any of the tankers plus or minus a percentage tolerance. The maximum tolerance recognised for nomination purposes is 5% of the volume. If the tolerance actually specified in a nomination exceeds 5%, the nominal volume nominated is then to be the specified volume plus or minus 5% (SI 1987 No 1338 (7)).

Revision of nominations
Amendment or withdrawal of nominations is permitted only within carefully defined limitations, which vary according to whether the nominated transaction is a sale, a supply or an appropriation.

Sales
Where a nomination is not fully satisfied by delivery under the contract of the participator's equity crude, that nomination can be amended or withdrawn if the failure was caused either by 'good commercial reasons' and not as a result of a tax avoidance arrangement, or by circumstances beyond the control of the participator or of any connected or associated person. The Revenue has to be satisfied that these conditions are met. If no oil is delivered under the contract in the month, the nomination may be withdrawn or, if some of the oil is instead delivered under the contract in the preceding or immediate following month, altered so as to be a nomination for the actual delivery month. Where a delivery is made for the month to which the original nomination relates but in an amount less than the nominal volume specified, the nomination may be amended as to nominal volume to the amount actually delivered.

Supplies and appropriations
The preconditions for amendment or withdrawal of a nomination are that the failure to fulfil the nominated transaction was caused by circumstances outside the control of the participator or of any person connected or associated with him or, if the participator is the field operator or the operator of a pipeline system transporting his blended oil, by his action in the interests of safety or prevention of pollution or otherwise in accordance with good oil field practice, not motivated by tax avoidance. If no equity oil is supplied or appropriated in accordance with the nomination, it may be withdrawn. If the nomination is partially fulfilled, the nomination may be amended as to nominal volume in line with the volume actually supplied or appropriated (FA 1987 Sched 10 (8) and SI 1987 No 1338 (11) – (17)).

Effect on chargeable profit

For each month in a chargeable period, a reconciliation is required between the quantity of equity crude nominated and the quantity actually delivered or appropriated against the nominations. The 'effective volume' nominated is, in general terms, equal to the nominal volume. If the aggregate of effective volumes of nominated transactions would exceed the amount of equity production for the month, the nominated transactions are taken to be reduced by cancelling a nomination or nominations or reducing the effective volume covered by a nomination as the case may be, on a last in first out basis.

Two parallel calculations are made:
(*a*) 'Aggregate nominated proceeds' is the sum of:
   (1) The proceeds of each nominated transaction. In general the proceeds are the effective volume nominated multiplied by the nominated price. This is so whether or not the transaction has been fully consummated as nominated: if a proposed volume for sale is satisfied by bought-in crude instead of equity crude, or is appropriated instead of being sold, the proceeds brought in are still stated by reference to nominated price and not be reference to actual proceeds or market value. If a quantity nominated for appropriation is instead sold at arm's length, the proceeds are the market value;
   (2) The market value of the excess of the equity production for the month over the effective volume covered by nominations.
(*b*) 'The proceeds of disposals and appropriations' in the month means the sum of:
   (1) The price received or receivable for disposals of the participator's share of equity crude in sales at arm's length and;
   (2) The market value of the remainder of his share.

The excess, if any, of (*a*) over (*b*) for each month is aggregated and added to the PRT gross profit for the chargeable period. The broad effect is that the volume of equity crude sold at arm's length which is not covered by nominations may be brought in at the higher of market value and realisation price: and where nominated arm's length sales contracts are satisfied not by equity crude but by bought-in or commodity crude, the tax base is the higher of the nominated price and the proceeds of sale of the relative volume of equity crude or its market value if it is not sold at arm's length (FA 1987 Sched 10 (9 – 11)).

Surcharge provisions

The nomination scheme qualifies but does not replace the underlying principles of measurement of income for PRT purposes under which one standard applies to sales at arm's length and a different standard to other disposals and appropriations. Alternation between the standards

6.7.3 UK Oil Taxation

follows the commercial decisions as to the means of disposing of equity crude. In recognition of the remaining scope available to some producers effectively to choose that standard which is likely to produce the lower measure, reserve powers are incorporated to the scheme which enable surcharge provisions to be invoked. The surcharge is not effective unless and until the Treasury makes an order, which must be preceded by approval of the draft order by the House of Commons. If an order is made, any excess of equity production over the effective nominated volume for a month is brought into the calculation of 'aggregate nominated proceeds' not at market value but at market value multiplied by a 'designated fraction' in the range between unity and $\frac{3}{2}$ (see Effect on Chargeable Profit above).

Secondly, the 'proceeds of nominated supplies and appropriations' are to be as provided in the main rules only if the volumes in question are actually applied for refining purposes, or if failure so to apply them is caused by circumstances beyond the control of the participator or of any company associated with the participator. Otherwise, the proceeds of the transaction in question are to be taken as market value of the effective volume multiplied by the 'designated fraction'.

The provisions are aimed particularly at opportunistic decisions taken after the relative transaction base date to satisfy nominated arm's length sales contracts by commodity rather than by equity crude at a price which may exceed the market value for the month, or to divert the nominated volume to a non arm's length disposal or to refining purposes. If an order were to be made, it would apply to all participators, whether or not they had undertaken the kind of manipulation which it is designed to counter, except that it does not apply to a participator who has not nominated any proposed arm's length sale for the month (F(No2)A 1987 Sched 8(5)).

The Treasury order which triggers the surcharge must be made before the end of the chargeable period to which it relates, and may apply to any month in that period: it may also have effect for a later period. The Government gave an undertaking on 4 December 1987 that, if an order were to be made while consultations were still in progress between the Revenue and the industry about the application of the nomination scheme to refinery movements, the surcharge would not apply to supplies or appropriations effected before the date of the order.

Blended oil
A person who is a participator in two or more fields utilising a common transportation system whose entitlement to equity production from the fields is blended oil may nominate proposed sales, supplies or appropriations of that oil having effect for all of the fields in question,

provided that he does not make a nomination for the same month which relates to only one of the fields. The regulations are modified accordingly (FA 1987 Sched 10 (12) and SI 1987 No 1338 (19)(20)).

6.7.4 Valuation of Gas

Most of the gas produced from UK fields, consisting in the main of methane, is sold to the British Gas Corporation (now British Gas). This continues to be the case despite the removal of the BGC's monopoly as a buyer (see 6.8.1) and its privatisation in 1986. Gas sold to the British Gas under pre-July contracts is exempt from PRT. Other sales to the British Gas are generally chargeable to PRT at selling prices as sales at arm's length.

Valuation is frequently required, however, of other constituents of gas production, which are commonly appropriated by the producer or disposed of in sales not at arm's length. The framework of assumptions to be made concerning the notional contract in relation to valuation of oil applies also, with certain modifications, to the valuation of gas. Prior to amendments introduced in the Finance Act 1980, there was considerable doubt whether the various gas fractions, methane, ethane, propane, butane and C5+ condensates, should be valued as one stream at some point before separation, and corresponding doubt about the extent of 'appropriate' initial treatment which had to be assumed. This was partly due to the fact that the original definition of initial treatment as it related to gas separation did not extend beyond 'separating oil so won and consisting of methane gas from oil so won and consisting of gas other than methane'. For chargeable periods ending after 31 December 1979 the valuation rules for gas are more specific. Initial treatment is not to be assumed as a condition of the notional contract if the gas has not actually been initially treated, either by the producer before disposal or appropriation or by the producer or a connected person after disposal or appropriation (Sched 3 (2A)(2)). In the more normal case, however, initial treatment is to be assumed and is to include the actual initial treatment which has been carried out. Each gas fraction or stream of a kind which is transported and sold in normal commercial practice is required to be valued separately from other fractions or streams (Sched 3(2A)(3)). The definition of initial treatment is expanded to include separation not only of gas from oil but also of gas fractions sold separately in normal commercial practice; liquefying for purposes of transporting; and otherwise processing to bring the gas to a condition in which it would normally be sold; but excluding refining or activities aimed solely or mainly at achieving a chemical reaction in gas, *cracking* (s 12). The treatment to be 'assumed' includes not only that

6.7.4 UK Oil Taxation

which has been carried out by or on behalf of the participator, but also that carried out by or on behalf of any person connected with the participator. This may mean that gas sold to an associated company has attributed to it a comparatively high value enhanced by initial treatment carried out by the associated company even though the expenditure borne by that company attracts no PRT relief.

6.7.5 Valuation of Ethane used for Petrochemical Purposes

An alternative mechanism is provided for the valuation of ethane which is sold other than at arm's length or appropriated and is thereafter to be used for petrochemical purposes. The need for this alternative arose because the normal rules for valuation, which apply separately to each monthly total of disposals or appropriations, could produce values for ethane which are inappropriate in the context of disposals under a specialised long term contract. It applies by election, which has to be made, in the case of ethane which is appropriated, by the participator or, in the case of sales, by the participator and the purchaser together. If the election is accepted by the Revenue, the values which emerge from the pricing formula proposed in the election are adopted for PRT purposes, in place of the values which would have resulted from application of the rules in Sched 3(2). The period for which the election applies may be up to fifteen years.

If it appears to the Revenue or to the participator, after the expiry of at least five years, that 'by reason of any substantial and lasting change in any economic circumstances . . . the market values determined in accordance with the price formula specified in the election are no longer realistic', either of them may serve notice that the election should cease to apply. The Revenue has the option in any event, after the five year point, of requiring the formula specified in the original election to continue in force or of accepting, if appropriate, a new pricing formula proposed by the party or parties to the election (FA 1982 s134 and Sched 18).

The operation of these provisions was examined in a rather surprising context, following an application by ICI for judicial review. The ethane content of associated gas produced from the Brent field, owned jointly by Shell and Esso, was intended to be transported to Mossmorran for separation and fractionation and for use as feedstock in a new ethylene cracker. Somewhat similarly, BP planned to use ethane from its Magnus field as feedstock in its ethylene cracker at Grangemouth. ICI was the only other ethylene producer in the UK, having three crackers at Wilton of which one was owned jointly with BP. The Wilton crackers used naphtha as a feedstock, ICI having no access to the alternative cheaper feedstock ethane. Following the steep rise in oil prices in 1979, the European demand for ethylene was much reduced compared with the demand forecast when plans for the Mossmorran project were made, and it was against this background that the alternative ethane valuation rules were introduced.

ICI contended that, on the premise that the Government had entered into a commitment with the oil companies which would result in their ethane production being charged to PRT and to ring fence CT at a value substantially below market value, such a result would constitute an aid under Articles 92 and 93 of the Treaty of Rome and would give the companies an unwarranted competitive advantage not available to ICI. The Court of Appeal found that, if the Revenue had accepted an election for the alternative basis of valuation in accordance with the evidence of the Revenue's approach to arriving at a market value of Brent ethane, resulting in a valuation substantially lower than that considered by ICI and the Court to be appropriate, it would have acted unreasonably. Persistence by the Revenue in the misapplication of the provisions would be ultra vires. Had an election been accepted on a valuation basis which was contrary to the law, such acceptance would be void and the terms of the election would require to be restated. (*The Queen* v *Attorney-General ex parte Imperial Chemical Industries Plc* [1987] 1 CMLR 72).

6.7.6 Alternative Valuation of Light Gases

An alternative to the normal valuation method is also available for certain other light gases. A participator may elect to be charged by reference to a price formula of his choice which will reflect values approximating to arm's length prices. The gas in question is gas of which the largest component by volume is methane or ethane or a combination of the two, which either results from fractionation before sale or appropriation or which is sold or appropriated without being fractionated: it excludes ethane to be used for petrochemical purposes. The election applies only to such gas which is sold on non arm's length terms or appropriated, and which is not subject to fractionation in the interval between disposal or appropriation and use for the purposes specified in the election; and it also covers gas stocks if they prove to be relevantly sold or appropriated after the end of the chargeable period. Fractionation in this context means treatment in order to separate one or more gases from a composite gas stream.

The provisions relating to elections for the alternative valuation of ethane used for petrochemical purposes apply for these purposes, subject to modifications. The election, which may have effect for up to

6.7.6   UK Oil Taxation

15 years, must specify the purposes for which the gas will be used. The price formula must have regard to the likely influence on prices of variations in the level of supply. The factors to be taken into account include consideration of whether it would be reasonable to assume that a contract for sale of the gas at arm's length would include take or pay or capacity payment clauses. If that would be a reasonable assumption, the price formula must then reflect the pattern of notional receipts arising under such clauses. The timing of the charge on those amounts is governed by the rules relating to actual receipts (see 6.7.9). The Revenue has power to withdraw acceptance of the election at any time if it appears that the out-turn of events is materially different from the forecasts on which the terms of the election were based, and other powers of review, exercisable after 5 years, may also result in cancellation or revision (FA 1986 s109 and Sched 21).

6.7.7 CIF Gas Sales

Under the general rules, sales on cost insurance and freight terms (c & f or cif) are charged to PRT by reference to the full price receivable. The selling price in these circumstances may be expected to include recovery of the related freight and, if appropriate, insurance costs together with some profit margin. Those costs, however, are not allowable for PRT purposes if they are incurred in exporting oil or gas from the UK. The seller will normally be able to avoid this inequity by arranging to sell on other terms, but in the case of sales of natural gas liquids (NGL), this may not be a practical option. Transport of NGLs requires specialised vessels which the seller, as a regular and long term producer, may be better able to supply than the buyer.

A special provision was introduced in 1982 to meet this difficulty. Where gas is sold at arm's length on terms which provide that the seller transports it from the UK to a non-UK delivery point or meets some or all of the costs of such transport, for PRT purposes the actual sale price is set aside. Instead, a deemed price is adopted which assumes that the contract is on terms identical to the terms of the actual contract except that it requires the gas be delivered at a point in the UK and does not require the seller meet any of the cost of transport from the UK. UK delivery point is, in the case of gas won onshore, the place at which the seller could reasonably be expected to deliver it or, if there is more than one such place, the one nearest to the field from which the gas was produced. The intention of this adjustment is to strip out of the sale price the element representing consideration for transport from the UK (s2 (5A)).

Petroleum Revenue Tax 6.7.8

For CT purposes, it is the actual sale price, not the PRT deemed price, which is taken into account.

6.7.8 Oil Stocks

In addition to sales and appropriations, the PRT gross profit also recognises stocks of oil held by the participator at the end of a chargeable period. The oil in question is production which has been neither sold nor appropriated, or which has been sold but is still held by the participator pending delivery.

One half of the market value of these stocks is taken into the gross profit. The general rules for establishing market value also apply here: the notional contract is assumed to be for sale of the whole of the stocks falling to be valued and for no other oil. A deduction is made in calculating gross profit of one half of the market value of oil stocks at the end of the previous period, that is, the amount included in the gross profit of that period in respect of closing stocks.

The value of stocks is the monthly average price for oil of the kind in question for the final month of the period (see 6.7.2). Since that figure is not known in most cases at the time when the PRT return is required, two months after the end of the period, but is derived later from relevant returns for the period and other sources, the return figure frequently differs from that adopted in the assessment. For the same reason, it is unlikely that the payment on account, due at the same time as the return, will match exactly the tax finally assessed.

Most of the stocks which need to be taken into account for PRT are those held in onshore storage pending delivery to a customer or appropriation by the producer (initial storage, see 6.15.6). Any element of tank contents which is not readily recoverable for sale, tank bottoms sediment and water, is in practice excluded from the volume to be valued. Offshore oil in the course of transport to the point of first landing in the UK is specifically excluded: this includes oil in pipelines from the field to shore and oil in tankers at the field or in transit from the field to the UK, and in practice also extends to oil in storage at an offshore production platform (see 6.8.3).

Because participators in jointly owned fields rarely take, or lift, oil on a schedule which precisely mirrors their *pro rata* entitlement, at the end of a chargeable period some may have taken more than that entitlement, or overlifted, while others may have underlifted. A participator which has overlifted is chargeable to PRT by reference to the oil actually lifted. Account cannot be taken in the computation, for example as negative stock, of any amount by which the overlifting exceeds the equity pro rata share of oil stocks. A participator which has underlifted is also chargeable by reference to actual liftings, subject to

6.7.8 UK Oil Taxation

adjustment for stocks. If the amount by which it has underlifted exceeds the closing stocks attributed to it, the amount for which it accounts for PRT purposes is stocks so attributed and not the larger amount of the underlift. Looking at the field as a whole, PRT is charged by reference to actual liftings and to oil physically in stock (s2(5)(*d*)).

6.7.9 Take or Pay Contracts and Capacity Payments

Contracts are sometimes made for purchase of production of gas from a field on 'take or pay' terms which allow some flexibility to the purchaser in the timing of deliveries taken under the contract. This type of arrangement is particularly relevant to production from certain fields which British Gas takes on an irregular basis in order to equalise national supply and demand. Where payments are made in respect of quantities of gas for delivery at particular times, delivery may be taken instead at later times for no further consideration. Those payments, so far as they relate to deliveries in the later period, are not brought into charge for the earlier period in which delivery did not take place but are treated as the sale price of the actual deliveries. If the full entitlement has not been delivered by the latest time allowed by the contract any balance of advance payment not otherwise brought into the PRT profit is then treated as the sale price for a deemed delivery.

These arrangements may incorporate provision by the purchaser of a 'capacity payment' as additional consideration to the producer for cooperation in irregular or seasonal supply. Such a payment is not dependent on delivery of gas at particular times. If it is not otherwise charged as an advance payment for gas, it is specifically brought in as part of the price for actual deliveries. It is included in the PRT calculation for the chargeable period in which it is paid or payable. If there are no deliveries in that period, it is treated as the price received or receivable for the equivalent of one tonne of oil deemed to be delivered in the period (FA 1984 s114).

6.7.10 Blended Oil

Oil produced from a number of offshore fields is co-mingled in pipeline systems through which it is transported to the UK. Where, 'for the purposes of commerce', the blended oil is allocated between the participators in the originating fields in accordance with an agreed method, the amounts so allocated are taken to be the participators' shares of oil won from those fields. The originating fields may include transmedian line fields or fields which are not in the UK sector of the continental shelf. The participators are required to provide to the Revenue details of the allocation method and of any change in method or material change in the constituents of the blend: this requirement is usually satisfied by the pipeline operator on behalf of the participators. Penalties are provided for non compliance and for provision of incorrect information.

The Revenue is entitled to reject the allocation method if it appears not to be just and reasonable for oil taxation purposes, and to propose amendments which render it acceptable. The allocation for tax purposes is then made in accordance with the amendments. Any of the participators may appeal against the proposed amendments, and all participators affected are then joined in the appeal proceedings. The appeal may be resolved by agreement or by determination of the Special Commissioners (FA 1987 s63 and Sched 12).

6.8 PRT Exemptions

6.8.1 Gas Sold to British Gas Corporation Under Pre-July 1975 Contracts

Gas sold to the BGC under a contract made before July 1975 is exempt from PRT (s10). Having regard to the BGC's position at that time as a monopoly buyer of natural gas, the price ruling under existing contracts was likely to be relatively low, and exposure of the profit to the rigours of PRT would have had a damaging effect on project economies. Once the shape and potential impact of PRT was apparent, a seller of gas was able, in negotiating a price under a new contract with the BGC, to seek to compensate for increased tax liabilities. The exemption benefits the participators in a number of Southern Basin gas fields and in the UK sector of the large Frigg field. It can also apply to sales of associated gas — that is, gas produced in association with production of oil — and significantly the substantial volumes of associated gas produced from the Brent field are sold under pre-July 1975 contracts. BGC's position as a monopoly buyer of gas production was terminated by the Oil and Gas (Enterprise) Act 1982, and the Corporation, now called British Gas, was privatised in 1986.

In 1981, the Government came to the view that, as a result of the PRT gas exemption, the direct yield to the Exchequer in respect of gas production was lower than its full potential, and introduced the Gas Levy. It is payable by the BGC on gas purchased or produced by it which is exempt from PRT, at a rate increasing to five pence per therm in 1983/84.

Many contracts for sale of gas to the BGC contain price revision

6.8.1 UK Oil Taxation

clauses which provide for negotiation of increases in price in limited circumstances such as the incurring of major additional capital expenditure on the field. Difficult questions of contract law sometimes arise as to whether sales under amended terms are sales under the original contract or under a new contract created by the amendments, and whether the contract is sufficiently extensible to accommodate particular quantities of gas.

Production of natural gas (methane) from a gas field is normally accompanied by production of quantities of NGL or condensates. If gas sold to British Gas is exempt from PRT by virtue of a pre-July 1975 contract, other production from the field is also exempt if the cumulative amount of that production does not exceed 5% of the total cumulative production including gas sold to British Gas. The calculation is in terms of weight not values, and for this purpose 1,100 cubic metres of gas at a temperature of 15 degrees centigrade and pressure of one atmosphere is equal to one tonne (s10(1)(*b*)).

Expenditure related to the production of gas which is exempt from PRT is not generally allowable for PRT relief (see 6.15.5). If it is incurred with a view to generating tariff or disposal receipts, however, it may be allowable against those receipts.

6.8.2 Oil used for Production Purposes

Oil which a participator appropriates to its own use is brought into charge to PRT at market value. Oil used for production purposes, however, is not oil 'relevantly appropriated', and is effectively excluded from the PRT charge. Production purposes are defined as carrying on drilling or field production operations, pumping oil from an offshore field to the UK or initial treatment, relating either to the field from which the oil is produced or to any other field in which the participator has an interest. Oil transferred from one field for production purposes in another field in the same ownership is not, therefore, charged (s12).

6.8.3 Oil in Transit

Oil in the course of being transported from an offshore field to the UK first landing point is excluded from opening and closing stocks which are taken into account in arriving at gross profit. Oil in transit for this purpose includes oil in tankers and offshore pipeline systems and oil in storage at the platform or offshore loading facility. In practice, oil in tankers in the course of transport direct from an offshore field to a foreign port may also be excluded from chargeable stocks (see also 6.15.6) (Sched 3(7)).

6.8.4 Royalty in Kind

Oil which is delivered to the Secretary of State as royalty in kind (see 5.5.2) is not charged to PRT and is disregarded in the calculation of oil allowance (Sched 3(4)). If it should prove that more oil has been delivered to the Secretary of State than represents his 12½ royalty entitlement, the excess is to be brought into account as though it were sold to the Secretary of State at arm's length, even though payment for it may not be received until a later period.

6.9 Gas Banking

Associated gas which is produced in significant quantities from offshore oil fields needs to be transported ashore or otherwise utilised in ways which are not wasteful of energy resources. At the same time, all offshore fields require substantial quantities of fuel for platform drilling and production operations, a need which can be most efficiently met from a convenient supply of gas won offshore. Some fields may produce more associated gas in the early years of field life than they require as platform fuel, while in later years gas production may be insufficient to meet those requirements. In response to these problems, complex commercial arrangements are sometimes made under which gas produced from one field is disposed of to the participators in another field, in consideration not for cash but for a return delivery of gas at some future time, either for use as platform fuel or for on-sale to a third party.

This kind of arrangement, known as 'banking', was not in mind when the Oil Taxation Act 1975 was drafted, and not surprisingly strict application of the Act would have exposed both parties to the transactions to serious inequities. For example, the producer of the banked gas might have been chargeable to PRT on that production by reference to a relatively high notional onshore landed value, even though consideration might not be received for some years, while the banker might find itself liable to PRT on the return deliveries of gas which in other circumstances would have been sold to the BGC under an exempt pre-July 1975 contract; and there were consequential CT difficulties.

The problems were met by the Oil Taxation (Gas Banking Schemes) Regulations 1982 (SI 1982 No 92), for which provision had been made in FA 1980 s108. If the participators in two fields involved in a gas banking scheme elect for the application of the Regulations, the normal

6.9 UK Oil Taxation

rules are modified. Gas which is 'banked' and gas which is supplied in return from the 'bank' is disregarded in calculating gross profit in relation to the field from which the gas was actually produced: instead, it is taken into account in each case in the gross profit in relation to the field to which it is transferred under the scheme. The consent of the Board to the making of an election has first to be sought in a joint application by the responsible persons for the two fields, and if that application is approved an election, to which all the participators in the field must be party, may then be made. The gas which is the subject of 'banking' under the scheme has to be associated gas, defined as gas which is 'won from the field at a rate dependent on that at which the oil other than gas is so won'; and the participators have to undertake that both the banked gas and gas delivered in return is either sold to the BGC, used for production purposes in the transferee field or, in emergencies, flared. An election continues in force during the currency of the particular gas banking scheme, so long as the Board does not revoke its consent.

The income tax and CT rules are also modified by the Regulations. Gas transferred under a gas banking scheme is not taxed as production from the transferor field but is instead treated as though it were produced from the transferee field by the participators in that field in the course of their ring fence trades. As regards royalties, consent to the making of an election for application of the Regulations is dependent on the participators undertaking to agree to variation of the terms of relevant licences in such manner that gas transferred under the scheme is disregarded in calculating liabilities in relation to the licensees of the transferor field and is instead brought into charge as though it were produced from the transferee field.

FA 1980 s108 includes provision for the making of regulations applying to international gas banking schemes, that is, schemes in which one of the fields concerned is not a UK field. To date no such regulations have been enacted.

6.10 Tariff and Disposal Receipts

6.10.1 General

Under the 1975 Oil Taxation Act, non oil income such as tariffs was brought to account only to the extent that it offset relative expenditure, and allowable expenditure on providing an asset was reduced by disposal receipts. Any profit or gain on those transactions was outside the scope of the PRT charge: at the same time, if the other parties to the transactions were participators, they were likely to qualify for relief on the full amount of the payments. Steps were taken in the 1983 Oil Taxation Act to stem this potential 'PRT leakage'. The scope of PRT was extended for chargeable periods ending after 30 June 1982 to include income and capital receipts derived from the use or disposal of field assets. The extension was associated with changes in the expenditure relief rules, which now permit full front-end relief for most field assets, whether they are to be used solely for the purposes of the field or to be shared by other fields under tariff arrangements.

6.10.2 Qualifying Assets

Tariff or disposal receipts are chargeable only if they are attributable to the provision or use of a 'qualifying asset'. A qualifying asset is a non mobile asset, or a mobile asset dedicated to a particular field, in respect of which expenditure incurred by the participator is allowable either under the old or the new expenditure relief rules. Assets are excluded which are not expected to continue in use in connection with the field after the end of the claim period of first such use. Also excluded are land and interests in land and any building or structure on land of a kind the cost of which is not allowable for PRT purposes (see 6.15.5). This exemption removes the possibility of charge, for example, on the sale price of a warehouse owned by an associated company and leased to a participator who has had relief on the lease rents. Arguably, a lease or similar right may itself be a qualifying asset, so that income received from other participators for sub-lease or hire is chargeable.

An asset may be a qualifying asset, giving rise to chargeable receipts, even though the field in question produces only exempt gas. In that case, however, mobile assets are excluded and, instead of the pre-condition that expenditure in respect of the asset 'is allowable or has been allowed', the hypothesis is made that expenditure 'would . . . be allowable or have been allowed' were it not for the fact that it related to exempt gas. The assumptions required in making that judgment are not entirely clear. Nevertheless, the possibility exists that substantial receipts attributable to exempt gas fields, such as insurance recoveries in respect of total loss an asset, could be subject to PRT.

Mobile assets not dedicated to a field are not qualifying assets. A mobile drilling rig, for example, is not likely to be dedicated to a field: in consequence, the proceeds of its disposal are not directly chargeable to PRT, though they may reduce allowances otherwise due for exploration and appraisal expenditure (OTA 1983 s8).

6.10.3   UK Oil Taxation

6.10.3 Tariff Receipts

Tariff receipts are defined as the aggregate of the amount or value of any consideration, whether of a capital or a revenue nature, received or receivable by a participator in any period (not including any amount actually received before 30 June 1982) in respect of:

(*a*) the use of a qualifying asset

(*b*) the provision, in connection with the use of a qualifying asset otherwise than by the participator itself, of services or other business facilities of any kind.

They do not include any part of the consideration which, from the point of view of the payer, is in respect of interest or other obligation related to obtaining a loan or credit. Since expenditure incurred in connection with deballasting of tankers is not allowable for PRT purposes, that part of a tariff receipt which is to any extent attributable to the use of an asset or to the provision of services or facilities in connection with deballasting is not chargeable, and any necessary apportionment is made on a just and reasonable basis. Apportionment is similarly made if in other circumstances receipts in respect of the use of an asset include an unquantified element which does not constitute a tariff receipt.

In general, the field to which tariff receipts are attributable for PRT purposes is that for which the expenditure in respect of the asset concerned is allowable. If it is allowable to the participator for more than one field, then:

(*a*) in the case of a mobile asset, no account is taken of a field to which it is not dedicated;

(*b*) if the asset is a qualifying asset only because expenditure on it is allowable under the associated assets rules (see 6.17.1), any receipts referrable to the 'associated' asset are attributed to the field which obtained the benefit of the allowance for expenditure on the 'main' asset with which it is associated; and

(*c*) subject to (*a*) and (*b*) above, receipts are attributed to that one of the participator's fields in relation to which a development decision was first made. Such a decision is treated as made when consent for development is granted by the Secretary of State for Energy in respect of all or part of a field, or when a programme of development is served on a licensee or is approved by the Secretary of State for all or part of a field. If development decisions are made at the same time for more than one relevant field, the first such decision is deemed to be that for the field for which it appears, at the time of the decision or when the asset in question is provided if later, that the greatest use of the asset will be made.

Tariff receipts, less any tariff receipts allowance, are brought into charge to PRT by inclusion in the 'positive amounts' which enter into the calculation of the profit or loss for the chargeable period. They were not liable to APRT (OTA 1983 s6).

6.10.4 Purchase of Oil at Place of Extraction

Instead of entering into tariffing arrangements for use of its field assets, a participator might buy oil offshore and resell it onshore having transported and treated it using its field assets. Provisions are made which are aimed at preventing the reduction in total PRT charge which could result from such arrangements. If a participator or an associated company purchases oil at the place of extraction, for example at an offshore platform, and transports, treats or stores it by means of assets which are qualifying assets of the participator's field, the participator is charged on notional tariff receipts. The measure of receipts in these circumstances is the difference between the purchase price and 'selling price' on the on-sale or appropriation of the oil. The 'selling price' means the actual sale price in relation to arm's length sales, or the market value in relation to non-arm's length sales or appropriations. The oil is treated as though it were won by the participator from the field to which the qualifying assets relate.

The provisions seem intended to apply to purchases offshore of oil produced from a field which is not the field to which the qualifying assets relate, but they might also apply where the participator purchases oil from a fellow participator in that field. They do not apply to:

(a) purchase and delivery of oil in pursuance of certain agreements between participators in the same field (chiefly, participation agreements under which oil is disposed of to BNOC or to OPA);
(b) oil which, before the 'selling price' would otherwise require to be determined, is either stored in the field to which the qualifying assets relate or used for the purpose of assisting the extraction of oil from that field; or
(c) oil the market value of which is taken into account in the calculation of the PRT profit or loss of a participator under the normal rules dealing with oil disposed of otherwise than in sales at arm's length (OTA 1983 Sched 2 (12)).

6.10.5 Tariff Receipts Allowance

An allowance is provided which exempts from PRT a certain amount of 'qualifying tariff receipts'. For each chargeable period, the participators in the field to which the tariffs are attributable (the 'principal

6.10.5   UK Oil Taxation

field') are entitled to a tariff receipts allowance of 250,000 tonnes in respect of each 'user' field. If in relation to a particular user field the tariffs derived from a contract made before 8 May 1982, the allowance in respect of that field was 375,000 tonnes for chargeable periods ending on or before 30 June 1987, reducing to 250,000 tonnes per chargeable period thereafter.

Qualifying tariff receipts
The allowance is available only in respect of 'qualifying' tariff receipts, and not in respect of other tariff receipts or of disposal receipts. Qualifying tariff receipts are those attributable to the use of an asset, or to the provision of services or business facilities in connection with its use, for extracting, transporting, initially treating or initially storing oil won otherwise than from the principal field.

Tariffs payable by a co-participator in the principal field for use of an asset or provision of services in connection with that field do not qualify (OTA 1982 s9).

Some or all of the participators in the user field may also be participators in the principal field, owning an interest in the qualifying assets. Arrangements adopted in these circumstances commonly constitute 'cross-tariffing', each participator concerned paying tariff partly to the other asset owners and partly to himself in proportions which reflect use of the proportionate shares in the assets. The payments are normally charged as tariff receipts, attracting tariff receipts allowance, and allowed in the user field, except for the self-tariff element.

A field may make use of the facilities of more than one other field, perhaps transporting oil through one pipeline system and gas through another. Each of the host fields is entitled to a tariff receipts allowance.

Tariffs which arise from use for the purposes of a non-UK production source may be qualifying tariffs (subject to the same criteria as apply to use for a UK field), provided that the Secretary of State for Energy makes an order specifying the non-UK source as a 'foreign field'. In the case of a transmedian field, the UK sector and the non-UK sector are treated as two separate user fields.

A number of fields in the Norwegian sector, including the Ekofisk complex and Heimdal, have been specified as foreign fields. By concession, tariff receipts allowance is backdated to cover receipts which arise from use in connection with a foreign field before the date on which the field is specified by the Secretary of State.

Calculation of the allowance
The allowance in respect of each user field for each chargeable period is

divided between the participators in the principal field according to their share of qualifying tariff receipts deriving from the user field and is then converted into a cash equivalent. Except in the circumstances described below relating to receipts under 'existing contracts', a participator's cash equivalent is calculated by the formula;

$$£A \times \frac{B}{C}$$

where:
A   represents the participator's qualifying tariff receipts from the user field for the chargeable period,
B   represents the tariff receipts allowance in respect of the user field in question, expressed in tonnes, and
C   represents the throughput of oil from the user field extracted, transported, initially treated or initially stored using assets which gave rise to the qualifying tariffs.

The fraction $\frac{B}{C}$ is not to exceed unity, so that the cash equivalent cannot exceed the participator's qualifying tariff receipts from the field.

Gas transferred to a user field under a 'gas banking scheme' (see 6.9) is treated for these purposes as won from that user field.

For chargeable periods ending not later than 30 June 1987, where some of the receipts from a user field are qualifying tariff receipts from 'existing contracts', that is, contracts which entitle the participators to the increased allowance of 375,000 tonnes, and other qualifying tariff receipts from that field do not arise from such contracts, a more complex formula applies. If the tariffs under the more recent contracts derive from the same oil, separate calculations of the tariff receipts allowance are made in respect of receipts and throughput under existing contracts and under later contracts, in the case of the former using 375,000 tonnes as the B factor in the formula. The tariff receipts allowance for the chargeable period is then the sum of the two resulting amounts.

If the tariffs under the separate contracts do not derive from the same oil, the calculation proceeds in stages:

Stage 1
In respect of the existing contract receipts, the formula is:

$$£A_1 \times \frac{B_1}{C_1}$$

where:
A_1 represents existing contract receipts;
B_1 is 375,000 tonnes; and
C_1 is the throughput of oil to which the receipts relate.

6.10.5 UK Oil Taxation

Stage 2

In respect of the other receipts the formula is:

$$£A_2 \times \frac{B_2}{C_2}$$

where:
A_2 equals those other receipts;
B_2 is 250,000 tonnes; and
C_2 is the throughput of oil to which the receipts relate.

Stage 3

The sum produced by the stage 1 formula is reduced by multiplying it by the fraction:

$$\frac{C_1}{C_1 + C_2}$$

and the sum produced by the stage 2 formula is reduced by multiplying it by the fraction:

$$\frac{C_2}{C_1 + C_2}$$

The cash equivalent of the tariff receipts allowance for the chargeable period is then the sum of the two amounts reduced as in stage 3 or the total amount of the qualifying tariff receipts if less (OTA 1983 Sched 3).

Tariff receipts referable to different periods

Qualifying tariff receipts may be receivable over a period of longer or shorter duration than the period of use of the asset to which they relate; for example, a commuted front-end tariff may be paid for a period of future use. In these circumstances the tariff receipts allowance for the period or periods in which the receipts are receivable and chargeable is not calculated as described above by reference to the throughput in those periods. Instead, for the purpose of calculating the allowance only, the receipts are spread over the period of use (up to a maximum of ten years), in proportion to the expected throughput from the user field, and a notional allowance is calculated for each chargeable period within the period of use, adopting the estimated tariff receipts and the projected throughput as the A and C factors in the formula:

$$£A \times \frac{B}{C}$$

The tariff receipts allowance in the period for which the tariffs are actually chargeable is then the sum of the notional allowances for each of the periods of use or the amount of the qualifying tariff receipts of the chargeable period if less. There are rules modifying this calculation where tariff receipts referable to use in different periods and also other 'normal' tariffs fall into the same chargeable period.

(Examples of the calculation of tariff receipts allowance are given at Appendix 2.)

6.10.6 Disposal Receipts

For chargeable periods ending after 30 June 1982, disposal receipts attributable to qualifying assets are brought directly into the PRT charge. The receipts in question are defined as the aggregate of the amount or value of any consideration received or receivable in respect of the disposal of a qualifying asset, or of an interest in such an asset. Any part of the consideration which, so far as the payer is concerned, is interest or an expense otherwise related to the obtaining of a loan or credit is excluded. Also disregarded is consideration given for the purpose of acquiring a direct or indirect interest in oil won or to be won from a field. The provisions which determine the chargeable field for the purposes of tariff receipts apply also to disposal receipts (see 6.10.3).

A disposal of an asset giving rise to a chargeable receipt may have an effect on the amount of supplement otherwise due on current expenditure (see 6.21.7).

Disposal receipts, like tariff receipts, are brought into the 'positive amounts' which enter into the calculation of PRT profit or loss. They were not liable to APRT (OTA 1983 s7).

6.10.7 Particular Disposals

(*a*) If a qualifying asset is disposed of more than two years after it ceases to be used in connection with any oil field or, if later, more than two years after it ceases to give rise to tariff receipts in the hands of the participator, the proceeds are not chargeable as disposal receipts. In such a case, the allowable expenditure on the asset is likely to be reduced or restricted, taking account of the remaining useful life of the asset; and if the amount of relief already allowed then proves to be excessive, the excess is brought in as a disposal receipt (see 6.17.1 – Assets taken out of field use) (OTA 1983 s7(4)).

(*b*) Insurance or other compensation receipts for the loss or destruction of a qualifying asset are brought into charge as disposal receipts. The disposal is deemed to take place at the time the payment is received or receivable (OTA 1983 Sched 2(7)). It follows that the receipts may be chargeable for a period earlier than the period for which relief is given on the cost of replacing the asset, if indeed it is replaced. This rule does not apply to insurance or other recoveries which relate for example, to damage but not to loss or destruction: in that case, the receipts are effectively offset against any expenditure occasioned by the event.

(*c*) The amount of receipts which are chargeable in relation to the disposal of a 'brought-in' asset is restricted, in recognition of the fact that allowable expenditure on the asset may also have been restricted (see 6.17.1). A brought-in asset is one which is used by the

6.10.7 UK Oil Taxation

participator or an associated company for some non-field purpose before being brought into use for the purposes of a field. The chargeable amount is a proportion of the disposal consideration corresponding to the proportion of the expenditure on the asset which qualified for relief (OTA 1983 Sched 2(9)).
(*d*) On the disposal of an asset which has been partly used in connection with the deballasting of tankers, any disposal receipt is reduced in accordance with the proportion of the expenditure on the asset which was allowable (OTA 1983 Sched 2(10)).
(*e*) Receipts or credits which arise from the redetermination of obligations or entitlements of the participators in a transmedian field, straddling the median line between the UK sector and another sector of the continental shelf, are treated as chargeable disposal receipts to the extent that they relate to a qualifying asset (OTA 1983 s7(3)). This provision does not extend to adjustments on redetermination of UK fields (see 8.12).

6.10.8 Non Arm's Length Receipts

Adjustments are required to the amount of tariff or disposal receipts chargeable to PRT where transactions take place with a connected person or otherwise than at arm's length. The transaction may be the disposal of a chargeable asset or provision of it under arrangements which might give rise to tariff receipts. If the other party to the non arm's length agreement is itself a participator in a field, it will be expected to claim a PRT allowance in respect of the payment: but that allowance may be restricted under the expenditure relief rules to the arm's length cost incurred by the disposer of providing the asset or service (see 6.26). In recognition of that restriction, the amount chargeable on the disposer is also restricted to that 'cost'.

If the other party to the non arm's length agreement is not a participator in a field, the recipient is charged on 'open market consideration' instead of actual consideration receivable. For example, the transfer of a floating production platform formerly used in a UK field to an associated company for use in a Norwegian field is deemed to take place at open market value (OTA 1983 Sched 2(5)).

6.10.9 Anti-avoidance Provisions

There are provisions which are designed to counter the diversion of receipts which, were they to arise to a participator, would be charged as tariff or disposal receipts. Where consideration deriving from use or

Petroleum Revenue Tax 6.10.9

disposal of a qualifying asset of a participator is received, not by the participator, but by a connected person, by virtue of a scheme or arrangements the main purpose or one of the main purposes of which is avoidance of PRT or CT, it is brought to account as a tariff or disposal receipt of the participator. This would be likely to apply, for example, where a participator company assigns the benefit of a tariff agreement to an associated company which is outside the scope of PRT. A company is connected with another company if, broadly, one has control of the other or both are under common control. The rule is modified to avoid double counting where, for example, tariff or disposal receipts are paid to an associated company and that company itself makes payments to the participator relating to use or disposal of the qualifying asset. In that event, only the excess of the receipts of the associated company over the actual payments to the participator is attributed to the participator for inclusion in its chargeable tariff or disposal receipts (OTA 1983 Sched 2(2)).

A provision of potentially wider application concerns receipt by a person of tariff or similar income for use of an asset which is not a qualifying asset of that person but which is used to any extent by a participator (the user) who is connected or associated with the recipient. Again, it is activated only if the arrangements have as the main purpose or one of the main purposes the avoidance of PRT or CT. The user is treated for PRT purposes as receiving the income which arises to the actual recipient or to any person connected or associated with him, leaving out of account any of it which the user provides. Such proportion of expenditure on the asset incurred by the actual recipient as it is just and reasonable to apportion to the use giving rise to the income is treated as though it were incurred by the user, for the purpose for which it was in fact incurred by the recipient. This attribution of expenditure does not apply to a mobile asset, such as a drilling rig, which is not dedicated to a field. If there is more than one user, the attributions of income and expenditure are apportioned between them on a just and reasonable basis (OTA 1983 Sched 2(11)).

One of the pre-conditions for application of this rule is that the 'user' is either connected with or associated with the recipient. For these purposes a participator company is associated with another company if the participator, by acting together with other participators in the same field or another field in which the asset in question might be used, would be able to secure or exercise control of the company. Thus, participators A B C and D, each owning 25% of the share capital and voting power in company X, are each associated with X: but if A owns 55% and B C and D together 45%, A is associated with X but B C and D are not associated with X. Since, under general tax rules applied to this provision (ICTA 1988 s839), the user is connected with the recipient if

75

6.10.9 UK Oil Taxation

the user acting together with one or more other companies is able to control it, any company which is connected with the recipient would also be associated with it. It might be argued that, if the proper construction of the definition of association is to impute potential to control rather than actual control, the ambit of association may be somewhat wider than connection.

The circumstances in which the Revenue would deem it appropriate to invoke this anti-avoidance provision are probably incapable of definition. It is possible to envisage an increasing number of bona fide commercial arrangements for the provision of assets, such as pipeline systems, by entities which are not participators but in which participators have at least a minority interest. The parties are likely to seek the Revenue's clearance in advance for such prospective arrangements. The consequences of the provision, if it were applied, are not without doubt. The general tenor and intent seems to be to place the participator concerned in approximately the same PRT position as would have obtained if it had incurred the expenditure on the asset itself; but on a less favourable interpretation of the rules, expenditure reliefs imputed to the participator may be inferior to those which would have applied to direct acquisition of the asset. In a simple case in which participator A controls a pipeline company B, the pipeline being used partly by A in field X and partly by unconnected participators in field Y, A would be charged on the tariffs received by B in respect of use for field Y, less tariff receipts allowance, and would be entitled to some relief on the cost of the pipeline in computing his field X profits. The question here is whether there is attributed to A the full cost of the asset and the attendant relief, including supplement if appropriate, or whether the attribution is restricted to that element of cost relating to use by field Y. On the latter construction, which seems the less likely, it may be that the expenditure relief would be given according to the remote associated asset rules (see 6.17.1); and title to supplement would be doubtful. Whether the tariff which A pays to B is allowable depends partly on whether or not a full attribution of the asset cost is made to A: in either case, the 'restriction to cost' rule is likely to come into play (see 6.26). These uncertainties may be magnified in practice since actual arrangements are likely to be substantially more complex.

Although the provision may be triggered by avoidance either of PRT or CT, the attribution of income and expenditure to a party which is not the actual recipient applies only for PRT purposes. The participator which is charged to PRT is entitled to deduct the PRT in calculating his CT liability. The actual recipient remains liable to CT under normal rules except that the income is specifically brought within the ring fence (see 7.8).

6.11 Receipts from Foreign Field Assets

6.11.1 Outline and Definitions

The Oil Taxation Act 1983 for the first time imposes a charge to PRT on certain receipts arising from assets of non-UK oil fields. The legislation relies on a bewildering series of definitions and cross-references, and the following analysis is an attempt to draw from it the essential framework. The charge is on the amount or value of any consideration, whether capital or revenue, received or receivable after 30 June 1982 by a participator (1) in a foreign field (2) in respect of either:

(*a*) UK use of a field asset (3); or
(*b*) provision of services or business facilities in connection with UK use of such an asset; or,
(*c*) disposal of, or of an interest in, such an asset where the asset has either been in UK use or could reasonably be expected after the disposal to be put to UK use (4).

Consideration so arising is a chargeable receipt only if:
(i) The field asset giving rise to the consideration is a chargeable asset (5) in relation to the participator; and
(ii) the consideration constitutes a receipt for which he is accountable (6).

Chargeable receipts are attributed to the foreign field for which the asset expenditure would have been allowable. If there is more than one such field, the receipts are attributed to the one in connection with which the asset would have been first used. In the case of receipts deriving from an asset used in association with a field asset, the appropriate field is that to which are attributed the chargeable receipts deriving from the field asset.

Definitions
(1) 'Participator' means, in essence, a licensee in the foreign field.
(2) A 'foreign field' is defined as an area not under UK jurisdiction but which is specified by the Secretary of State for Energy to be a foreign field. A number of Norwegian fields, including the Ekofisk complex and Heimdal, have been so specified. In the case of a transmedian field, the UK and non-UK sectors of the field are treated for these purposes as two separate fields.
(3) A 'field asset' is one which is not mobile; which is situated in the UK, the territorial sea or a designated area of the UKCS; and which has been or is expected to be used in a way which, if the foreign field were a UK field, would be used in connection with the field. This definition is extended to include an asset which, though not itself used or expected to be used in connection with the foreign field, is

6.11.1 UK Oil Taxation

used in association with an asset which is a field asset. The extension applies only where the associated asset gives rise to consideration which would be chargeable if the asset were a field asset, and where its useful life is expected to extend more than six months after the first receipt of the consideration.

(4) 'UK use' means, in relation to a field asset, its use in connection with the exploration or exploitation of the sea bed and subsoil and their natural resources situated in the territorial sea of the UK or a designated area of the UKCS.

(5) An asset is a 'chargeable asset' if expenditure on it would, assuming the field to be a UK field, be allowable for PRT purposes under either the old or new rules for expenditure relief (see 6.16.1 and 6.17) and, broadly, the asset is expected to be a long-term asset.

(6) The receipt is a 'receipt for which the participator is accountable' if, were the asset a qualifying asset in a UK field, the consideration would constitute a tariff or disposal receipt of the participator attributable to the field.

6.11.2 The Charge to Tax

A participator in a foreign field is liable to PRT in respect of chargeable receipts by reference to six month chargeable periods, the profit or loss being calculated under normal PRT rules with certain necessary modifications and assumptions. Tariff receipts allowance is given against receipts which, if arising in respect of a UK field asset, would be qualifying tariff receipts; and allowable expenditure is deducted from the net receipts. The oil allowance (see 6.28) is not given but the safeguard limitation on the tax payable applies (see 6.30). Tax payable on chargeable receipts is due on the dates applicable under general PRT rules. Provision is made to prevent a double charge on any consideration which would otherwise be brought into charge both as a tariff or disposal receipt of a participator in a UK field and as a chargeable receipt of a participator in a foreign field.

Expenditure is allowable if it is incurred on a foreign field asset which gives rise, or is expected to give rise, to chargeable receipts and is incurred with a view to giving rise to such receipts or to enhancing the value of the asset prior to disposal. There are provisions for the appointment of a responsible person (see 6.15.2) for the foreign field. Claims for foreign field expenditure are made by the responsible person on behalf of the participators unless, exceptionally, it is confidential expenditure, in which case it may be claimed separately by the participator concerned.

A foreign field participator having chargeable receipts is required to make a return, within two months of the end of each chargeable period, showing details of the receipts and of the assets giving rise to them. The responsible person is also obliged to make a return, one month after the end of the chargeable period, of the particulars necessary to enable the participators' shares of the tariff receipts allowance to be calculated.

6.11.3 Double Taxation Relief

Chargeable receipts arising to a participator in a foreign field which are liable to PRT, whether or not they are also liable to UK income tax or CT, may be within the charge to tax in the State in which the field is situated. For example, a participator in a Norwegian field who is liable to UK tax on tariffs derived from a pipeline used to transport oil from the field to the UK may also be chargeable to Norwegian income tax and special tax in respect of the same income. If the participator is a resident of Norway, the double taxation agreement between the UK and Norway provides relief from double taxation in Norway. The double taxation agreements between the UK and other countries bordering the North Sea similarly provide double taxation relief to residents of those other countries who are liable to UK tax on chargeable receipts. If the participator in question is not a resident of the State in which the foreign field is situated, the double taxation agreement between the UK and the foreign State does not prevent a charge to both UK tax and tax in the foreign State in respect of the chargeable receipts.

6.12 Chargeable Sums: Conveying and Treating Contributions

Where the Secretary of State takes royalties in kind from licensees under the first to fourth offshore licence Rounds, he makes cash payments representing the allowable costs of conveying and treating the oil so taken. The payments were not specifically catered for by the 1975 Oil Taxation Act, though they were in practice brought into the PRT computation either by inclusion in the royalty debit or credit calculation or by offset against expenditure reliefs. The PRT treatment was regularised by FA 1981 s118. All sums received from or paid to the Secretary of State after 31 December 1980 'by reference to a relevant licence' are brought into the PRT computation as positive amounts or negative amounts except:

(*a*) royalties or periodic payments falling to be taken into account in the licence debit or credit calculation, or other payments under or for the purpose of obtaining a licence, which are available for expendi-

6.12 UK Oil Taxation

ture relief (see 6.15.6);
(*b*) interest;
(*c*) repayment of royalty under PSPA 1975 s41(3) (discretionary repayments made to facilitate or maintain production from a licensed area);
(*d*) any payment relating to exempt gas.

Payments relating to a licence which covers more than one field are to be apportioned between the fields on a just and reasonable basis, not excluding the possibility that it may be reasonable to attribute them wholly to one of the fields. The 'subsidy' provision does not apply to chargeable sums, which arguably might otherwise need to be offset against the relative expenditure claimed for PRT allowance (Sched 3(8)).

Chargeable sums are taken into account in the chargeable period in which they are received, regardless of the period in which they accrue.

6.13 Relief for Royalty Payments

Royalties payable in cash to the Secretary of State are deducted in the PRT computation. The calculation of the deduction for a chargeable period is illustrated in the following example:

Chargeable period 1 July 1987 – 31 December 1987

				£m
	1	Royalties payable for the period, as shown in the participator's return		40
Add	2	Royalties paid in the period		35
Add	3	Periodic payments other than royalties, paid to Secretary of State in the period		3
				78
Less	4	Royalties payable for the previous period (as 1 for the previous period)	34	
	5	Royalties repaid by the Secretary of State in the period	NIL	34
		Licence debit (credit if negative)		44

The effect of this formula is to give relief on an accruals basis while bringing in repayments on a receipts basis. It allows the debit or credit to be established as soon as the participator's PRT return for the period is made, without the need to adjust it in the light of the final royalty liability for the period when that eventually emerges. The periodic payments referred to in the example are chiefly annual licence rentals.

Repayments to be taken into account do not include repayments made under PSPA 1975 s41(3) (discretionary repayments), which are exempt from PRT and CT.

Royalties are levied by reference to a licence, not by reference to a field. Where a licence covers an area which encompasses more than one field, there should normally be no problem in apportioning the royalties for PRT allowance, since the royalties for which relief is given are royalties in respect of the participator's share of oil won from the field. Relief for periodic payments, other than royalties, is given for payments under any 'relevant licence', which means any licence held or previously held by the participator in respect of a licensed area wholly or partly included in the field (s12). This suggests that the full amount of periodic payments under a relevant licence may be claimed even though substantial parts of the licensed area are not included in the field.

Oil which the Secretary of State takes as royalty in kind is not charged to PRT (see 6.8.4) and that oil is not included as royalty paid in the calculation of the licence debit or credit.

6.14 Relief for Expenditure: General

6.14.1 Outline

Relief is given for what might be termed field expenditure, that is expenditure incurred by a participator in searching for and appraising the field area, providing the production and transportation facilities, producing and disposing of the oil and finally closing down the field. The expenditure has to be incurred for a purpose which is within one of the defined qualifying purposes. It is not enough that it is incurred for bona fide commercial reasons, nor does allowance for CT purposes signify that it will be allowed for PRT. It may be in the nature of revenue or capital, though particular rules apply if it relates to the provision of a long term asset. Certain categories of expenditure are specifically excluded from allowance. Among these, the most important is interest, for which some alternative relief is provided in the supplement granted on particular categories of expenditure. Claims for field expenditure are normally made by the responsible person, on behalf of all of the participators in the field. Expenditure which is confidential to a participator, however, may be claimed separately by that participator.

In addition to field expenditure, relief is available for the cost of exploring and appraising areas not related to a field. The condition that such expenditure be shown to be 'abortive' was removed in respect of

6.14.1 UK Oil Taxation

expenditure, other than the cost of acquiring a licence interest, incurred after 15 March 1983. Allowance is also made for research expenditure not related to the field and for 10% of certain expenditure relating to other fields.

PRT is fundamentally different from other taxes in the timing of expenditure relief. No relief is given until the Inland Revenue indicate in a decision on a claim that the expenditure is admissible. Allowance is given in the next assessment to be made after that decision, which may or may not be the assessment for the period in which the expenditure was incurred. Claims are made by reference to claim periods of either six or twelve months. In recognition that an assessment for a chargeable period might be made before the Revenue has allowed some or all of the expenditure incurred in the period, a minimum provisional allowance is provided, based on a percentage of the income for the period. The main reason for these timing rules was probably the Government's wish to see that delays in making claims and in the agreement of allowances for expenditure should not hold up the flow of tax to the Exchequer. That concern has been largely overtaken by events, in that early and regular payment of tax is now secured by the arrangements for payment of PRT liabilities by instalments commencing in the chargeable period in question. On appeal against an assessment, a participator may withhold payment of tax but only to the extent that it relates to the difference, broadly, between the amount of income assessed and the participator's estimation of what that income should be.

6.14.2 Expenditure Incurred

Relief is given for expenditure incurred. The Oil Taxation Acts provide no guidance as to whether or when expenditure is incurred. In contrast, for the purposes of income tax and CT capital allowances the date on which expenditure is incurred is precisely defined, normally to mean the date on which the obligation to pay becomes unconditional (FA 1985 s56). In practice, the interpretation applied for PRT purposes derives largely from UK accounting principles. Expenditure incurred includes accruals provided on a reasonable and consistent basis, relating both to work invoiced but not paid for and work performed but not yet invoiced.

6.14.3 Capital or Revenue

The allowance of expenditure is not normally affected by the question of whether it is capital or revenue. The main relief sections include references to expenditure 'whether or not of a capital nature'. Particular rules apply to expenditure on long term assets, and claim forms require such expenditure to be distinguished.

The availability of supplement may in some instances depend on whether the expenditure is incurred in the provision of an asset. The main rule likely to afford supplement on expenditure incurred after production has commenced requires as a pre-condition that the expenditure be incurred for the purposes of 'carrying out works for or acquiring an asset or an interest in an asset' (s3(5)(c)). A proper attribution of indirect costs to relevant assets may then have a material effect on liability.

6.15 Field Expenditure

6.15.1 Claim Periods

Claims are made for claim periods, which are fixed independently of chargeable periods (6.5). A claim period is a period of twelve months or, if the responsible person so elects, six months, ending 30 June or 31 December: the first claim period, however, includes an unlimited time prior to the determination of the field (Sched 5(1)). The duration of a claim period can be changed from one period to the next. Whether the length of the period is six or twelve months, there is no requirement that all expenditure to be claimed be included in one claim for the period; as many claims may be made as the claimant finds necessary to encompass all of the expenditure. For example, if the claim period is twelve months, claims may be made to cover the two half years separately, and expenditure omitted, inadvertently or otherwise, from those claims may be included in further claims for the period.

The choice of length of the claim period may have a material effect on overall liability, and will almost certainly affect the timing of liability. Some provisions are geared to the ending of a claim period. The time limit for making claims is six years from the end of the claim period in which the expenditure is incurred (Sched 5(2)): and the time allowed for the making of an appeal against a decision on a claim is three years from the date of the claim (Sched 5(5)). The provision which allows the Revenue to adjust the amount of oil allowance to take account of expenditure claimed late is also tied to the date on which a claim period ends (Sched 3(11)). In general, adoption of a twelve month period will delay the effective allowance of expenditure incurred in the first half of that period. In most cases, this is not a beneficial result, but there are circumstances in which the delay may reduce overall liability. In

6.15.1 UK Oil Taxation

particular, it may accelerate the utilisation of oil allowance or defer allowance from a chargeable period in which effective relief is negated by safeguard to a later period in which the full PRT rate applies. In practice, election is usually made for adoption of six monthly periods.

6.15.2 The Responsible Person

Each field has a 'responsible person'. Its responsibilities are chiefly to render a return for each chargeable period relating to field production and tariff receipts (see 6.31.1), and to make claims for expenditure on behalf of the field participators. All field expenditure is claimed by the responsible person except that which is confidential to a particular participator, which that participator may claim on its own account.

The responsible person must be a company resident in the UK or a partnership the members of which are resident in the UK, but it does not have to be a participator. It is to be nominated by the field participators within 30 days of the notice of determination of the field and the Board has to approve the appointment. If the Board does not approve the nominee or if no nomination has been made within the time limit, the Board appoints one of the participators. It also has the power to approve a replacement nominated by the participators or to revoke approval and to appoint its own nominee (Sched 2(4)).

In most fields, the responsible person is the participator which holds the largest interest and acts as the field operator. This is a sensible enough arrangement since the need to formulate claims and to conduct negotiations with the OTO demands familiarity with the data. Where that person is a company not resident in the UK which holds its interest by virtue of an Illustrative Agreement (see 8.11), the responsible person may be the associated licence holder.

6.15.3 The Purpose Test

The key test of admissibility of expenditure is one of purpose — is the expenditure incurred for a purpose within one of the qualifying categories (s3(1))? Although there is no requirement that expenditure is 'necessarily' incurred for the particular qualifying purpose, it may be relevant in some instances to consider the motivation of the expenditure. At the extreme, it might be argued that expenditure incurred with the aim of avoiding tax is incurred for that purpose and not for a qualifying purpose. Where expenditure is incurred partly for a qualifying purpose and partly not, it is to be apportioned on a just and reasonable basis (s3(6)). The most common application of this dual purpose rule is in the allocation of expenditure of a field which produces both exempt and non-exempt oil.

Special considerations apply to expenditure on long term assets. For such expenditure, the test is one of use — is the asset used or expected to be used in connection with a field? Use in connection with a field is defined as 'use in connection with that field for one or more of the purposes mentioned in s3(1) of this Act (excluding section 3(1)(*b*), (s12(2)). Such proportion of use of an asset as gives rise to tariff receipts is treated as qualifying use (s3(7)).

There are differences also in the time at which the test has to be applied. The judgment of purpose should normally be that which would have been made had it been exercised at the time when the expenditure was incurred. The more objective test of long term asset expenditure is to be made as at the end of a particular claim period, in most instances the claim period in which the expenditure is incurred. The use of the asset not only establishes whether any allowance is due, but respective field and non-field use while in the participator's ownership may determine how much of the expenditure is allowable.

The test which expenditure has to meet in order to qualify for supplement is firmly a test of the purpose for which the expenditure is incurred.

6.15.4 Indirect Expenditure

Expenditure which is incurred for a qualifying purpose includes the indirect costs which are fairly attributable to it. During the passage of the Oil Taxation Bill in 1974, a Treasury Minister said 'Any directly attributable onshore control and back-up costs will be allowed: subsection (5) [now s3(6)] provides for the apportionment where necessary.' This assurance is regarded as endorsement both of onshore costs which are directly incurred for a specific field purpose and of overhead or support costs, but it raises the question — what is 'directly attributable'?

Ideally, indirect costs should be allocated to a project or cost-centre on a field or licence basis as the expenditure is incurred. In practice this is often not practicable. A major company is likely to have a complex of support departments, and it may receive support also from affiliated companies with equally involved accounting arrangements. Attribution of indirect costs may be achieved by a succession of charges from indirect to direct departments, and some exercise of hindsight may be required. Costs of the central overhead type may nevertheless constitute a part of the larger expense on a qualifying project, provided that there is a discernible thread connecting it to that larger whole. The onus

6.15.4   UK Oil Taxation

is on the claimant to demonstrate that all costs are generated by a qualifying purpose. The OTO is likely to reject claims for costs related to the maintenance of the company, such as long term planning and public relations, as not incurred for a specific field purpose.

6.15.5 Expenditure not Allowable

Certain categories of expenditure which would otherwise qualify for relief are specifically proscribed.

Interest
The PRT rules prohibit allowance for expenditure in respect of interest or any other pecuniary obligation incurred in obtaining a loan or any other form of credit (s3(4)(*a*)). They provide instead a proxy interest relief in the form of supplement on certain qualifying expenditure. The main reason for adoption of this course lay in the formidable difficulties which were expected to be involved in policing the level of interest charged against field profits, difficulties already apparent in the realm of CT which would have been exacerbated in a field-based PRT system. A relatively simple supplement allowance seemed to be a better alternative. In the light of the complexity endemic in the operation of the supplement provisions, however, there must be a question mark against the wisdom of the choice made in 1975.

Interest of all kinds is disallowed including interest on late paid invoices. The prohibition also extends to any expenditure relating to the obtaining of credit, such as commitment and guarantee fees and relative legal costs. It probably does not apply in relation to expenditure which may have its origin in credit obligations of the supplier or contractor (see 6.19.10).

Land
The cost of acquiring land or an interest in land is not allowable. Land is not defined, but for general tax purposes it means not only the land itself but also what lies under the land and what is emplaced on it, such as buildings. This rule does not prevent allowance for annual or periodic payments such as rent, which are made to maintain an interest in land, nor the cost of rights of access (s3(4)(*b*)).

Buildings or structures on land
The cost of acquiring or erecting any building or structure on land is not allowable unless it is within one of four permitted categories. These are buildings or structures:

(1) subsequently placed on the sea bed, for use in connection with a field;
(2) for use in the production or metering of oil from an onshore field;
(3) for use in initial treatment or initial storage of oil won either offshore or onshore.
(4) for use in the transportation of offshore oil from the point of first landing in the UK to the nearest reasonable UK delivery point (s3(4)(c)).

Buildings and installations at onshore terminals serving offshore fields largely fall within the permitted categories, relating either to initial treatment, initial storage or transportation. They include buildings which house the terminal plant, control and administration buildings and loading jetties. It is unlikely, however, that the building or acquisition cost of a participator's general offices will be seen by the OTO as qualifying for PRT relief.

Payments pro rata to production
No relief is available for 'any expenditure wholly or partly depending on or determined by reference to the quantity, value or proceeds of, or the profits from, oil won from the field' (s3(4)(d)). The chief effect of this provision is to disallow payments made by a participator to the holder of a subordinated interest in production from the field under overriding royalty, production interest or similar arrangements. The recipient will not normally be a participator within the charge to PRT in respect of such payments. Tariffs or similar payments for services are not regarded as caught by this provision.

Licence acquisition costs
No relief is available for the cost of acquiring an interest in oil won or to be won from a field, unless it is a payment to the Secretary of State. The prohibition includes the cash cost of buying an interest in a licence and related agreements such as the Joint Operating Agreement, whether the acquisition is made before or after the licensed area is determined as a field. It is not in practice extended to the cost incurred by a farmer-in in satisfying work obligations undertaken as consideration for transfer of the interest (s3(4)(e)). There are special rules relating to the transfer of an interest in a determined field (see 8.10).

Contractors tax
Licencees may be required to pay amounts equal to unpaid UK tax, and interest thereon, levied on contractors not resident in the UK who performed services in the licenced area. No PRT or CT relief is available for such payments (s3(4)(f)).

6.15.5 UK Oil Taxation

Exempt gas expenditure

Gas sold to the British Gas Corportion under a pre-July 1975 contract is exempt from PRT, as is other production from the same field not exceeding a 5% *de minimis* amount (see 6.8.1). Expenditure relating to such 'excluded oil' is not allowable.

In the case of expenditure which would otherwise be allowable under the provisions in s3(1)(*a*) (*b*) or (*c*) (exploration, payments other than royalties to the Secretary of State or appraisal), allowance is given only for a proportion, being the proportion which the original reserves of oil not subject to sale under the pre-July 1975 BGC contract bears to the total original reserves. The reserves estimates for this purpose have to be approved by the Secretary of State (s10(3)(*a*)). Expenditure falling under s3(1)(*i*) (closing down the field) is similarly apportioned, except that the division is made not by reference to the original reserves but by reference to the cumulative production of excluded oil and of all oil including excluded oil respectively (s10(3)(*b*)). This formula is likely to produce unfair results, particularly where field assets used for the purposes of excluded oil are also used to generate tariff income.

For all other costs, the disallowance is achieved by deeming excluded oil not to be oil as recognised for PRT, so that expenditure on excluded oil is not incurred for a qualifying purpose. Any necessary apportionment is then made on a just and reasonable basis (s10(2)).

It follows that use of an asset in connection with excluded oil is not regarded as use in connection with the field giving title to PRT allowance. Expenditure on the asset is, if necessary, apportioned on a just and reasonable basis between that non-qualifying use and any qualifying use, which may include use giving rise to tariff receipts (OTA 1983 s4(1)).

Prevention of double allowance

Expenditure is not allowable for a field if, or to the extent that, it has been allowed as field expenditure for any other field, or has been allowed under the exploration and appraisal or abortive exploration expenditure provisions for the field in question or any other field. This provision applies also if the expenditure is long term asset expenditure (s4(10) and OTA 1983 s3(6)). However, prior allowance of expenditure under the exploration and appraisal rules does not prevent a claim for allowance as field expenditure provided that the claimant is not the participator which made the exploration and appraisal claim (s3(3)). The OTO takes the view that this provision merely enables a responsible person to make a field claim for the expenditure on exploration or appraisal incurred by participators, even though the claim will not be allowed if the expenditure was previously allowed under the exploration and appraisal rules. It is questionable whether that view is correct.

In some circumstances, the cost of acquiring an asset does not qualify for relief if another participator in the field has had relief for its expenditure in providing or enhancing the same asset (see 6.17.1).

6.15.6 Allowable Field Expenditure

The rules relating to relief for expenditure on long term assets are now contained mainly in the 1983 Oil Taxation Act. Broadly, relief depends on the asset's use or expected use in connection with the field or to give rise to tariffs, and use in connection with the field means use for one or more of the purposes defined in s3(1). For other expenditure, the test is whether it is incurred for one or more of the purposes defined in s3(1). It may be incurred before the incurrer becomes a participator, and may include, for example, the cost of surveys undertaken before a licence for the field area is granted. The qualifying purposes are dealt with in the following paragraphs.

Searching for oil

> Searching for oil anywhere within the area of the field as subsequently determined under Schedule 1 to this Act or not more than 5,000 metres beyond the boundary of that area (s3(1)(*a*)).

This provision caters mainly for seismic surveys and exploration drilling and related expense. In addition to works undertaken directly by the participator on its own account, including those undertaken to earn an interest in a licence, it may cover also participation in works undertaken by others in the relevant area.

It does not extend to the reimbursement of prior costs incurred by a farmer-out, though those costs may still qualify in their own right for inclusion in a field claim to be made by the responsible person. The apportionment of seismic costs, which may be necessary because the works extend beyond the qualifying area, is usually made by reference to numbers of miles shot.

The reference to the area of the field 'as subsequently determined' may suggest that the provision is apt to cover only expenditure incurred prior to the determination of the field. While it is possible that that was the premise on which the provision was drafted, the better view is that determination does not bring an end to the possible application of the provision to the field in question.

While the test of whether expenditure is incurred for a particular purpose should normally be made as at the time when the expenditure

6.15.6 UK Oil Taxation

is incurred, that proposition needs modification in relation to searching, appraising and licence acquisition costs (s3(1)(*a*) (*b*) and (*c*)). Much expenditure of these types which may prove to be allowable is incurred before the area is revealed as a field, and the exercise of hindsight seems to be inevitable in deciding whether the expenditure was incurred for a requisite purpose.

Licence payments to the Secretary of State

> Making to the Secretary of State any payment under or for the purpose of obtaining a relevant licence, not being a payment by way of royalty or other periodic payment (s3(1)(*b*)).

Payments to the Secretary of State to acquire a licence are allowable if the licence is a 'relevant licence'. They may include premium or auction payments. Relevant licence 'in relation to a participator in an oil field means any licence held or previously held by him in respect of a licensed area wholly or partly included in the field' (s12). So long as the field lies partly within the licensed area, the licence is a relevant licence, even though much of the area may be quite unconnected with the field, and payments relating to the licence may be claimed in full without apportionment.

Royalties and other periodic payments under a licence are excluded from relief under this provision and allowed separately in the calculation of licence debit or credit (see 6.13).

Appraisal expenditure

> Ascertaining (whether before or after the determination of the field under Schedule 1 to this Act) the extent or characteristics of any oil-bearing area wholly or partly included in the field, or what the reserves of oil of any such oil-bearing area are (s3(1)(*c*)).

The site of the appraisal works may lie either within or without the field boundary, so long as the works are carried out for the purpose of appraising 'any oil-bearing area wholly or partly included in the field'. Oil-bearing area is not defined, but what may be contemplated is a separate geological structure which is known to contain oil. Partly because of the vagueness of the physical concept, the precise confines of this provision are not easy to establish. Unlike the searching provision, s3(1)(*a*), it does not limit the distance between the site of the works and the field boundary, so that if the cost of a well drilled more than 5,000 metres from the field is to qualify as field expenditure, it may do so under s3(1)(*c*) if the purpose is to test an oil-bearing structure which lies partly within the field boundary. The two provisions are not, however, alternatives offering a choice of claim. Which, if either, of the two is

Petroleum Revenue Tax 6.15.6

appropriate depends on the participator's intent and state of knowledge when the expenditure is incurred; and on whether the works are in the nature of wildcat exploration or appraisal of a known oil-bearing structure.

The relationship between expenditure claimed under either of these provisions as field expenditure and exploration and appraisal expenditure which is not related to a field is dealt with in paragraph 6.22.

Winning of oil

> Winning oil from the field (s3(1)(*d*)).

The bulk of expenditure relating to a field is likely to fall within this head. It includes both the major capital outlays on fabrication and installation of production facilities and the drilling of production wells, and the ongoing production operating costs. There may be a tendency to think that it is so compendious as to encompass all field-related expenditure which is not specifically within one of the other qualifying purposes, but it is probably more correct to regard expenditure incurred for the purposes of winning oil as that directly geared to the provision of the production apparatus and to production of oil.

The cost of insuring the field production facilities is usually a very significant proportion of production expenditure. It is accepted as a cost of winning oil qualifying for relief provided that the insurance policy is on normal commercial terms covering damage, loss or destruction. The cost of loss of profits cover, however, is unlikely to be allowable.

Metering

> Measuring the quantity of oil won or to be won from the field (s3(1)(*e*)).

The cost of providing metering equipment and of metering operations, whether on the production platform or at the onshore receiving point, is allowable. The reasons for inclusion of the reference to oil 'to be won' is not clear, since measurement of the quantity of that oil appears to be an operation already encompassed within appraisal activities under s3(1)(*c*)

Transportation of oil

> In the case of oil won from the field that was so won from strata in the sea bed and subsoil of either the territorial sea of the UK or a designated area, transporting it to the place where it is first landed in the UK or to the place in the UK at which the seller in a sale at arm's length could reasonably be expected to deliver it or, if there is more than one place at which he could reasonably be expected to deliver it, the one nearest to the place of extraction (s3(1)(*f*)).

6.15.6 UK Oil Taxation

The general concept is that expenditure incurred in transporting offshore oil to the UK is allowable. Before the provision was changed in 1979, it provided for transporting oil from offshore fields to 'the place where it is first landed in the UK'. Difficulties arose in the case of some fields from which the oil was transported ashore by pipeline since a cut-off of relief at the point of first landing rather than a delivery point left unrelieved substantial expenditure, particularly on terminal loading facilities. This lack of 'coincidence' between the taxing point and the point to which necessary expenditure could qualify for relief was recognised in the amendment now reflected in the expanded provision quoted above. The rule as amended now allows relief for the cost of transportation either to the UK point of first landing or to the nearest reasonable point in the UK at which the seller in a sale at arm's length could reasonably be expected to deliver the oil. It thus embraces terminal loading facilities and puts beyond doubt the admissibility of certain onshore pipelines which transport offshore oil to the nearest reasonable delivery point. The Revenue accepts that if the point of first landing is further removed from the field than the nearest reasonable delivery point, as it might be in the case of oil transported from the field by tanker rather than by pipeline, relief for the actual transportation costs will not be restricted.

The 1979 amendment adopts, in the nearest reasonable delivery point, the point of delivery which has to be assumed in the notional contract for oil to which the market value rules apply (see 6.7.2). For the purposes of the expenditure relief provision, however, it is immaterial whether or not the oil is sold at arm's length, or whether it is appropriated by the producer.

The law provides relief for the cost of transporting oil only to the UK, and it follows that, strictly, no relief would be available if the oil were shipped direct from the field to a country other than the UK. It is a condition of the licence that oil is landed in the UK, but that condition is sometimes waived. Since the measure of income for PRT in respect of oil is the selling price inclusive of any consideration for freight or, in the case of sales not at arm's length or appropriations, the UK landed value, equity demands some relief in these circumstances for actual or notional transportation costs. The Revenue accepts, by concession, that where oil is directly exported from a field by tanker and is not delivered to the UK, the cost of transportation to the actual point of delivery is allowable, up to the amount which would have been allowable if the oil had been landed in the UK. In determining the notional landing point in the UK, the usual approach is to take the place in the UK at which the participator in question would most probably have landed the cargo having regard to the pattern of actual deliveries to the

UK by that participator. In the event that the length of the actual voyage exceeds that of the notional voyage to the UK, the allowance for the transportation costs is restricted. The method of calculating the restriction may depend on the circumstances, but in general a disallowance of incremental costs related to the excess distance is acceptable to the OTO.

The insurance of cargoes in transit from field to shore might be regarded as indemnity against loss of profits rather than a transportation cost. It is understood that, in practice, relief is given for the insurance cost provided that the participator accepts that any recoveries under the policy will be within the charge to PRT.

No relief is provided for the costs of transporting oil won onshore. The presumption seems to be that onshore oil will be sold at the place of extraction, which is also the delivery point assumed in the notional contact for oil sold not at arm's length or appropriated (see 6.7.2). It is possible to envisage circumstances in which that presumption would not be valid.

Initial treatment

> The initial treatment . . . of oil won from the field (s3(1)(g)).

The definition of initial treatment is found in s12. It was amended in 1980 in conjunction with enactment of revised rules governing the valuation of gases (see 6.7.4). The scheme of the 1975 provision is, broadly, to permit the treatment of crude up to the point at which it could be safely stored or safely accepted by a refinery. It includes 'separating oil won from the field and consisting of methane gas from oil consisting of gas other than methane', and excludes 'any activities carried on as part of, or in association with, the refining of oil'. It became apparent that in its application to gas the definition left substantial areas of doubt which FA 1980 s109 sought to remove. The revised definition (which is dealt with in more detail in 6.7.4) is wide enough to encompass all costs of stabilisation and fractionation whether offshore or at onshore receiving terminals.

The definition of both initial treatment and initial storage specifically excludes deballasting, and it is generally accepted that there is no avenue of PRT relief for deballasting expenditure. Since deballast facilities at onshore terminals normally also play a role in the dewatering of crude received from the field and in the treatment of terminal effluent, a proportion of the relative capital and running costs may be allowable. Deballast recovery oil is not chargeable to PRT.

6.15.6 UK Oil Taxation

Initial storage

> Initial storage of oil won from the field (s3(1)(g)).

The definition of initial storage is contained in s12. It covers the storage of oil won from either onshore or offshore fields. The oil may be stored in the UK, the territorial sea or a designated area of the UKCS, but initial storage onshore is limited to ten times the maximum daily rate of production, as planned or achieved, whichever is greater. The limit should be set by reference to the effective usable capacity of the facilities. Initial storage does not include storage in connection with the operation of a refinery, conveying oil in a pipeline, or deballasting.

Disposing of oil

> Disposing of any oil won from the field which is disposed of crude in sales at arm's length (s3(1)(h)).

The original Oil Taxation Bill did not provide relief for selling costs, an omission remedied during passage of the Bill through parliament. Doubts have often been expressed about the scope of the provision. At first sight, it is rather more compendious than appears on closer examination. It refers only to disposals which are sales at arm's length, so excluding costs related to any sale which, for whatever reason, fails to satisfy the arm's length test (see 6.7.1). Apart from the obvious effect, the exclusion may be said to colour the nature of the provision: since it is necessary to know whether a particular disposal was a sale at arm's length before any title to relief on the costs of disposal can arise, it is difficult to argue that front-end costs of setting up disposal facilities can satisfy the test.

It is clear enough that incidental costs of selling at arm's length, such as salary and running costs of an oil selling department, qualify for relief. Oil may be sold, particularly where small quantities are involved, on terms under which the buyer charges a handling fee or marketing fee to the seller. Such a fee is normally accepted by the OTO to qualify for relief, provided of course that the sale is a sale at arm's length. Further doubts may arise in the area in which the responsibilities of the seller and the shipper meet, in which a seller will need to demonstrate that expenditure falling on it is a direct cost of disposing of oil rather than, say, part of the overall cost of the shipping operation.

Closing down the field

> Closing down the field or any part of it, but only if and to the extent that the expenditure is incurred for the purposes of safety or the prevention of pollution (s3(1)(i)).

The precise nature of the work which licensees will be required to undertake in closing down a field has still to be determined. It is reasonable to expect that that part of it which relates to abandonment of offshore facilities will be wholly within the safety or prevention of pollution categories; this may include plugging and abandoning wells, removal of the whole or part of platforms and perhaps removal of pipelines. The continuing cost of inspection and maintenance of facilities which are left in place or partially removed should also qualify.

The removal of a related onshore terminal and restoration of the site poses more difficult questions. The Revenue accepts that such works are capable of coming within the meaning of expenditure incurred for the purpose of 'closing down the field or any part of it'. Removal of plant and buildings and making good should satisfy the safety or prevention of pollution criteria, but some of the cost involved in reinstatement of the site and removal of access roads, which may be required as a condition of the lease rather than under the terms of the licence, may not qualify.

Any scrap or other disposal proceeds of assets in respect of which expenditure relief has been given will be chargeable as disposal receipts (see 6.10.6). In many cases, the closing down of the field will not entail abandonment of the terminal but rather disposal or tariffing to participators in other fields.

Statutory redundancy payments

Redundancy payments under the Employment Protection Acts which are allowable under ICTA 1988 s577 (2) for CT purposes also qualify for PRT relief, provided that the CT deduction falls to be given in calculating the participator's ring fence profits. The amount of any recoverable rebate is deducted from the allowable expenditure. The relief may be claimed against any field in which the payer is a participator, without the need for apportionment if there is more than one such field (s3 (2)).

6.16 Expenditure on Assets: The Background

Major changes were made in 1983 in the scheme of relief for expenditure on assets. In general terms, the new rules apply to expenditure incurred after 30 June 1982. The assets in question are long-term assets, that is, assets having a useful life which continues after the end of the claim period in which they are first used in connection with the field. The expenditure may be either revenue or capital, though in practice

6.16 UK Oil Taxation

almost all of it is likely to be capital. The prohibition on allowance of certain types of expenditure applies both to expenditure on assets and to other expenditure (see 6.15.5).

The old rules provided relief in proportion to the extent of use or expected use of the asset for the purposes of the participator's field. In most cases, relief was given for the full cost at the outset, though this was subject to review and possible adjustment for each succeeding claim period in the light of changing circumstances of use. As the number of North Sea fields increased and the actual and potential sharing of production and transportation systems proliferated, the asset relief regime became increasingly uncertain in application and cumbersome to operate. The new rules introduced in 1983 provide secure front-end relief for assets dedicated to a field, including those which may be used by other participators in return for tariff payments, and remove the need for automatic review in each succeeding period. Relief for assets not dedicated to a field is given on a *per diem* basis according to qualifying use over the asset's life. The counterpart of these changes is the extension of the PRT charge to receipts deriving from the use of assets otherwise than by the owner and to gains on asset disposals.

Under both old and new rules, there is an escape clause providing that the long-term asset provisions are not to apply if the Board consider that their application would have only a negligible effect on the total expenditure allowable for the field. The effect then is that the expenditure is considered under the general rules for full allowance as it is incurred. This provision, which is very rarely invoked, is thought to be intended to obviate the trouble of operating the relatively complex long term asset rules where only small amounts of expenditure are involved (OTA 1983 s3(2)).

The old rules are summarised in 6.16.1, the new rules are dealt with in more detail in 6.17, and the transitional provisions are discussed in 6.18.

6.16.1 The Old Rules: Expenditure Incurred Before 1 July 1982

Expenditure on a long-term asset which is used or expected to be used for a qualifying field purpose is in general allowed for the claim period in which the expenditure is incurred, provided that:
(*a*) after the expenditure is incurred, the asset is in that period used, if at all, only in connection with the field: and
(*b*) at the end of that period it is reasonable to assume that the asset will from then until the end of its useful life be used only in connection with the field: and
(*c*) the asset is not a mobile asset.

Unless all of the conditions are satisfied, a proportion of the expenditure is allowed for the claim period in which it is incurred, under one of two alternative formulae:
(1) if it is possible to make a reasonable estimate of field and non-field use to which the asset will be put during its lifetime, a proportion of expenditure is allowed corresponding to the proportion which estimated field use bears to total use; or
(2) if such an estimate is not possible, the allowance for the claim period is the proportion which actual field use in the period bears to total lifetime use.

The application of the formula in (1) may still achieve 100% allowance for the claim period in which the expenditure is incurred. For example, in the case of a mobile asset such as a tanker which is acquired for dedicated use in a field, the lifetime use may be estimated to be solely for that purpose. For mobile assets which have been put to other use before field use, allowances are restricted so as to exclude the wasted element of cost relating to prior non-field use. For other 'brought-in' assets, there is no such restriction, but allowance is given for the claim period in which the asset is first put to field use.

Whether full front-end relief is allowed or whether a proportion only of the expenditure is allowed for the first relevant claim period, the allowance entitlement is reviewed for each succeeding claim period. If then the estimates of future field and non-field use respectively indicate that allowances already given are excessive, a reduction is made, normally netted off against other expenditure allowances for the period; alternatively, the revised estimates may require that a further tranches of expenditure on the asset be allowed (s4).

Disposal of the asset generally triggers a balancing adjustment, the total qualifying expenditure on the asset being reduced by the amount of disposal proceeds. In the case of a disposal to a connected person, however, the adjustment is made not by bringing in the sale price but by revising the proportionate allowance, the remaining life of the asset after sale counting as non-field use. In neither case is any profit on the sale brought into PRT charge (Sched 4(4)).

6.17 Expenditure on Assets – The New Rules

6.17.1 Non-Mobile Assets and Mobile Assets Dedicated to a Field
The main asset rules apply to long-term assets which are either not mobile or, if mobile, are dedicated to a field. Relief is given for expenditure incurred by a participator in a field, or by that company before it becomes a participator, in acquiring, bringing into existence or enhancing the value of a long-term asset which, at the end of the

6.17.1 UK Oil Taxation

relevant claim period, is in use in connection with the field or is expected to be so used in the future (OTA 1983 s3(1)). Use in connection with the field means use for one of the qualifying purposes referred to in s3(1) (s12(2)). Use of an asset which gives rise to tariff receipts attributable to the field for which any of the expenditure is allowable under general rules is itself treated as qualifying use in connection with that field (s3(7)). References to an asset include an interest in an asset.

In relation to these assets, expenditure is generally allowable in full for the claim period in which it is incurred. In the case of a brought-in asset (that is, an asset which was used for some other purpose before being brought into use in connection with the field), the allowance is due for the claim period in which it is first used in connection with the field. For a mobile asset the expenditure is allowable, if not otherwise allowable for an earlier period, for the claim period in which the asset becomes dedicated to the field, subject to reduction on account of early allowances given under the rules relating to non-dedicated assets.

Dedicated mobile assets

There is no definition of mobile for these purposes. The dictionary definition 'movable' is probably wider than the context requires. What is perhaps contemplated is an asset which is inherently capable of movement for use for a succession of fields and likely to be so used unless it is 'dedicated' to one of them. A semi-submersible drilling rig is one of the more obvious examples: a rig emplaced on a platform for production drilling purposes may also be mobile. Nor is dedication to a field precisely defined. Instead, dedication is taken to begin when a number of conditions are satisfied. A mobile asset not already dedicated to a particular field becomes dedicated in a claim period if:

(1) It is used in connection with the field during at least part of the period; and
(2) It is reasonable to assume that at the end of that period it will be used in that connection during the whole, or substantially the whole, of the period from the end of the claim period to the end of its useful life or the end of the life of the field if earlier (whether or not it is used concurrently for another field); and
(3) Its main use during that period will be in connection with that field or two or more fields of which that field is one.

In some circumstances, an asset may be regarded as dedicated to a field in a claim period before that in which it is first used in connection with the field (OTA 1983 s2).

A shuttle tanker owned by the participators and used solely to transport oil from an offshore field to the UK is likely to be dedicated to the field. A semi-submersible rig used for exploration or appraisal

Petroleum Revenue Tax 6.17.1

drilling is unlikely to be a dedicated asset. A floating production platform, as a mobile asset, is probably dedicated to the field on which it is employed since the period for which the assumption of field use is required ends at the end of the life of the field, if earlier than the end of the asset's useful life.

Determination of whether a mobile asset is dedicated to a field is important because the reliefs available for expenditure on its provision are more favourable than those applying to a non dedicated asset. Generally, the expenditure is allowed in full for the chargeable period in which it becomes dedicated, whereas allowances for the cost of a non dedicated asset are phased over the asset's life. As a corollary, receipts derived from a dedicated mobile asset are chargeable to PRT as tariff or disposal receipts, while those attributable to a non dedicated asset are not within the PRT charge (see 6.10.2).

If expenditure has been partly relieved under the non dedicated asset provisions for periods before the asset becomes dedicated to a field, the amount then qualifying for relief under the dedicated asset rules is reduced accordingly. This does not apply in the case of a 'brought-in' asset in respect of which the allowable expenditure is reduced so as to exclude the proportion attributable to use prior to dedication to the field (OTA 1983 Sched 1 (9)).

Assets acquired for two or more fields
Where the purchaser of an asset is a participator in more than one field and it appears that the asset is used, or is expected to be used, in connection with more than one such field, the expenditure is apportioned between the fields on a just and reasonable basis, not excluding the possibility that it may be just and reasonable to attribute all of it to one of the fields. The test is applied at the end of the 'relevant claim period', generally the claim period in which the expenditure is incurred. Strictly, account should apparently be taken of fields determined at that time, not including prospective developments for which no field determination has been made. There is no provision for re-allocating expenditure relief between fields once the initial split has been made (OTA 1983 Sched 1 para 5 (1)).

If use of such an asset in connection with one of the fields gives rise, or is expected to give rise, to tariff receipts which are chargeable in another of the fields, the expenditure which is attributable to the use giving rise to the tariffs is apportioned to the chargeable field. Tariffs are chargeable in that field for which development consent was given first (see 6.10.3).

If, in addition to use for two or more of the participator's fields, the asset is also used, or is expected to be used, to any extent for other purposes, the amount of expenditure which is fairly attributable to that

6.17.1 UK Oil Taxation

other use is apportioned to the field for which development consent was given first. This may apply, for example, in the case of a mobile asset which, although satisfying the test of dedication to a field, is expected to be employed to a minor extent outside the UK sector. Use which is expected to give rise to tariff receipts is generally treated as use in connection with the participator's chargeable field (OTA 1983 Sched 1 para 5(3)).

If no apportionment is required under the foregoing provisions, the whole of the allowable expenditure is attributed to use in connection with the participator's field or, if there is more than one such field, the field for which development consent was given first (OTA 1983 Sched 1 para 6).

Associated assets

Allowance is available in some circumstances for expenditure on assets which are not themselves field assets but which may give rise to receipts. If a non-mobile asset which is not used at all in connection with the field in question (the principal field) is used or expected to be used in association with another asset which is, or is expected to be, so used, and the first (associated) asset gives rise to receipts which, if it were a qualifying asset, would be chargeable as tariff receipts, then use of that asset to produce those receipts is treated as use of the asset in connection with the principal field. An asset is only treated as used in association with a principal field asset if it is in fact used in a way which constitutes use in connection with another field (or would constitute such use but for the exemption from PRT of gas sold to the BGC under a pre-July 1975 contract), or is used in connection with a field which is not within UK jurisdiction. Then, that part of the expenditure on the associated asset which is attributable to the use in question is treated as allowable for the principal field. (OTA 1983 Sched 1 (1)).

Remote associated assets

Relief for associated assets is restricted if they are 'remote' from the principal field asset, that is, if some part of the asset is more than 100 metres from the nearest part of the principal field asset. A spur pipeline used to connect another field to the principal field's pipeline system is such a remote asset. Expenditure allowable on a remote associated asset may not be taken into account in ascertaining PRT liability for a chargeable period earlier than the first period in which tariff or disposal receipts from the asset are included in the calculation of profit or loss. Even then, the amount allowed for any period may not exceed the aggregate of tariff receipts, net of any tariff receipts allowance, and disposal receipts derived, wholly or partly, from the asset in that period. Where tariff receipts of the period are reduced by tariff receipts

Petroleum Revenue Tax 6.17.1

allowance and derive partly from remote associated assets and partly from other assets, the tariff receipts allowance is, for this purpose, divided pro rata between the two categories of tariff (OTA 1983 Sched 1 (2)).

Assets used for exempt gas or deballasting purposes
Where an asset is used, or expected to be used, in connection with a field, and part of the use relates to gas which is exempt from PRT on a sale to the BGC under a pre-July 1975 contract, the allowance is reduced to a just and reasonable proportion. A similar proportionate reduction is made if part of the use, or expected use, relates to deballasting. Where an asset is used in connection with exempt gas and is also used, or expected to be used, in a way giving rise to tariff receipts, the latter use is treated as qualifying use in connection with the field. Use of an asset, for these purposes, includes the provision of related services or business facilities.

Expenditure may be incurred in enhancing the value of an asset with a view to its subsequent disposal, or to the disposal of an interest in it, in circumstances giving rise to disposal receipts. If the expenditure would not otherwise be allowable because the asset is used for exempt gas purposes, a just and reasonable proportion of it is allowable as though attributable to use in connection with the field (OTA 1983 s4).

Brought-in assets
If, in the period between the participator's incurring the expenditure and first use of the asset in connection with a field (discounting, in the case of a mobile asset, any use while the asset was not dedicated to that field), the asset is used by the participator or a connected person for a non-field purpose, the allowable expenditure is reduced in the proportion which the estimated life of the asset after the first use in connection with the field bears to its estimated total life in the hands of the participator. No expenditure on an asset is allowable if it is used in connection with an exempt gas field prior to non-exempt field use, and it was not reasonable to expect when the asset was acquired or brought into existence that it would be used for a qualifying field purpose (OTA 1983 Sched 1 (7)).

Assets acquired from a participator in the same field
Under the old rules (see 6.16.1), expenditure incurred in providing a long-term asset was not allowable if expenditure previously incurred by another participator in the field in acquiring, bringing into existence or enhancing the value of the asset had been allowed for the field (Sched 4 (1)). Under the new rules, if the purchase consideration provided to a fellow participator, or to a company associated with it, constitutes tariff

6.17.1 UK Oil Taxation

receipts or disposal receipts chargeable to PRT, it may qualify for relief (OTA 1983 s5(4)).

Assets taken out of field use
Where a field asset ceases to be used in connection with a UK field without giving rise to disposal receipts and is, or is expected to be, used in some other way, the allowable expenditure is reduced. This may apply, for example, where an asset is taken out of the UK field for use in a non-UK field in the same ownership. Use giving rise to tariff receipts is treated for this purpose as use in connection with a UK field. The expenditure remaining allowable is the fraction $\frac{A}{B}$.

where:
A represents a reasonable estimate of the time beginning with first use by the participator in connection with a field or, if earlier, first use giving rise to tariff receipts, and ending when the asset is first used, or is expected to be first used, other than for the purpose of the UK field; and
B represents a reasonable estimate of the useful life of the asset in the hands of the participator or, if it was a brought-in asset, so much of that useful life as falls after its first use in connection with a field.

If the expenditure already allowed exceeds the amount allowable as reduced in this way, the excess is treated as a disposal receipt to be brought into the calculation of profit or loss of the chargeable period in which field use ceases. If the expenditure was allowed for more than one field, the notional receipt is taken into account for the field in which the asset was last used by the participator, or in which it last gave rise to tariff receipts.

Similarly, if allowance has been given for expenditure on an asset which is expected to be brought into qualifying use and, that expectation having ceased to apply, the asset is then used or expected to be used for other purposes without being disposed of, the allowance is recaptured (OTA 1983 Sched 1(8)).

Assets no longer in field use
If expenditure is incurred on a non-mobile asset which has already been used, or was expected to be used, in connection with a field, and
(a) at the end of the claim period in which the expenditure is incurred the asset is no longer used, or expected to be used, in connection with the field; and
(b) the expenditure gives rise, or is expected to give rise, to tariff receipts or is incurred with a view to disposal of the asset or of an interest in it,
any use which gives rise to tariffs is treated as use in connection with the field; and if receipts would arise on a disposal, the asset is treated as used in connection with the field throughout the claim period in which

Petroleum Revenue Tax 6.17.2

the expenditure is incurred. The effect is, for example, that expenditure is allowable which relates to assets which continue to be tariffed after the principal field ceases production (OTA 1983 Sched 1(3) as amended by FA 1988 s139).

6.17.2 Non-Dedicated Mobile Assets

More restrictive relief rules apply to mobile assets which are not dedicated to a field. The amount of expenditure allowable for the first relevant claim period (in practice, the claim period in which the asset is first used in connection with a field) is calculated according to the formula;

$$A \times \frac{B}{C}$$

where:
A   is the expenditure incurred;
B   is the length of time the asset has been used in connection with the field in the period between the incurring of the expenditure (or the asset's first use in connection with the field, if later) and the end of the claim period; and
C   is the length of time between the incurring of the expenditure and the date when the useful life of the asset is reasonably likely to end. If the asset is not used for any purpose between the incurring of the expenditure and its first use in connection with the field, the expenditure is treated as having been incurred on the date on which the asset is first used in connection with the field.

For each subsequent claim period a further tranche of the expenditure is allowed using a similar formula. In this case, however, B represents the length of time the asset has been used in connection with the field in that period and all earlier periods, and expenditure previously allowed is deducted from the resulting figure.

Restrictions apply if a non-dedicated mobile asset becomes dedicated to the field for which these allowances have been given or is, or becomes, dedicated to another field. Expenditure is not allowable under the proportionate write-off rules described above for a claim period for which it is allowable under the rules for dedicated assets (see 6.17.1), nor for a claim period which falls wholly or partly within a claim period of another field to which the asset is, or becomes, dedicated if the expenditure is allowable under those rules for the latter period. Where expenditure in relation to the asset becomes allowable under the rules for dedicated assets, no part of that expenditure is eligible for proportionate write-off for any claim period ending less than six months before the end of the claim period for which the expenditure is allowable under those rules.

The provisions under which the proceeds of disposal of an asset are brought into the PRT charge do not apply if the asset is a mobile asset which is not dedicated to a field. Instead, the old rules continue to apply to the disposal of such an asset (see 6.16.1). The effect is, broadly, that

6.17.2 UK Oil Taxation

the total allowable expenditure on the asset is reduced by the amount of disposal consideration (OTA 1983 s1).

6.18 Transitional Provisions

Expenditure on assets, other than non-dedicated mobile assets, which is incurred after 30 June 1982 is generally allowable under the new rules described in 6.17.1. The old rules apply, with certain modifications, to expenditure incurred in a 'transitional claim period' which ends before 1 July 1982, or which begins before 1 July 1982 and ends after that date but not later than 31 December 1983 (that is, either a twelve month claim period ending on 31 December 1982 or a first claim period for a field which ends between 30 June 1982 and 31 December 1983). In the case of a period straddling 1 July 1982, however, the responsible person could elect, before 30 June 1984, that the part of the claim period ending on 30 June 1982 and the part falling after that date be treated as separate periods. In such a case the new rules apply to expenditure incurred after 30 June 1982. Where a field has a first claim period ending after 31 December 1983 which includes expenditure incurred before 1 July 1982, such expenditure is treated as incurred on that date, so that the new rules apply to the whole period (OTA 1983 s13).

For the transitional claim period, a modified version of the old rules applies to expenditure on long-term assets. The expenditure allowable is the proportion which, according to the 'best estimate reasonably practicable at the end of the period', the time for which the asset will be used in connection with the field bears to its total useful life. This formula applies both in respect of expenditure incurred in the transitional claim period itself, and to the review of allowances for expenditure incurred in earlier periods. Use of an asset which has given rise, or is expected to give rise, to tariff receipts attributable to a field is treated for the purposes of the transitional claim period review as use in connection with that field. Tariffs which were received or receivable before 1 July 1982, and thus do not enter into the PRT calculation, are attributed for this purpose to the field to which they would have been attributed if they had been received or receivable after that date.

After the transitional claim period, no further review is made of allowance for expenditure incurred in that or earlier periods. The old rules would have required a review of allowances for each subsequent claim period, whether the expenditure had been allowed in full or by proportionate write-off (OTA 1983 Sched 5).

Participators were able to claim a reduction of tax for chargeable periods ending before 1 December 1983 (the date of passing of the 1983 Oil Taxation Act) to the extent that the amount of expenditure actually allowable under the old rules is exceeded by the amount which would have been allowable if the modifications to the old rules made for the purpose of the transitional claim period review had always applied (OTA 1983 Sched 5 (5)).

Where no claim was made in respect of a particular item of expenditure for a period earlier than the transitional claim period, because the old rules did not afford any relief, a claim could be made for that expenditure for the transitional claim period. (OTA 1983 Sched 5 (7)).

6.19 Supplement

Certain categories of field expenditure qualify for supplement, an additional allowance commonly referred to as 'uplift'. It is intended to provide a substitute relief for interest, which itself is specifically disallowed (see 6.15.5). The same rate allowance, presently 35%, applies to all qualifying expenditure regardless of the stage in the field project at which the expenditure is incurred; but expenditure incurred after the end of the chargeable period in which 'payback' occurs does not qualify (see 6.19.9). The qualifying expenditure may be either capital or revenue, but in practice the great bulk of it is capital; and most of it is likely to be incurred before commencement of production.

Supplement is a very important relief. Apart from the obvious benefit of the addition to expenditure allowance, whether greater or smaller than the real interest cost, agreement that expenditure qualifies for supplement is the key to inclusion in the 'accumulated capital expenditure' for the purpose of calculating safeguard (see 6.30); and supplement itself is treated as an expense in the calculation of payback, which fixes the number of periods for which both safeguard and supplement can apply. Qualification for supplement is a precondition of a claim for cross-field allowance.

In order to qualify for supplement, expenditure has to be incurred for one or more of the purposes which are defined in s3(5). These rules are a fertile source of contention, partly because some of the tests call for subjective judgment rather than objective proof.

6.19.1 Bringing about Commencement of Production or Transportation

> Bringing about the commencement of the winning of oil from the field or the commencement of the transporting of oil won from it to the UK (s3(5)(*a*)).

With very few exceptions, field expenditure incurred before the field begins to produce qualifies for supplement. This includes the costs of

6.19.1 UK Oil Taxation

exploration leading to discovery, the fabrication and installation of production and transportation systems and the drilling of initial development wells. Appraisal expenditure is separately provided for (see 6.19.2). The cost of acquiring from the Secretary of State the licence for the field area should also qualify, even though, as in the case of exploration expenditure, the purpose test is made with some degree of hindsight. Purpose should be distinguished from reason: the reason why pre-production expenditure is incurred in one form or at one time rather than another form or time may be commercial or fiscal, independent of the operational business of bringing about commencement of production, but the purpose test should be applied aside from these considerations.

First production of oil does not bring an abrupt end to the possible application of this provision. Substantial expenditure on construction and installation of facilities is likely to continue to be incurred after the oil begins to flow, either because the project schedule is so designed or because the expenditure is incurred late. For some time after production operations begin, considerable outlay may also be incurred in rectifying faults in the systems. In considering qualification for supplement, the OTO is understood to accept in principle that expenditure on these types of construction overrun is incurred for the purpose of bringing about commencement of production.

Assets may be acquired before commencement of production which are surplus to immediate requirements or are intended for use in later production phases. Delay in bringing the assets into use does not normally prejudice allowance of the expenditure, but in considering supplement it may not be possible to demonstrate that the expenditure is incurred for the purpose of bringing about first production or transportation. Title to supplement will then depend on the expenditure satisfying one of the other tests (see 6.19.2 to 6.19.4).

6.19.2 Appraisal

> Ascertaining (either before or after the determination of the field under Schedule 1 to this Act) any of the matters mentioned in Section 3(1)(*c*)(s3(5)(*b*)).

Exploration or appraisal drilling and survey work within the field area or its environment which is carried out before production begins generally qualifies for supplement either as appraisal expenditure or in bringing about the commencement of production. The status of that which is undertaken in the production phase may be less clear. If it consists in appraisal of a known oil-bearing area wholly or partly within the field, the expenditure is allowable under the ascertaining head s3(1)(c) and accordingly also qualifies for supplement. If, on the other hand, it is in the nature of pure or wildcat exploration, it may be allowable under the searching head s3(1)(a) but it does not then qualify for supplement. The participator's state of knowledge and intentions at the time are vital factors in the establishment of the category into which the expenditure falls.

There is also a frontier, which is often indistinct, between production operations and appraisal. Logging and related activities aimed at monitoring the performance of the reservoir and maximising recovery of oil are a normal feature of production, which are unlikely to be seen by the OTO as carried out for the purpose of ascertaining within s3(1)(c). Specific appraisal programmes may be undertaken, however, which have a qualifying purpose in their own right. Alternatively, if they are undertaken in order to determine how and where a development or injection well should be drilled, they may be in essence part of the drilling project which itself qualifies for supplement.

6.19.3 Improving the Rate of Production: Preventing or Reducing a Decline in that Rate

> Carrying out works for, or acquiring an asset or an interest in an asset to be used for the purpose of, substantially improving the rate at which oil can be won or transported to the UK from the field, or preventing or substantially reducing a decline in that rate (s3(5)(c)).

Interpretation of this provision leads to the greatest controversy. It recognises three purposes:
(1) substantially improving the rate at which oil can be won or transported to the UK;
(2) preventing a decline in that rate;
(3) substantially reducing a decline in that rate.

As a pre-condition, the expenditure must be incurred either in carrying out works or in acquiring an asset or an interest in an asset. There should not normally be much doubt whether expenditure is within the second of these categories, but questions do arise as to whether particular operations constitute the carrying out of works. In the context of oil operations, the expression has an engineering connotation implying some alteration in state or nature.

The improvement in rate, or reduction in the decline in rate, has in either case to be 'substantial'. It is tempting to think that the test is in terms of an increase or decrease which is absolute rather than relative to the subsisting rate, but it is not certain that this is so. Fortunately, perhaps, title to supplement rarely turns on the meaning of substantial.

Apart from these peripheral difficulties, there is the more funda-

6.19.3 UK Oil Taxation

mental problem of deciding the purpose of expenditure. It is in the nature of virtually all oil field expenditure that it is directed towards improving the rate of production. The OTO, however, emphasises that the rate in question is the rate at which oil *can* be won or transported: and it suggests that this implies consideration of the field's potential rate of production at the time, assuming the facilities to be properly operational. In consequence, expenditure which it sees as maintaining the potential by restoring actual production to that level, such as expenditure on repairs or renewals, is not regarded as qualifying for supplement. Workovers fall into the area of controversy. Those involving major alteration to the structure of a well may be accepted as qualifying, but most are likely to be rejected as repair or maintenance works.

Aside from the areas of debate, large amounts of expenditure incurred during the producing phase are accepted to qualify for supplement under this provision. Many fields are developed in phases, additional production platforms being brought on stream at intervals or major additional systems being installed some time after first production. All expenditure of this nature is likely to qualify. So also does the cost of development wells and water or gas injection wells, including casing and other hardware and intangible drilling costs.

6.19.4 Providing for Initial Treatment or Initial Storage

> Providing any installation for the initial treatment or initial storage of oil won from the field (s3(5)(*d*)).

This provision caters primarily for facilities at onshore receiving terminals including the structures and plant used to stabilise crude and fractionate gases and tanks used to store oil or gas pending sale or appropriation. It also covers offshore storage and systems on offshore platforms which process oil produced from the field before transmission ashore, and initial treatment and storage facilities used in connection with onshore fields.

Unlike the provision relating to 'bringing about commencement' (see 6.19.1), there is no explicit timing qualification attaching to the provision of initial treatment or initial storage facilities. It is clear that the costs of constructing and setting up the initial infrastructure for treatment and storage are costs of 'providing' installations. To what extent subsequent capital outlay is expenditure on providing, rather than altering or maintaining, is largely a question of degree.

6.19.5 Assets Giving Rise to Tariff Receipts

Where expenditure on an asset is incurred partly for purposes carrying title to supplement and partly for the purpose of enabling the asset to be used in a way which gives rise to tariff receipts, the tariff-related part of the expenditure is also treated as qualifying for supplement. Expenditure on exempt gas field assets may also qualify for supplement to the extent that it is incurred in order to enable the asset to be tariffed. However, expenditure which is incurred solely for the purpose of generating tariff receipts does not qualify for supplement (s3(5A)).

6.19.6 Hiring

The proviso to s3(5) reads: 'but expenditure incurred in hiring an asset shall not so qualify unless the asset is used in carrying out works for a purpose mentioned in paragraph (*a*), (*b*) or (*c*) above or works for the provision of any such installation as is mentioned in paragraph (*d*) above'.

Hiring expenditure does not qualify for supplement unless the asset in question is used in carrying out works for a qualifying purpose. The restriction, which is regarded as applying equally to leasing or chartering costs, aims to prevent or reduce duplication of effective relief for underlying interest costs. Since a hire charge would be expected to incorporate recovery of the asset owner's financing costs, the grant of both allowance for the charge and supplement thereon would provide in essence a double relief for the interest element. The alternative remedy of denial of any relief on the interest element might have been logical, but it would have been a good deal more cumbersome to operate.

Many assets hired or chartered for oil operations are in fact used for carrying out works for a qualifying purpose. Thus, for example, the costs of chartering a drilling rig used in field exploration or appraisal or a derrick barge used in platform installation operations will qualify for supplement. The long term charter of a production platform, on the other hand, is not likely to qualify.

6.19.7 Asset Disposals: Restriction of Supplement

The disposal of an asset does not result in withdrawal of any supplement which has been allowed in respect of expenditure on the asset. However, if the disposal of a qualifying asset gives rise to disposal receipts (see 6.10.6), any supplement which would otherwise be allow-

6.19.7 UK Oil Taxation

able on other expenditure in the claim period in which the disposal takes place is restricted by reference to those receipts. A qualifying asset is a non-mobile asset or a mobile asset dedicated to a field, in respect of which expenditure is allowable under either the old or the new rules relating to long-term assets (see 6.16.1 and 6.17.1). The restriction does not apply if the 'new' expenditure qualifies for supplement under the transitional rules which preserved title to supplement on expenditure incurred before 1 January 1983 under pre-1981 contracts regardless of the intervention of payback (6.19.9). Where the restriction does apply, the amount of expenditure qualifying for supplement is reduced to:

$$A \times \frac{B}{C}$$

where:
A   is the total amount otherwise qualifying for supplement,
B   is the disposal receipts or, if less, the amount of expenditure originally allowed in respect of the asset or interest disposed of; and
C   is the total amount of expenditure allowable to the participator in respect of field expenditure in the claim period.

The rationale for the restriction is presumably that financing costs of expenditure incurred in the period will be reduced to the extent that expenditure can be met out of the disposal proceeds, so that supplement, as a proxy relief for interest, should be proportionately reduced (OTA 1983 s7).

This provision applies to disposals made after 30 June 1982. Under the old rules relating to long-term asset expenditure, a similar supplement restriction followed reduction of allowances due to disposals or change of use of assets.

6.19.8 Rates of Supplement

The rate of supplement depends on the date on which the expenditure is incurred and, in respect of expenditure after 1 January 1979, on the date of the contract under which it is incurred. For expenditure incurred before 1 January 1979, the rate is 75%. For expenditure incurred after 31 December 1978 under a contract made:

    before 1 January 1979 – the rate is 75%
    before 1 January 1979, but the expenditure relates to a 'change order' made later – the rate is 66 ⅔%
    after 31 December 1978 – the rate is 35%.

The Oil Taxation Bill introduced in 1974 had provision for a 50% rate of supplement which was considered by the Government to give fair recognition of interest costs attaching to field development. During the passage of the Bill through parliament the rate was increased to 75% as part of a package of measures designed to provide encouragement particularly for the development of marginal fields.

The rate was reduced in 1979 to 35% in respect of expenditure incurred under contracts made after 31 December 1978, subject to transitional arrangements. The reduction was associated with an increase in the rate of PRT to 60% compared with the original 45%, the Government evidently taking the view that relief of 105% (60% × 175) for supplemented expenditure would be unduly generous. Expenditure incurred after 31 December 1978 in pursuance of a contract made earlier continued to attract supplement at 75%. If, however, that expenditure is 'attributable to a request for an alteration or addition made, or other instruction given, on or after that date by or on behalf of the person incurring the expenditure to another party to the contract', the rate is 66 ⅔%, giving effective relief of 100% (60% × 166 ⅔%) (F(No2) A 1979s19). There is no term to these provisions; so long as qualifying expenditure continues to be incurred in pursuance of pre-1 January 1979 contracts, it attracts supplement at 75% or 66 ⅔% as appropriate. Not surprisingly, the meaning of 'in pursuance of' raises many questions; whether, for example, indirect costs attaching to a construction project are incurred in pursuance of the contract under which the direct expenditure is incurred. Difficult areas of contract law may also be involved, as in the question of whether the extension of the term of a particular contract constitutes mere continuation or the making of a new contract. Some of these issues are also relevant to the transitional arrangements included in the provision which terminates supplement by reference to payback (see 6.19.9)

6.19.9 Cut-off of Supplement: Payback

Even under the Revenue's relatively narrow interpretation of the provisions, a good deal of expenditure incurred well into the production phase is likely to qualify for supplement. By 1981, the government had decided that continuation of the allowance was not justified in respect of expenditure to which no significant financing cost attached, particularly expenditure incurred after cumulative field costs had been recovered out of production. It was also concerned about the scope for 'wasteful expenditure' which, through a combination of supplement and consequent addition to the safeguard base, might yield substantially more in tax relief than the expenditure itself.

Expenditure incurred after the end of the chargeable period in which payback occurs – the 'net profit period' – does not now qualify for supplement (FA 1981 s111). The calculation of payback is made separately for each participator. The net profit period is the period in which

6.19.9 UK Oil Taxation

the cumulative total of a participator's assessable profits for periods up to and including that period exceeds the aggregate of:
(*a*) the cumulative total of its allowable losses, and
(*b*) the total amount of APRT paid by it in respect of the field.
For this purpose, the APRT taken into account does not include any which is repaid unless it is a repayment made after the end of the net profit period of an excess of APRT credit which remained unabsorbed by set-off against PRT when the APRT charge expired (31 December 1986; see 6.37).

Tariff and disposal receipts arising after 1 July 1982 are included in the calculation of profit or loss: for payback purposes, the gross amounts are taken into account before reduction by tariff receipts allowance. Reliefs for: abortive exploration expenditure; exploration and appraisal expenditure; research expenditure not related to the field; cross-field allowance; unrelievable losses of other fields; which have been allowed in the computation of profit or loss are removed in the payback calculation, thereby taking out elements which are extraneous to the field and bringing the calculation back onto a field basis. The effect of the spreading of expenditure relief is also disregarded (see 6.25).

Field expenditure incurred in the net profit period or earlier which is allowed, with related supplement if appropriate, in the calculation of profit or loss of a later period is brought back into the net profit period calculation if the effect of so doing would be to postpone the net profit period. This does not include expenditure on brought-in assets or mobile assets becoming dedicated to the field which is allowed for a claim period beginning after the end of the net profit period; and expenditure on remote associated assets is taken into account for this purpose only if they give rise to tariff or disposal receipts before the end of the net profit period (See 6.17.1).

The net profit period cannot in any case be earlier than the first chargeable period ending after a development decision has been made for any part of the field area in which the amount of oil won and saved exceeds 1,000 tonnes (or in which gas production exceeds 1,100 cubic metres at 15 degrees centigrade and pressure of one atmosphere). Except for this provision, an artificially early payback might be reached, with consequent loss of supplement and safeguard benefits, where appreciable amounts of oil are won before the main development expenditure is incurred (FA 1985 s91).

The payback provisions do not disqualify for supplement any expenditure incurred before 1 January 1981, nor expenditure incurred after 31 December 1980 but before 1 January 1983 in pursuance of a contract made before 1 January 1981 (FA 1981 s111(7)). The meaning of 'in pursuance of a contract' was considered in *Mobil North Sea Ltd* v *CIR*

([1987] STC 458). Mobil had made a contract with Bechtel on 25 July 1979 under which Bechtel was to perform certain procurement work and to manage the construction, hook-up, testing and commissioning of the second production platform on the Beryl Field. The House of Lords upheld the company's contention that the platform expenditure, including that incurred by virtue of contracts entered into by Bechtel as agent for Mobil after 31 December 1980 was incurred in pursuance of the 25 July 1979 contract.

A participator might reach payback but then revert to a position of cumulative net loss because of heavy or exceptional expenditure incurred after the end of the original net profit period. If the reversion takes place within three years of the end of the net profit period, the title to supplement is restored in respect of expenditure incurred before the end of the revised net profit period. The revised net profit period also replaces the original net profit period for the purpose of fixing the length of time for which safeguard may be available (FA 1981 s113).

6.19.10 Contractor Financing

Steps were taken in 1981 to counteract what was seen as circumvention of the prohibition of relief for interest. In fixing the price of goods or services, the supplier will seek to recover his financing costs, though the price itself does not thereby consist to any extent of interest. If a participator could so arrange matters that the financing costs relating to the goods or services which would normally fall on it were instead absorbed by the supplier, in return for a corresponding increase in the price, it might expect to obtain relief on the full price and in addition, assuming the expenditure to be incurred for a qualifying purpose, supplement on that price. A turnkey contract for, say, construction of a major part of a field project might have produced such a result, albeit made for commercial reasons unconnected with avoidance of tax.

FA 1981 s115 attacks 'contractor financing' by denying supplement on expenditure incurred under contracts with extended or deferred terms of payment. As in the case of the restriction of supplement on hiring costs (see 6.19.5) the more logical remedy would have been denial of all relief on the part of the price representing consideration for interest, but that route was presumably regarded as impracticable. The provision, which applies to contracts made after 1 July 1980, prescribes a yardstick of payment terms against which the actual contract is to be judged: if the test is failed, none of the expenditure incurred under the contract qualifies for supplement.

There are two important categories of contract which are exempt from the test: first, a contract under which the expenditure to be paid by

6.19.10 UK Oil Taxation

the person incurring it is less than £10 million; and second, a contract of which it is reasonable to expect, at the time when it is made, that not less than 90% of the price will be paid within nine months of commencement of the work. In considering the first of these categories, potential increases in price due to cost escalation or design changes may be ignored. All other contracts are then measured against the prescribed yardstick. The measurement is a matter of judgment to be exercised at the time when the contract is made as to whether 'it is reasonable to expect' that the payments will meet the standard. The central theme of the requirement is that payments should be made, within certain tolerances, in step with the performance of the work. The yardstick is that payments are required, within six months of commencement of work and at intervals not exceeding six months thereafter, of not less than 75% of amounts which are proportionate to the progress of the work. It recognises the time which in the real world may elapse in the rendering of invoices and in payment, and allows a further three months to cover this.

In the case of a contract which provides for stage payments geared to separate strands of work, the expected payment schedule attaching to each strand may be separately measured; if each of the notional separate contracts would pass the test, then the contract itself does so. If, however, some of the notional separate contracts pass the test but one or more does not, the contract as a whole fails, so that none of the expenditure qualifies for supplement.

In the case of a field in shared ownership, the participators may contract jointly or through the field operator as agent. Doubts may arise as to whether, for the purpose of the £10 million exemption referred to above, the price to consider is the contract price or each participator's share of it. Argument that each participator's price is considered separately is likely to be resisted by the OTO.

6.20 Exploration and Appraisal Expenditure

PRT liability is calculated on a field basis, but in addition to relief for field expenditure allowance is also available for certain expenditure not related to the field. The relief for exploration and appraisal expenditure introduced in 1983 is very much less restrictive than the abortive exploration relief which it replaces. It is available against any field in which a participator has an interest, and there is no time limit for making a claim. It extends to any expenditure, whether capital or revenue, which:

(*a*) is incurred after 15 March 1983 by a participator or an associated company; and

Petroleum Revenue Tax 6.20

(*b*) at the time it is incurred does not relate to a field for which a development decision has previously been made; and

(*c*) is incurred wholly and exclusively for one or more of the qualifying purposes which are;

  (1) searching for oil in the UK territorial sea or a designated area of the UKCS;

  (2) ascertaining the extent or characteristics of any oil-bearing area in the UK territorial sea or a designated area;

  (3) ascertaining the reserves of oil of any such oil-bearing area;

  (4) making any payment to the Secretary of State for Energy under or for the purpose of obtaining a licence (other than a payment by way of royalty or other periodic payment).

Allowance for a payment to the Secretary of State, within (4) above, is available only if at the time of claim the licence concerned has expired or has been determined or revoked, or part of the licensed area has been surrendered: in the latter case, only such proportion of the expenditure is allowable as corresponds to the area surrendered (s 5A).

For the purposes of this provision a development decision is made when consent for development is granted by the Secretary of State or a programme of development is served on the licensee or approved by the Secretary of State for the whole or part of a field. Development in this context means the erection or carrying out of permanent works for the purpose of getting oil from the field or the purpose of transporting offshore oil to land, or winning of oil otherwise than in the course of searching for oil or drilling wells. The Secretary of State's approval of an extended production test prior to development of a field would probably not constitute the making of a development decision for this purpose.

If the expenditure in question is incurred at a time when the area to which it relates has not been determined as an oil field, but a notice of proposed determination has been given, the area is treated as having become an oil field at the time of the notice if, when the actual determination is made, the area is included in the field.

It may not always be clear whether particular expenditure 'relates to' a field. The Revenue has indicated that it will not ordinarily regard exploration or appraisal of an area outside the boundary of a field as related to that field. The concept is, nevertheless, physical: expenditure on the drilling of a well within the boundary of a field in which the participator concerned has no economic interest is related to the field and outside the scope of exploration and appraisal relief.

The scope of the relief is not quite as wide as the industry might wish. While it is apt to cover appraisal of the extent and characteristics of an oil reservoir, it stops short of the preliminary feasibility and design work for production systems for the prospective field. That expenditure

6.20 UK Oil Taxation

may be allowable as field expenditure if the development goes ahead, or as research expenditure not related to a field (see 6.23).

Associated companies
Relief is available if the expenditure is incurred by the participator or by 'a company associated with it in respect of the expenditure'. Companies are so associated if throughout the period (during which both are in existence) from the date on which the expenditure was incurred to the end of the chargeable period in which it was incurred, or the end of the earliest chargeable period in which the participator company was a participator in the field:
(*a*) One is a 51% subsidiary of the other and the other is not a 51% subsidiary of any other company; or
(*b*) Each of them is a 51% subsidiary of a third company which is not itself a 51% subsidiary of any other company.

The OTO takes the view that a claim is not valid in respect of the expenditure of the associated company until the end of the relative chargeable period is reached, since it is not possible conclusively to demonstrate until that time that the conditions of association are fulfilled.

Exclusion of onshore exploration and appraisal
The relief enacted in 1983 extended to exploration and appraisal in both offshore and onshore areas. With effect for expenditure incurred after 31 March 1986, works in 'onshore' areas no longer qualify for exploration and appraisal relief. Since abortive exploration relief, which was overtaken by the more generous exploration and appraisal relief in 1983, is not restored, PRT relief for onshore expenditure is available, with the possible exception of allowance for research costs, only if it qualifies as field expenditure. A payment to the Secretary of State to acquire an onshore licence is not excluded from relief, but such payments are likely to be small.

For oil taxation purposes, however, the territorial sea is now deemed to include certain areas which are commonly covered by water and which are for other purposes part of the UK rather than the territorial sea. These are areas lying between the landward boundary of the territorial sea and the shoreline of the UK. The shoreline is the high water line, except that particular rules apply in drawing the line across the mouths of bays and estuaries. The effect is that relief continues to be available for works carried out in the areas in question. (FA 1985 s90 and FA 1986 s108).

Expenditure on assets
Relief is available for the cost incurred by the participator, or the

associated company if appropriate, in providing an asset having an expected life of at least a year which is used for one of the qualifying exploration and appraisal purposes. The allowance is given by proportionate write-off over the expected useful life of the asset, the appropriate fraction of the expenditure being deemed to be incurred on each day of qualifying use.

The disposal of the asset brings an end to the write-off allowances and, depending on the circumstances of disposal, may cause a recalculation of the total allowances due. On a sale at arm's length for market price, the denominator of the write-off fraction is altered to represent the life of the asset up to the date of the disposal rather than total expected life, and allowances are adjusted by applying the revised fraction to the net cost after deduction of the receipt. If the asset is sold to a connected person, or at a price less than market value, the receipt is brought in to offset the cost, but the write-off schedule is not revised. In this case also, allowances are recalculated by reference to the net cost. If the sum of allowances given proves to be excessive, the excess is charged as a receipt. The procedure by which effect is given to additional allowances is less clear: in practice, they may be incorporated in a decision on a current claim (s5(2)).

Set-off of associated receipts
The general rule is that sums received by the participator or a connected person which are generated by expenditure otherwise qualifying for exploration and appraisal relief are offset against that expenditure, causing a corresponding reduction in the allowance. It does not bring into charge any profit element. The offset is not required if the receipt is consideration for the assignment of a licence interest or rights: one effect of this exclusion is that a farmer-out who receives reimbursement of his drilling cost from a farmer-in does not lose title to relief on the relative cost.

Receipts for the arm's length disposal of oil won in the course of exploration and appraisal operations, such as a pre-development production test, are specifically brought in against the relative expenditure. If such oil is disposed of otherwise than in sales at arm's length, or is appropriated to refining or other use apart from field production operations, deemed receipts are brought to account equal to the market value of the oil, to the exclusion of any actual receipt. The normal valuation rules apply with certain modifications (see 6.7.2). The effect of this provision is to secure, by reduction of allowable expenditure, the effective charge to PRT of oil won from an area which might not be determined as a field. If the area does become part of a field, the oil won before determination of the field is chargeable for that field in the normal way (see 6.4): this should not constitute a double charge

6.20 UK Oil Taxation

because the exploration and appraisal expenditure which has been offset will be claimable as field expenditure.

If, as result of the offset of receipts, the amount of expenditure allowed proves to have been excessive, the excess is brought into the calculation of profit or loss for the chargeable period in which the receipts arise.

Prevention of double allowance
Expenditure does not qualify for exploration and appraisal relief if it has already been allowed for any field either under those or other provisions. A claim for relief as field expenditure, however, is not precluded if the same expenditure has been allowed on a claim for exploration and appraisal relief by a different person (s3(3)) (see 6.15.5).

6.20.1 Restriction of Relief: Interests Acquired in Mature Fields

On 13 September 1983, the Chancellor of the Exchequer announced the Government's intention to introduce legislation which would prevent the utilisation of past exploration and appraisal expenditure, abortive exploration expenditure and unrelievable field losses against interests acquired in mature fields. The announcement was made shortly after the publication by BP of an offer to sell interests totalling approximately 10% in the large and highly profitable Forties field.

Exploration and appraisal expenditure incurred before a company's qualifying date in relation to a field is not available for claim against that field; but this does not apply if the qualifying date falls before 14 September 1983 or before the end of the first chargeable period of the field.

The qualifying date means, broadly, the earliest of the following:
(a) the date on which the company becomes a participator in the field:
(b) the date on which an associated company becomes a participator in the field; and
(c) the date from which the company is treated as a participator in the field by virtue of rights under an Illustrative Agreement (see 8.11) or, if later, the date on which the associated licensee company becomes a participator.

If, on transfer of a field interest, the transferee becomes entitled to claim for exploration and appraisal relief expenditure incurred by the transferor or an associated company, the transferor's qualifying date is also taken into account; if that date preceded 14 September 1983 or the end of the first chargeable period, the expenditure may still be claimed by the transferee even though the transfer in question takes place later.

Petroleum Revenue Tax 6.22

These restrictions apply also to abortive exploration and research expenditure reliefs (see 6.21 and 6.22)(FA 1984 s113).

6.21 Abortive Exploration Expenditure

The relief for abortive exploration expenditure relates only to expenditure incurred before 16 March 1983, being replaced by the exploration and appraisal relief in respect of later expenditure.

Qualifying expenditure is that incurred wholly and exclusively for the purpose of searching for oil in the UK, the territorial sea or a designated area of the UKCS which 'is not, and is unlikely to become, allowable for any oil field'. In contrast to exploration and appraisal relief, allowance is not due for expenditure as incurred, but is dependent on satisfaction of the test that it is unlikely to become allowable as field expenditure. The provision affords much scope for argument, claimants tending to see the test as requiring no more than a balance of probability at the time of claim that the area to which the expenditure relates will not be developed as an oil field, the OTO arguing the need for positive evidence that the area is unlikely ever to be developed.

In other respects, most of the provisions applying to the allowance of exploration and appraisal expenditure apply also to this relief (see 6.20). The allowance may be taken against any field in which the participator has an interest, and claims are not now subject to any time limit. The expenditure may be incurred by the participator or by an associated company. The rules relating to expenditure on assets and to the treatment of associated receipts also apply, except that for the purposes of abortive exploration relief sums received for assignment of rights or interests in a licence are not excluded from receipts which fall to be offset against allowances (s5).

6.22 Research Expenditure

Research projects may be undertaken with the aim, in whole or in part, of increasing the efficiency or enhancing the volume of oil production in the UK or the UKCS. Applicants for offshore licences in the ninth Round onwards have been required to demonstrate some commitment to research and development effort. Since allowance as field expenditure depends on the expenditure having been incurred, at least in part, in connection with a particular field, expenditure which cannot be related to a field does not generally qualify. However, a delayed allowance is available for research expenditure not related to a field.

There is no definition of research for this purpose. The Revenue has indicated that it will accept a fairly broad interpretation not necessarily

6.22 UK Oil Taxation

akin to the meaning of scientific research used in the CT capital allowances code. It may include, for example, research into secondary or tertiary recovery technology as well as design of new production systems.

The qualifying expenditure is research expenditure incurred by a participator after 16 March 1987 for a purpose such that, if it had been incurred in relation to a particular field, it would have been allowable for that field. It excludes expenditure incurred for a purpose which would endorse allowance as exploration and appraisal relief, or which would do so but for the fact that it relates to UK onshore areas. Also excluded is expenditure which is incurred for the purpose of a particular field: the participator does not have the option, for example, of refraining from a claim for relief as field expenditure in a low tax or non liable field in favour of a claim for research relief against a high tax field. Expenditure which might be expected to relate to exempt gas production is disregarded. The expenditure must be incurred at least partly for purposes relevant to a UK area, whether that area is onshore or offshore: any non UK element is excluded by just and reasonable apportionment. The bar to relief for exploration and appraisal expenditure incurred after 31 March 1986 relating to onshore areas does not extend to research relief.

Assuming that the expenditure satisfies all of these conditions, it does not become available for relief until the expiry of three years from the date on which it was incurred. Then, it is necessary to establish that it 'has not become allowable' as field expenditure related to any field. The premise of this further condition is that, although the expenditure does not satisfy a field purpose test at the time when it is incurrred, subsequent developments could bring it within a category of allowable field cost. This might occur, for example, where research is undertaken into the feasibility of applying a particular production technique to a potential field development and, within three years, the area in question is determined as a field. In this context, the timing of the determination of a field may be important.

A number of the provisions relating to exploration and appraisal relief apply also to the research allowance. Expenditure on a qualifying research asset is allowed by proportionate write-off over the expected useful life of the asset, beginning not earlier than the third anniversary of the date of incurral; and the allowance may be offset by certain disposal proceeds. Other receipts by the participator or by a connected person which are attributable to research expenditure are also brought to account as a reduction of the amount of expenditure otherwise allowable or, if the allowance has already been taken into account in a PRT computation, as an item of income for the period of receipt. A receipt attributable to expenditure which was incurred partly for UK purposes and partly not is apportioned in line with the apportionment of the expenditure. Receipts derived from intellectual property or other fruits of the research come into the reckoning but any amount in excess of the relative expenditure is not chargeable.

In contrast to exploration and appraisal relief, the research allowance does not extend to expenditure incurred by a company associated with the participator. Expenditure, therefore, needs to be borne by the participator itself. This requirement is satisfied if the participator pays for research which he undertakes directly or which he commissions, or if he shares the cost of research authorised by a licensee group of which he is a member. The purchase of certain data for use in the prosecution of a relevant research project should also qualify. In general, however, the purchase of the fruits of another's research or the charge to a participator of costs relating to a project carried out by an associated company which appears, with hindsight, to have relevance to UK development may not represent expenditure 'incurred for the purpose of research '. Relief is prohibited for research expenditure incurred before the acquisition of an interest in a producing field (see 6.20.1). The benefit of unrelieved expenditure is inherited in some circumstances by a successor in the event of a transfer of an interest in a field (see 8.8.1) (FA 1987 s5B and Sched 13).

6.23 Cross-Field Allowance

The cross-field allowance is intended to provide an incentive for the development of new fields. Relief for up to 10% of certain expenditure incurred for the purposes of a new field may be taken, by election, against the profits arising in another field rather than the new field: the allowance offers the prospect of earlier and more certain relief, particularly where the level of production from the new field may prove to be insufficient to attract PRT liability (FA 1987 s65 and Sched 14).

The trigger for setting in train a cross-field allowance is determination by the Secretary of State of the new field, the 'field of origin'. That event may pre-date any request for, or approval of, development consent in respect of that field area. Until the field is determined, the expenditure cannot be included in a claim so as to receive the necessary endorsement that it is allowable and qualifies for supplement. An early determination, therefore, may be desirable if the participators are looking to cross-field allowance as the primary avenue of relief; on the other hand, if they wish to make the most use of the research allowance for pre-development expenditure, a later determination is likely to be preferred.

6.23 UK Oil Taxation

Qualifying expenditure

The qualifying expenditure is that incurred after 16 March 1987 which is allowable under normal rules as expenditure incurred in connection with the field of origin, and which qualifies for supplement in relation to that field. It follows that it must be incurred before the end of the net profit period in relation to the field of origin (6.19.9). The cost of leasing or chartering production or transportation facilities is unlikely to qualify (see 6.19.6). The expenditure must be incurred by the participator who makes the election or by an associated company which is a participator in the field of origin. For this purpose, a company is associated with the participator if one of them is a 51% subsidiary of the other or both are 51% subsidiaries of a third company which is not itself a 51% subsidiary of any company. The relationship must subsist throughout the 'relevant period', ending on the date of the election and beginning with the claim period in which the expenditure is incurred or, if that is the first claim period for the field of origin, when any part of the field was determined as a field by the Secretary of State.

The field of origin must satisfy certain conditions. It is a field:
(a) 'no part of which lies in an area to the east of the UK between latitudes 52° and 55° north, and is not an onshore field;
(b) for no part of which consent for development has been granted by the Secretary of State before 17 March 1987; and
(c) for no part of which a programme of development has been served on the licensees or approved by the Secretary of State before 17 March 1987.

For these purposes, a consent for development or a programme of development is disregarded if it relates in whole or in part to another field which was determined before the determination of the new field in question and a consent or programme relating to the new field is given or approved after 16 March 1987. Development means the erection or carrying out of permanent works for the purpose of getting oil from the field or of transporting offshore oil to land, or winning oil other than in the course of searching for oil or drilling wells: consent for development does not include consent limited to the purpose of testing the characteristics of an oil-bearing area not involving the erection or carrying out of permanent works.

Elections

The expenditure in question has to be claimed, and claimed as qualifying for supplement, for the field of origin. An election for cross-field allowance cannot be made until a final decision has been made by the OTO that the expenditure does indeed qualify for supplement. That may happen either when the OTO issues a notice agreeing the supplement claim or, following refusal of the claim, supplement allowance is agreed on appeal or the claim is upheld by the Special Commissioners or the Courts.

Then, an election in respect of particular expenditure must be made before that expenditure is taken into account in an assessment or determination of loss for the field of origin, notice of which is given to the participator. If the supplement claim is allowed only after an appeal, the time limit for an election is extended to thirty days after final settlement of the appeal.

More than one election may be made in respect of the same expenditure, provided that the total amount elected does not exceed cumulatively 10% of the expenditure. The election or elections may apportion the relief between more than one receiving field. Elections for cross-field allowance are irrevocable.

Relief cannot be taken in the receiving field for expenditure incurred before the claimant's 'qualifying date' in respect of that field (broadly, the date of acquisition of an interest in the field) unless that date precedes the end of the field's first chargeable period.

Effect in receiving field
The allowance is taken into account, in the same way as expenditure allowed for the receiving field itself, in the assessment or determination of loss for the chargeable period of the receiving field made next after the date of the election or, if the election is made within thirty days of the decision by the OTO allowing the supplement claim, after the date of that decision. If a successful appeal is made against refusal of supplement, the relevant assessment or determination is that made next after the date of that appeal. The allowance is left out of account in the calculation of payback in the receiving field, and is added back in calculating adjusted profit of that field for safeguard purposes.

The amount of cross-field allowance may be altered if the decision on the relative expenditure and supplement claim in respect of the field of origin is varied (see 6.32.3). In the case of a reduction in the amount allowed on the claim, the election is treated as specifying a cross-field allowance not exceeding 10% of the reduced amount. If the variation increases the amount allowed on the claim, a further election for cross-field allowance may be made as though the increase were a separate amount of expenditure.

6.24 Provisional Expenditure Allowance

In recognition of the fact that relief for expenditure is not allowed on an incurred basis but only when the expenditure is agreed by the Revenue,

6.24 UK Oil Taxation

provision is made for a minimum provisional expenditure relief. The relief can be illustrated as follows:

Chargeable period to 30.6.1988

(1) 5% of	(a)	the price received for arm's length sales in the period and the market value of non-arm's length sales in the period, and	
	(b)	the market value of appropriations in the period (s2(9)(a))	A
(2) *less*		the amount of field expenditure incurred in the period which is taken into account in the calculation of profit or loss of the period (s2(11))	B
(3)		Provisional allowance (nil if (1) does not exceed (2))	C

The base figures are those derived from the participator's return. The return requires in regard to arm's length sales, the price received or receivable, whereas the 5% allowance is calculated by reference to the price received: the difference probably has no practical significance. In many cases, the restriction (see (2) above) means that no provisional allowance falls to be made. However, in profitable fields in which the level of expenditure is low in proportion to income, the provisional allowance may be due with some regularity especially in periods of peak production, a phenomenon probably not envisaged when the provision was enacted.

6.24.1 Reversal of Provisional Allowance

The provisional allowance is reversed out in the next but one chargeable period (s2(8)(b)). But this is subject to some complicated fine-tuning. If the amount of field expenditure taken into account in the calculation of profit or loss of that period includes expenditure incurred in the preceding period, the amount of the reversal is increased by the lesser of that expenditure and the provisional allowance of the preceding period. For example:

Chargeable period to 30.6.1989

(1)		Provisional allowance in the period to 30.6.1988	C
(2) *Add*		the lesser of	
		(a) field expenditure allowed in the calculation of profit or loss of the period 30.6.1989 which was incurred in the period to 31.12.1988	
and			
		(b) provisional allowance in the period to 31.12.1988	D
		Amount of reduction in allowances	E

If an addition to the reversal is made in this way, the amount of that addition is deducted from the reversal to be made for the next period, in this example, to 31 December 1989 (s2(8)(*b*) and s2(10)).

6.25 Spreading of Expenditure Relief

In general, allowable expenditure qualifies for 100% write-off, with the exception of expenditure on non-dedicated mobile assets which is allowed over asset life. The availability of supplement increases the front weighting of PRT reliefs. While this characteristic of the system normally benefits participators, there are circumstances in which a participator may wish to delay allowances so as to bring forward and even out the PRT liabilities over the life of the field. In particular, companies not resident in the UK, or resident both in the UK and in another state, which are liable to tax in the UK and in the other state in respect of production operations may need to equalise the measure of profits for UK and foreign tax purposes in order to optimise double taxation reliefs. Some scope is provided to spread forward certain expenditure reliefs.

Relief for expenditure qualifying for supplement, together with the supplement attaching to it, which would be taken into account in the calculation of profit or loss of a chargeable period may, on election, be taken partly in that period and partly in later periods. The election by the participator has to be made within three months of the end of the chargeable period or, if later, within twenty-seven months of the end of the first chargeable period. The participator specifies the maximum amount of the relief in question which it requires to be taken into account in the period. The balance of the relief is carried forward for incorporation in twenty equal tranches in the calculation of profit or loss for the next twenty chargeable periods. The participator may instead nominate in the election an alternative schedule, taking the balance of relief in equal tranches over three, five, ten or fifteen chargeable periods. Furthermore, the participator may, within the same time limit, make a secondary election in relation to any of the periods in the write-off schedule, requiring the whole of the remaining balance to be utilised in that period. Tax which becomes payable or repayable for any of the first four chargeable periods of a field in consequence of an election to spread expenditure relief does not carry interest up to the date of the election (Sched 3 (9)).

The effect of an election to spread expenditure relief is disregarded for certain purposes. The calculation of oil allowance is made as though no election had been made: it is not, for example, possible to take oil allowance in a period in which the existence of an assessable profit rather than a loss is attributable only to the spreading of expenditure

6.25 UK Oil Taxation

relief. Similarly, the safeguard limitation is calculated as though no election had been made (Sched 3 (10)).

Example of spreading election

Field begins production 1.11.1985	£ m
First chargeable period 31.12.1985	
Expenditure and supplement to be taken into account in first chargeable period	135
Election made 31.3.1988 (last possible day) requiring to be taken into account for first chargeable period 31.12.1985 not more than	55
Election specifies that the balance is to be allowed in 10 succeeding periods	
30.6.1986	8
31.12.1986	8
30.6.1987	8
31.12.1987	8
Election made 30.9.1988 (last possible day) requiring remaining balance to be allowed in chargeable period 30.6.1988	48

6.26 Transactions not at Arm's Length

Relief may be restricted if expenditure is incurred either in a transaction with a connected person or otherwise not at arm's length. The PRT rule does not follow the CT precedent of applying a market value limitation. Instead, the allowance for expenditure in acquiring an asset in such a transaction is restricted to the amount of expenditure incurred in an earlier arm's length transaction in acquiring, bringing into existence or enhancing the value of the asset. A company is connected with another company if, broadly, one has control over the other or both are under common control. In the original 1975 provision, connected persons included co-participators in a field, but this extended meaning was repealed in respect of expenditure incurred after 31 December 1978.

A somewhat similar restriction applies 'with any necessary modifications', to expenditure incurred in leasing or hiring and for provision of certain services or facilities. Difficult questions may arise as to what modifications are necessary in particular circumstances and what is the measure of comparable third party expenditure (Sched 4 (2)).

Technical amendments were made to the provisions in relation to expenditure on the aquisition of an asset after 31 March 1983, or expenditure in respect of use of such an asset or provision of services or facilities in connection with its use (OTA 1983 s5).

6.27 Contributions to Expenditure

No allowance is due for expenditure which has been or is to be met, directly or indirectly, by the Crown, any government or public or local authority in the UK or elsewhere, or any person other than the participator. This provision precludes relief for expenditure to the extent that it is to be covered, for example, by government grants or subsidies or by contributions by co-participators or others. It also denies relief for expenditure to be met out of insurance recoveries, unless the recovery relates to the loss or destruction of an asset: in that case, it is not offset against the cost of replacement but is brought into the calculation of profit or loss as a disposal receipt (see 6.10.6) (Sched 3 (8)).

6.27.1 Regional Development Grants

The grants and subsidies to be offset against expenditure (6.27) originally, excluded regional development grants made under Part I of the 1972 Industry Act and certain grants made under corresponding Northern Ireland provisions. Now, where such grants, or grants made under Part II of the 1982 Industrial Development Act, are received in respect of expenditure incurred after 9 March 1982, they are to be offset for PRT purposes against the relative expenditure. Consequential restrictions are made in CT allowances (FA 1982 s137).

6.28 Oil Allowance

The oil allowance is one element in the package of reliefs intended to provide particular assistance to small or marginal fields which were introduced during the passage of the Oil Taxation Bill through parliament in 1975. The allowance is given as a reduction of the assessable profit. For each field for which development consent was given before 1 April 1982, there is an allowance of up to 250,000 tonnes per chargeable period, approximately equivalent to production at a rate of 10,000 barrels per day. The allowance is divided between the participators in proportion to their shares of oil won and saved from the field in the period. It is available for an indefinite number of chargeable periods, but it runs out when the cumulative allowances of all participators reach 5 million tonnes: if the maximum allowance per period were utilised, therefore, the oil allowance would last for 20 consecutive periods. Any balance of allowance which is not utilised in a chargeable period is carried forward as part of the pool of allowances, but it does not increase the allowance for a later period above the 250,000 tonnes limit (s8).

These chargeable period and cumulative limits apply in respect of

6.28 UK Oil Taxation

periods ending after 31 December 1978. For earlier periods, the limits were 500,000 long tons and 10 million long tons respectively. An increased allowances applies in certain new fields and a reduced allowance in other new fields (see 6.28.1 and 6.28.2).

The amount of the reduction in assessable profit is the cash equivalent of the participator's share of the weight allowance, calculated by the formula;

$$£(A \times \frac{B}{C})$$

where:
A is the gross profit for the period (broadly, oil sales and appropriations, adjusted for stock)
B is the participator's share of the allowance, in tonnes
C is the participator's share of oil won and saved in the period (not including excluded oil — see 6.8.1).

The value of the allowance therefore increases with the price of oil.

Example
P has a 40% share in the field. His share of oil won and saved in the chargeable period ended 31 December 1987 is 600,000 tonnes and his gross profit £48,000,000. The cash equivalent of his share of allowance for the period is:

$$£48,000,000 \times \frac{100,000}{600,000}$$
$$= £8,000,000$$

Doubts have arisen as to whether division of the allowance between the participators 'in shares proportionate to their shares of oil won and saved from the field during the period' should be made in proportion to their equity entitlement or in proportion to the quantity of oil which each takes, or lifts, during the period. The two methods may produce materially different answers because, although an underlift may be reflected as stock in the calculation of gross profit, it comes in only at one half of market value. The equity basis is probably technically correct, though in practice a liftings basis has sometimes been applied in particular circumstances. In either case, the OTO would expect all participators in a field to adopt the same basis.

The meaning of 'oil won and saved' has also been the subject of some debate. Oil in transit is excluded from the PRT charge (see 6.8.3) but it is not specifically excluded from oil won and saved for the purposes of the oil allowance calculation. Similarly, oil used for production purposes related to the field is not charged to PRT: it is clear that it is oil won but less clear that it is saved. The OTO takes the view that elements which are produced from the reservoir, including water and inert gases which may depress the quality of the saleable oil or gas produced, must be taken into account as oil won and saved.

Petroleum Revenue Tax 6.28

Adjustment for final periods
For the chargeable period in which the final balance of remaining allowance falls to be used, the allocation of that allowance between the participators is a matter to be decided by them and notified to the Board by the responsible person. Failing that, the Board has the power to make the allocation.

However, the imbalance in the amounts of oil allowance utilised by each participator may be so substantial that the residue is insufficient to permit equitable adjustment to be made in the final period. In that case, adjustment may be made in both that and the preceding period. The responsible person may give to the Revenue, not later than 6 months after the end of the final oil allowance period, a notice of apportionment of the allowance for both final and penultimate periods. The apportionment must be designed to achieve 'so far as practicable' a cumulative sharing of the allowance which is proportionate to the relevant participator's shares of oil won and saved. The responsible person has discretion in making the proposal to take into account fewer than the total number of chargeable periods in which oil allowance has been given in assessments, and to exclude from the calculation oil won and saved before the commencement of the periods which are taken into account. The proposed apportionment need not relate to all of the participators in the field.

If the apportionment proposal is accepted by the OTO, oil allowance for the final and penultimate periods is shared accordingly. Rejection of the proposal is subject to a right of appeal of the responsible person to the Special Commissioners, whose decision thereon is final. Participators other than the responsible person have no right to be heard in appeal proceedings (FA 1987 s66).

Alternative calculation: gas
If production from the field includes gas (other than gas exempt from PRT), the participator may elect for an alternative calculation of the cash equivalent of its share of oil allowance. Use of the alternative method may enable the oil allowance to be attributed primarily to that element of production, either oil or gas, which has the higher relative value, so yielding a higher cash equivalent. Whether election for this basis will be beneficial depends on those relative values and on the effect of the conversion formula applied to particular kinds of gas.

If the share of oil won and saved other than gas exceeds the share of the oil allowance, the cash equivalent is calculated using as the A factor only that part of the gross profit attributable to oil other than gas.

If the share of oil won and saved other than gas is less than the share of oil allowance, the cash equivalent is the sum of two amounts, produced by applying separate calculations to that part of the oil

6.28 UK Oil Taxation

allowance up to the tonnage of oil other than gas and to that part in excess:
(a) in relation to the part not exceeding oil, the A factor is that part of the gross profit attributable to oil other than gas;
(b) in relation to the excess of the oil allowance, over oil other than gas, the A factor is that part of the gross profit attributable to gas.

In either case, the Revenue accepts by concession that, in order to produce the result apparently intended, the gas or oil, as appropriate, which is left out of account in the A factor should also be excluded from oil won and saved in the C factor (s8(4)).

1,100 cubic metres of gas at a temperature of 15° centigrade and pressure of one atmosphere is treated as equivalent to one tonne of oil.

6.28.1 Increased Oil Allowance for Certain New Fields

The maximum oil allowance for a chargeable period and the cumulative maximum allowance are doubled, to 500,000 tonnes and 10 million tonnes respectively, for certain new fields. A relevant new field is a field:
(a) no part of which lies in an area under a landward licence or in an area to the east of the UK and between latitudes 52° and 55° North (that is, in the area known as the southern basin of the North Sea); and
(b) for no part of which consent for development had been granted by the Secretary of State before 1 April 1982; and
(c) for no part of which a programme of development had been served on the licensees or approved by the Secretary of State before that date.

In applying these criteria, no account is taken of a consent for development granted before 1 April 1982 or a programme of development served or approved by the Secretary of State before that date if:
(1) in whole or in part, that consent or programme related to another field which was determined before the new field was determined; and
(2) on or after 1 April 1982, a further consent has been granted or a programme served or approved which relates in whole or in part to the new field.

Development for this purpose is defined as the erection or carrying out of permanent works for the purpose of getting oil from the field or for the purpose of conveying oil won from the field to a place on land, or the winning of oil from the field otherwise than in the course of searching for oil or drilling wells (FA 1983 s36).

Those fields which qualify for the increased oil allowance are also exempt from royalties (see 5.2).

6.28.2 Reduced Oil Allowance for Certain New Fields

Fields in the Southern Basin of the North Sea and onshore, for which development consent is first given after 31 March 1982 or for which a programme of development is first served or approved after that date, qualify only for a reduced oil allowance. The allowance is 125,000 tonnes for chargeable periods ending after 30 June 1988, and the cumulative maximum allowance for the field is 2.5 million tonnes. The fields are identified by the reverse of the definition of relevant new fields for the purpose of the increased oil allowance (see 6.28.1): that is, they are fields any part of which lies in a landward area or in an area to the east of the UK and between latitudes 52° and 55° North. No acccount is taken of a consent for development or a programme served or approved before 1 April 1982 if it related wholly or partly to another field which was detemined before the field in question and after 31 March 1982 a consent for development is granted or a programme of development is served or approved which relates wholly or partly to the field in question. Development has the same meaning as for the increased oil allowance (FA 1988 s138).

The fields in question are exempt from royalties (see 5.2).

6.28.3 Interaction of Oil Allowance and Expenditure Relief

Oil allowance is given as a mandatory reduction of assessable profit, or of assessable profit as reduced by any loss relief. Assessable profit is, broadly, the income of the period less expenditure allowances agreed before the assessment is made. In some cases, more oil allowance may be given in an assessment than would have been given if the assessable profit had been smaller; and if the reason for the larger profit is the absence from the calculation of profit of expenditure relief which would have been taken into account had a claim been made and allowed earlier, the oil allowance may be adjusted retrospectively. If the Board so directs, the allowance is reduced to what it would have been if field expenditure which is claimed, whether by the responsible person or by the participator, later than the anniversary of the end of the claim period (the relevant time) had instead been claimed before and allowed at the relevant time (Sched 3 (11)).

The Act offers no guidance as to the circumstances in which the Board might make a direction under this provision, nor has the Board

6.28.3 UK Oil Taxation

indicated what it considers to be the relevant criteria. It is assumed, however, that a direction might be made to counteract a deliberate attempt by a participator to obtain a tax advantage by delaying an expenditure claim. The effect of a direction could be fairly draconian. The gap created in the assessment by the reduction in oil allowance is not filled by the expenditure relief which occasioned the adjustment; that is taken into account under the normal rules of computation in the next assessment to be made after the Board notifies agreement of the claim. There may, therefore, be a resulting tax liability for the period for which the adjustment is made, carrying interest from two months after the end of the period. The displaced oil allowance is added to the remaining pool, to be shared between the participators: whether the participator concerned ultimately achieves its cumulative field share of allowance may depend on the scope for adjustment in the final periods (see 6.28).

The construction of this anti-avoidance provision ensures in any case that it has fairly limited potential application. The adjustment envisaged is made by reference to expenditure which could have been 'claimed before and allowed at the relevant time'. This means that the provision can have no application to an assessment which is made earlier than that time (twelve months after the end of the claim period). In the case of a field well into production, assessments will normally be made within five months of the end of the relative chargeable period, tax being due six months after the end of the period.

The possible impact of the provision is associated with the question of whether the scheme of the Act recognises that oil allowance may be given in priority to expenditure relief. Many participators would wish to utilise reliefs in that order at the front end of field life. By doing so, the benefit of expenditure relief could be carried forward so as to delay the incidence of tax. Furthermore, in the case of small or unprofitable fields, failure to maximise oil allowance in early chargeable periods may mean not only earlier tax liability but also absolute loss of some oil allowance benefit, whether because of the impact of safeguard or otherwise. The OTO has sought to resist attempts to secure early oil allowance. In practice, it has not made assessments for the early chargeable periods of a field until much of the front-end expenditure has been claimed and allowed, so that for those periods little or no assessable profit emerges against which oil allowance can be utilised.

In *Amoco UK Exploration Company* v *IRC* [1983] STC 634, the company appealed against a determination of loss for the first chargeable period and assessments for the next three periods (for which the assessable profits were covered by losses brought forward) on the grounds that there ought to have been assessable profits covered by oil allowance had assessments been made at the 'proper' time. The appeal was dismissed, Walton J finding that the Revenue was entitled to make assessments at any time within the general six years time limit and was not, as had been contended by the company, bound to make assessments forthwith on receipt of a participator's return for a chargeable period.

6.29 Loss Relief

The PRT computation for a chargeable period may produce an allowable loss instead of an assessable profit. This occurs where the sum of the negative amounts exceeds the sum of the positive amounts; in broad terms, where expenditure exceeds income.

The main loss relief rule is that a loss is allowed, automatically and not subject to a claim, as a reduction of the assessable profit in the succeeding period: if that profit is insufficient to absorb the whole of the loss, any balance is relieved against the next assessable profit and so on until the loss is exhausted(s7(1)). The participator may, however, make a claim to carry back loss for relief against assessable profits of earlier periods, beginning with the latest such period. If a claim is made under this provision, it takes precedence over the main carry forward rule. There is no specific time limit for a claim and the period of carry back is unlimited. It is not possible to claim to carry back only part of the loss, nor to carry back only to specified periods: if a claim is made, all assessable profits for earlier periods must be extinguished if the loss is sufficient, any remaining balance of loss then being available to carry forward (s7 (2)).

A third rule requires that if, when the winning of oil from the field has permanently ceased, a loss remains after the maximum relief under either of the rules indicated above, it is to be treated as reducing any available assessable profits from the field, beginning with later periods and working backwards. The purpose of this provision is presumably to ensure that a field loss is utilised to the maximum extent within the field so that only the irreducible residue is available for claim against assessable profits of another field under the unrelievable field loss rules (s7(3)). It is not clear to what extent account should be taken of tariff income which may arise after production from the field ceases in deciding whether the loss is relievable by carry forward (see also Interaction with Tariffing 6.29.1).

Loss relief is given by reducing assessable profit, and oil allowance is applied to any assessable profit remaining after reduction by loss relief.

6.29.1 UK Oil Taxation

6.29.1 Unrelievable Field Loss

If, at the end of the life of a field, a residue of loss remains after all of the participator's assessable profits from the field have been relieved, it may be allowed in the calculation of profit or loss from another field in which the participator has an interest. Before an unrelievable field loss can be established, the Board has to confirm to the responsible person, in response to an application, that the winning of oil from the field has permanently ceased. The responsible person has a right of appeal if the application is rejected.

Once the Board's confirmation is received, a participator may make a claim for allowance of the unrelievable field loss against another field. The procedures relating to the claim and its agreement and allowance in an assessment or determination are similar to those applying to field expenditure. The time limit for the claim is six years from the date of agreement that the winning of oil has permanently ceased or from the date of determination of the other field, whichever is later. (s6 and Sched 8).

If a field is determined but cumulative production never reaches the amount required to trigger the first chargeable period (see 6.5), it is still possible to have a loss established as an unrelievable field loss for relief elsewhere.

An unrelievable field loss may be claimed by a company which is associated with the participator which incurred the loss. Companies are associated for this purpose if:

(*a*) throughout that part of the relevant period in which both were in existence, one was a 51% subsidiary of the other which itself was not a 51% subsidiary of a third company, or

(*b*) each of them was, throughout that part of the relevant period in which it was in existence, a 51% subsidiary of a third company which was not itself a 51% subsidiary of any other company.

The relevant period begins with the chargeable period in which the loss accrued and ends with the end of that period or the end of the first chargeable period in which the claimant company is a participator in the field against which the loss is claimed.

Relief is no longer available for an unrelievable field loss against an interest acquired in a producing field unless the winning of oil from the loss-making field ceases after the 'qualifying date' (broadly, the date of acquisition of the interest in the producing field – 6.20.1 (FA 1984 s113)).

Because oil allowance is given as a reduction of any assessable profit remaining after the allowance of loss relief, the existence of an unrelievable field loss at the end of field life means that the participator has not utilised any of its share of the field oil allowance. By the same token, oil allowance taken in assessments cannot create or augment an unrelievable field loss.

It seems to be envisaged that an unrelievable field loss will be claimed wholly against one field, and cannot be apportioned between two or more fields. However, an unrelievable field loss may be established in more than one chargeable period where, for example, abandonment costs are incurred over an extended time: each such loss would be claimed against a different field. An unrelievable field loss may itself create or augment an unrelievable field loss in the claimant field.

There are some potential anomalies relating to unrelievable field losses in the field transfer rules (see 8.8.1).

Interaction with tariffing

The unrelievable field loss rules were not altered in consequence of the introduction in 1983 of the tariff receipts provisions. Assessments on tariffs relating to a field may continue for a number of years after production of oil from the field has ceased. The OTO is understood to take the view that an unrelievable loss cannot be claimed against another field so long as there is the prospect that tariff receipts chargeable on the field will arise in the future, and that the loss must be reserved for relief against those profits. Arguably, however, the legislation contemplates that a loss subsisting at the time of cessation of production may be established for possible use against another field, assuming agreement of a notice that the winning of oil has ceased and maximum offset against earlier profits. That loss remains relievable against future tariff profits if it is not exported under the unrelievable loss rules.

6.30 Safeguard

The amount of PRT payable in the early years of field life is not to exceed a level such as would reduce the participator's after-tax profit below a minimum return on investment in the field. This safeguard relief was introduced as a safety net for the benefit of less profitable fields, and in its original form was available throughout field life. Given a PRT rate of 45%, it was expected that the incidence of safeguard would be comparatively low, occurring towards the end of field life if at all. The profile of the relief was significantly changed by increases in the PRT rate, and again by the 1985 collapse in oil prices, (s9).

The period for which safeguard may apply is now restricted. The maximum number of chargeable periods for which the tax may be limited by safeguard is the number between the first chargeable period and the net profit period (payback) inclusive, plus one half of that

6.30 UK Oil Taxation

number, counting any fraction as a whole period (FA 1981 s114). For example:

first chargeable period	31 December 1983
net profit period	31 December 1986
number of periods to payback = 7	
total periods for safeguard = 7 + 4 = 11	
last chargeable period for safeguard	31 December 1988

In arriving at the number of periods in the base, there are excluded any periods in which the amount of oil won and saved from the field does not exceed 1,000 tonnes (or an equivalent amount of gas). The main purpose of this provision is to prevent establishment of an artificially extended safeguard term where, in particular, the first chargeable period is triggered by a production test, followed by a substantial interval before the field is developed (FA 1985 s91).

6.30.1 Safeguard Calculation

For those periods to which safeguard is applicable, tax is limited to: 80% × ('adjusted profit' minus 15% of accumulated capital expenditure). If the adjusted profit is less than 15% of the accumulated capital expenditure, no tax is payable for the period. Otherwise, in order to determine whether any limitation of the tax charged is appropriate, it is necessary to do two parallel calculations, one under normal PRT rules and the second under safeguard rules. If the tax figure resulting from the first calculation is greater than that resulting from the second, the difference reduces the tax charged in the assessment. It will seen that the marginal rate of tax in this safeguard limitation zone is 80%. The two elements in the safeguard computation are arrived at as follows:

Adjusted profit
(1) Assessable profit (before any reduction for losses or oil allowance) or allowable loss 0

Add back
(2) Field expenditure allowed which qualified for supplement 0
(3) Supplement on expenditure in (2) 0
(4) Abortive exploration expenditure allowed 0
(5) Exploration and appraisal expenditure allowed 0
(6) Research expenditure allowed 0
(7) Cross-field allowance 0
(8) Unrelievable field loss allowed 0

Deduct
(9) Excess allowances charged as income (6.20)
Adjusted profit 0

The broad effect is to arrive at operating profit, having left out of account capital expenditure and expenditure and losses extraneous to the field.

Petroleum Revenue Tax 6.30.2

Accumulated capital expenditure is the cumulative amount of field expenditure allowed as qualifying for supplement, whether claimed by the responsible person or by the participator itself, which is taken into account in the calculation of profit or loss of the chargeable period in question and all earlier chargeable periods. If a restriction of supplement is made in respect of disposal receipts (see 6.19.7), only the restricted amount of the relative expenditure is added to accumulated capital expenditure.

Expenditure incurred in the period in question or in earlier periods which is allowed late and taken into account in calculating the profit or loss of a later period is not then added to the amount of accumulated capital expenditure ruling at the end of the period in which the expenditure was incurred although it is carried back for the purpose of calculating payback (see 6.19.9). If the expenditure itself is allowed in time to be included in the calculation of profit or loss of the period in which it was incurred but the claim to supplement in respect of it is agreed later, the expenditure is apparently added to accumulated capital expenditure of the period in which the supplement is reflected in the profit or loss calculation and not in the period for which the expenditure was allowed.

6.30.2 Interaction of Safeguard and Other Reliefs

Supplement and the expenditure to which it relates are disallowed in the calculation of adjusted profit for safeguard purposes, but that expenditure is added to the accumulated capital expenditure not only for the period in the profit or loss of which it is reflected but for all later periods for which safeguard may run. No benefit is obtained from supplement as such allowed in the profit calculation of a period in which tax is limited by safeguard. Tax relief on expenditure qualifying for supplement allowed in a period to which safeguard does not apply is, at the current PRT rate of 75%,
$$(100 + 35) \times 75\% = 101.25\%$$
The same expenditure and supplement allowed in a safeguard period would give relief only by increasing the accumulated capital expenditure, thus:
$$(100 \times 15\%) \times 80\% = 12\% \text{ with a further } 12\% \text{ for each subsequent safeguard period.}$$

This disparity is not normally of concern since expenditure incurred after the end of the net profit period cannot now qualify for supplement. In the exceptional case where a PRT liability arises in the payback period, limited by safeguard, the responsible person would

6.30.2 UK Oil Taxation

need to decide whether to make a claim for supplement. A similar dilemma may present itself in relation to expenditure incurred in the payback period or earlier which is allowed late. In partial alleviation of these difficulties, the responsible person is able to claim supplement on part only of the expenditure claimed, allocating the supplement only to those participators wishing it claimed on their behalf.

The safeguard computation also negates the benefit of exploration and appraisal or abortive exploration allowances which have been taken into account in the 'normal' PRT calculation. This means that a participator will normally wish not to have such expenditure allowed for a period for which safeguard applies, but rather to carry the allowance forward to a later period. If, however, the potential safeguard reduction is small, the participator may still wish to utilise available exploration and appraisal or abortive exploration expenditure relief in order to effect a bigger reduction in tax calculated under the normal rules. Research allowance, cross-field allowance and unrelievable field losses are similarly eliminated, that is, added back in arriving at adjusted profit for safeguard purposes.

The calculation of oil allowance proceeds independently of safeguard. Any allowance due under the normal rules is actually used, reducing the pool of the field's remaining quota, even though no benefit accrues from it because the tax payable is limited by safeguard.

Because adjusted profit for the purpose of the safeguard calculation is not reduced by losses brought forward or carried back from other chargeable periods, the amount of tax payable under safeguard is unaffected by those losses. No effective relief is obtained for losses allowed in the period to which safeguard would otherwise apply unless the effect of the allowance is to reduce the amount of tax under the normal calculation below the safeguard limit.

The Government became concerned about the facility available to participators to defer claims for expenditure incurred in periods in which it would attract no effective relief because of safeguard, and to take the allowances in a later period. It announced in December 1987 – 'Nevertheless, the Government has decided, in the light of representations received during the review and in the current situation in the oil market, not to bring forward legislation in next year's Finance Bill to prevent extra relief from being obtained by means of deferring expenditure claims'. It added that the Revenue would not seek to counteract such benefits by deferring assessments.

6.31 Returns

Two main types of PRT return and one supplementary return are called for, relating chiefly to the establishment of income. They are entirely separate from claims for expenditure.

6.31.1 Return by Responsible Person

The responsible person is required to deliver for each chargeable period a return in respect of the field, within one month of the end of the chargeable period. The return is to contain a declaration that it is correct and complete and to state:
(*a*) the quantity of oil won and saved from the field during the period;
(*b*) the respective interests of the participators in the field in that oil;
(*c*) each participator's share of that oil in accordance with those interests; and
(*d*) such other particulars as the Board may require (Sched 2 (5)).

For chargeable periods ending 31 December 1983 or later, additional details are required relating to the calculation of tariff receipts allowance if appropriate.

If the responsible person fails to make the return in time, he is liable to a penalty not exceeding £500 plus a further penalty not exceeding £100 for each day that the failure continues after it is declared by the Special Commissioners or the court: but no penalty is chargeable if the failure is remedied before penalty proceedings are commenced (Sched 2 (6)). If the responsible person fails to make a return, or the Board is dissatisfied with the return, the Board may require him to deliver such accounts relating to the field or to production from it as is specified in the Board's notice, or to make available for inspection such books, accounts and documents relating to the field or to production as are specified (Sched 2 (7)). The submission of an incorrect return, or an incorrect statement or declaration in connection with an expenditure claim, carries a maximum penalty of £2,500 or, in the case of fraud, £5,000 (Sched 2 (8)).

A responsible person who, having realised that an error was made by a predecessor in that position, then fails to remedy it without unreasonable delay is himself deemed to have made the submission negligently (Sched 2 (9)).

6.31.2 Return by Participator

A participator is required to make a return for each chargeable period within two months of the end of the period. The return is to contain a declaration that it is correct and complete, and give the following

6.31.2 UK Oil Taxation

information relating to the participator's share of production from the field:

(a) in the case of each delivery of oil disposed of crude, the quantity of the oil, the person to whom the oil was disposed of, and the price received or receivable or, in the case of sales not at arm's length, the market value;

(b) in the case of each relevant appropriation of crude oil, the quantity and the market value;

(c) in the case of crude oil delivered to the Secretary of State as royalty in kind, the total quantity of that oil;

(d) in the case of crude oil which at the end of the period has either not been disposed of and not relevantly appropriated or has been disposed of but not delivered, the quantity and the market value (Sched 2 (2)).

Following the introduction of the nomination scheme, further information is required:

(e) the excess of nominated proceeds for the period, if any;

(f) details of nominated transactions which were not fulfilled, or were not fulfilled by the participator's equity production from the field.

For each month, a reconciliation is required between the nominated volume of equity crude and the volume delivered in pursuance of the nominated transactions; but, for any month in which oil forming part of equity production was delivered, supplied or appropriated as proposed in nominations and no other such oil was delivered under arm's length sales contracts, a detailed reconciliation is not necessary.

Returns are required to include details of tariff and disposal receipts, and of royalty, periodic payments and other amounts payable to or by the Secretary of State in respect of the relevant licence.

The first return for a field which a participator makes is also required to give details of how much exploration and appraisal expenditure incurred in an area related to the field has been claimed by the participator or an associated company or by a participator from which the field interest was transferred, and similar details of research expenditure.

If a participator fails to make a return in time, it is liable to a penalty not exceeding £500 or, if the return is more than six months late, £500 plus the amount of tax assessed for the chargeable period. In addition, a further penalty not exceeding £100 is chargeable for each day on which the failure continues after it has been declared by the Special Commissioners or the court. The offence can be purged by rendering the return before penalty proceedings are commenced. This does not apply, however, if the claim is more than six months late, and it must be assumed that a participator will take great care not to expose itself to the risk of this draconian penalty (Sched 2 (3)).

Petroleum Revenue Tax 6.32

As in the case of a responsible person's return, if the return is not delivered or if the Board is not satisfied with the return the Board may order production of accounts and records (Sched 2(7)).

Where a participator fraudulently or negligently submits an incorrect return, or accounts statement or declaration in connection with a claim for relief, it is liable to a penalty not exceeding £50 plus the amount by which the tax payable was reduced by reason of the error (or twice that amount in the case of fraud) (Sched 2(8)). Where a return or accounts, statement or declaration required by a Board's notice is incorrect though not submitted either negligently or fraudulently, it is treated as having been submitted negligently if the participator, having realised the error, fails to remedy it without unreasonable delay (Sched 2(9)).

6.31.3 Additional Return by Participator

A participator is also required, within two months of the end of a chargeable period, to render an additional return of 'relevant sales of oil'. If two or more participators in the field are in the same group of companies, one return only may be made covering the relevant transactions of all of them. The sales in question are arm's length sales for delivery in the chargeable period to which the participator, or any company associated with the participator which is resident in the UK, is a party whether as seller, buyer or otherwise: but they exclude sales of less than 500 tonnes and sales of gas consisting mainly of methane or ethane, and any sales which are included in the main PRT return for the period. For this purpose, two companies are associated if one is controlled by the other or both are under common control. For each sale, the details required are the date of contract and delivery, the buyer and seller, the amount of oil sold and the sale price: the Board may prescribe additional details (FA 1987 s62).

The Board also has the power to direct a participator to make available similar information relating to transactions by companies associated with a participator which are not resident in the UK (FA 1984 s115).

6.32 Claims by Responsible Person

All field expenditure is claimed by the responsible person except that which is confidential to a participator, which may be claimed by that participator on its own account (see 6.33). Claims are made for claim periods, in respect of expenditure incurred in those periods (see 6.15.1); but expenditure incurred by a person at a time before he becomes a participator in the field is to be included in a claim for the

6.32 UK Oil Taxation

claim period in which he becomes a participator. The time limit for a claim is six years from the end of the claim period.

A claim must indicate what part, if any, of the expenditure claimed is also claimed to qualify for supplement. If different elements of it are considered to qualify at different supplement rates, the claim must make the appropriate distinctions. Where one or more participators, having passed payback, are not entitled to supplement, the claim is made for supplement which would be due were it not for the intervention of payback; but if it appears to the responsible person that, because of the payback cut-off, none of the expenditure is likely to qualify for supplement, he need not make a supplement claim (FA 1981 s111 (6)). The OTO accepts that the requirement that expenditure be allocated between the participators in accordance with their field interests does not necessarily mean that supplement on that expenditure must be similarly allocated. The responsible person may claim supplement on part only of the expenditure and allocate the whole of the supplement on that part to one or more particular participators, not exceeding their proportionate entitlement.

The claim must also show 'the shares in which, in accordance with their respective interests in the oil field, the participators propose to divide between them' the expenditure and supplement. The Board is not bound to accept that division (see 6.32.1).

If a claim is made in respect of expenditure on a non-dedicated mobile asset (see 6.17.2), claims for subsequent periods are required to include all information necessary for calculation of the proportionate further allowance or claw-back of earlier allowances as appropriate. If a claim is not made for a subsequent period within twelve months of the end of the period, the Board may proceed to make such adjustments to the allowances in respect of the asset as seem to the best of its judgment to be necessary (Sched 5).

6.32.1 Decisions on Claims

A participator may take credit in calculating its payment on account (see 6.37.2) for any expenditure and supplement which has been claimed, but none of it can be included in the calculation of profit or loss by reference to which tax for any period is formally charged before it is allowed by the Board. Allowance is notified in a notice of decision which has to state:

(*a*) the amount of expenditure allowed;
(*b*) the amount, if any, allowed as qualifying for supplement;
(*c*) the shares in which, in the Board's opinion, the expenditure and supplement allowed is divisible between the participators (Sched 5(3)).

Petroleum Revenue Tax 6.32.1

If the decision relates to part only of the expenditure claimed, or claimed as qualifying for supplement, one or more further notices is given in relation to the remainder. There is no time limit within which a decision on the whole of the claim must be made, although, since any appeal against a decision must be lodged within three years of the date of the claim, it is evidently envisaged that a full decision will be made within that time.

It frequently happens, particularly in relation to claims for the first claim period, that the first notice of decision relates to part only of the claim, followed by further notices. The OTO finds it expedient to proceed in this way, enabling it to notify acceptance of part of a claim even though at that time it finds itself unable to make a decision on the remainder, whether for lack of information or otherwise. The parts of a claim not covered by the notice or an earlier notice are sometimes referred to as reservations. The notice should make clear what part of the expenditure and supplement claimed has been decided upon, and of that part, how much is allowed. The Act does not actually require the Board to show how much is 'disallowed', though in practice this is normally done in order to clarify the extent of a claim which is covered by the notice.

Notices relating to supplement make appropriate distinctions if parts of the expenditure are claimed at different rates. The decision as to how much of the expenditure qualifies for supplement is made without regard to the effect of one or more of the participators having passed payback. If a participator disagrees with an assessment on the grounds that supplement to which it is entitled is, in the view of OTO, barred by the payback provisions, it must seek remedy through appeal against the assessment rather than appeal against the decision on the claim.

In the case of a claim for allowance of both expenditure and of related supplement, the decision as to expenditure may be given in one notice and the decision as to supplement in a separate notice. It is not suggested that this practice is non-statutory, but the consequence of taking expenditure and the related supplement into account in assessments for different chargeable periods raises a doubt as to whether the Act was designed to operate in this way (see, for example, the effect on safeguard, 6.30.2).

The manner in which allowances are divided between the participators can be a matter of contention between the OTO and the participators. The OTO takes the view that division 'in accordance with their respective interests in the oil field' requires in strictness division according to their respective equity interests in oil to be won. It has opposed allocation of relief according to the proportions in which the participators bear the expenditure, partly on the practical ground that it carries the risk of distorting the total amount of field safeguard benefit.

6.32.1 UK Oil Taxation

It has, however, conceded some degree of flexibility. In particular it has accepted that exploration and appraisal expenditure relating to a field which is incurred before the commencement of production may be apportioned between the participators in such manner as they agree. There may also be other circumstances in which allocation in line with 'disproportionate cost sharing' is considered appropriate. For example, the application of the 1983 Oil Taxation Act rules to inter-field use of an asset, owned by one participator and made available to other participators in the field in return for tariff payments, is not consistent with allocation of relief for the cost of the asset between the participators.

6.32.2 Appeals Against Decisions

The responsible person has a right of appeal to the Special Commissioners, within three years of the making of the claim, against the Board's decision if
(a) the amount or total of amounts of expenditure, or the amount or total of the amounts of supplement, allowed in the notice or notices of decision is less than the amount claimed; or
(b) the division of allowances between the participators differs from the manner of division proposed in the claim. If the appeal is on this second ground, any of the participators is entitled to be heard in appeal proceedings, but otherwise the responsible person alone is responsible for prosecuting the appeal.

Effect is given to the notice of decision regardless of the appeal: that is, any allowance notified in it is available for inclusion in the calculation of the assessment or determination of loss next made (Sched 5 (5)).

The appeal may be settled by agreement before it is determined by the Special Commissioners, or one of the grounds (*a* or *b* above) may be settled leaving the other for determination by the Commissioners. If the amount of expenditure allowance, or the amount of supplement if appropriate, is settled by agreement, the amount allowed in excess of that allowed in the notice is treated as having been allowed by the Board on the date on which the appeal was made. If agreement is reached on the manner in which allowances should be divided between the participators, effect is given to that agreement in all notices of decision given on the claim in question. The responsible person may at any time abandon an appeal; and an appeal settled by agreement is treated as abandoned (Sched 5 (6)).

If an appeal is heard by the Special Commissioners, they have the power to vary the decision, whether or not the variation is to the advantage of all or any of the participators. This might in theory extend to their reducing allowances notified in the Board's decision. They may decide what amounts of expenditure or supplement in dispute are allowable. Those amounts are then treated as having been allowed on the date on which the appeal was made, and any consequential adjustments of assessments or determinations are to be made (Sched 5 (7)).

Provision is also made for the appeal to be heard by the High Court if either party is dissatisfied with a determination of the Special Commissioners. Again any expenditure or supplement allowed by the court in excess of amounts already allowed by the Board or the Commissioners is treated as having been allowed on the date of the appeal. If allowances are reduced, any tax payable in consequence carries interest from two months after the end of the chargeable period to which it relates (Sched 5(8)).

Because expenditure or supplement allowed in consequence of an appeal against the Board's decision is treated as having been allowed at the date of the appeal, it is taken into account in the assessment or determination of loss next made after that date. It is, therefore, normally in the interest of a participator that, if an appeal is to be made, it is made as early as possible. Difficulties can arise where the notice or notices of decision cover part only of the expenditure or supplement claimed, the remainder being 'reserved' pending a further notice. If an appeal cannot be made against the lack of allowance until a decision on the amount 'reserved' is made, the participator may not be compensated in interest on tax saved as a result of allowance eventually agreed. Worse still, supplement claimed before payback but allowed later may be effectively lost because it falls into a period in which the safeguard limitation applies. In the case of a late agreement of supplement in principle, the amount of the supplement claimed may be reduced, the reduced amount then being allocated only to those participators which can benefit from it.

There is some difficulty in construing the provisions relating to the form of the Board's decision on a claim. A notice may cover part only of the expenditure or supplement claimed, leaving the remainder for a later notice or notices (Sched 5 (3)). There is a doubt whether there can be only one decision on a claim, albeit notified in more than one notice. In practice, the OTO regards each notice as a decision, or at any rate a part decision, in respect of which there is a right of appeal, subject to provisos. In the OTO's view, no right of appeal arises unless, of that part of expenditure or supplement claimed on which the decision is made, some is not allowed; or unless the responsible person disagrees with the manner in which the notice divides the allowances between the participators. It does not accept that an appeal may be made against the decision on grounds that part of the expenditure or supplement claimed is 'reserved' and is therefore not allowed.

6.32.2 UK Oil Taxation

The industry has expressed dissatisfaction with a system in which delays in the making of full decisions on claims, and consequently in the triggering of a right of appeal, can have arbitrary and significant effects on liabilities. Within the practical and statutory constraints, the OTO has sought to operate the provisions as fairly as possible.

6.32.3 Variation of Decisions on Claims

Provision was introduced in 1983 to enable the Board to rectify decisions which prove to be incorrect. It applies to decisions made after 15 March 1983 on claims for field expenditure made by the responsible person or by a participator: it applies also, in respect of decisions made after 16 March 1987, to claims by a participator for exploration and appraisal relief, abortive exploration expenditure relief and research relief (FA 1987 s 67).

If the Board discovers, within three years of the date of the notice of decision, that the decision was incorrect, it can issue a notice of variation which sets out what it considers to be the correct position. The provision is presumably intended to rectify over allowance, though capable of dealing also with an under allowance. The error may be either in the amount of expenditure allowed or the amount of expenditure allowed as qualifying for supplement. The notice of variation is subject to a right of appeal within 30 days of issue. The appeal may be settled by agreement or otherwise abandoned, and the Board may withdraw the notice of variation before it becomes effective. If the appeal is heard by the Special Commissioners, they may confirm, quash or vary the notice.

The notice becomes effective on expiry of the appeal period or on settlement of an appeal if appropriate. The decision in respect of which the variation is made is then treated as amended in terms of the notice of variation and as having been made in the amended form on the date on which the actual decision was made. Any increase or decrease in the allowance of expenditure or supplement is presumably allocated between the participators, in the case of a claim by a responsible person, in accordance with the proportions adopted in the original decision. All necessary adjustments to assessments or determinations of loss are then made (Sched 5(9)).

6.33 Claims for Field Expenditure by Participators

If a participator 'satisfies the Board that, for reasons of trade secrecy, it would be unreasonable for him to have to provide the responsible person with the information necessary for the making of a claim', the participator may make a claim for the expenditure on its own account (Sched 6). The machinery relating to such a claim follows very closely that laid down for claims by the responsible person (though there are certain necessary modifications such as deletion of references to allocation of expenditure between participators). Expenditure is claimed for the claim period in which it is incurred or, if it is incurred before the claimant becomes a participator in the field, for the claim period in which it becomes a participator. The time limit for claims is six years after the end of a claim period. Under this Schedule, there are no provisions for fixing claim periods, and it appears that the claim periods adopted for the purpose of the field claims by the responsible person apply also for the purpose of claims by any of the participators.

Whether expenditure satisfies the trade secrecy test is entirely a matter within the Board's discretion. The types of expenditure which are commonly claimed by participators on their own account include costs of insurance arranged separately rather than through the operator, overhead and support costs attributable to the participator's interest in the field but not chargeable as consortium expense, and certain tariff payments.

6.34 Claims for Exploration and Appraisal Expenditure

A participator may make a claim in respect of exploration and appraisal expenditure incurred by itself or by an associated company (see 6.20). There is no time limit for such a claim, and there are no rules as to the period for which a claim should be made. Most claims are in practice made for periods of six months or a year, but they may be for longer or shorter periods.

Most of the provisions relating to a claim by a responsible person are applied to claims for exploration and appraisal expenditure. These include the making of decisions on claims and rights of appeal. In contrast to claims for field expenditure, however, it is provided that if the claimant discovers that an error or mistake has been made in a claim, it may make a supplementary claim (Sched 7).

Expenditure incurred by a participator may be allowed in an assessment for a chargeable period even though it is incurred after the end of that period. The OTO normally accepts for consideration with a view to such allowance claims for expenditure incurred up to three months after the period end, provided that the claim is made not later than four months after the period end. It does not accept that such a claim is permissible in respect of expenditure incurred by an associated company, since the test of association must be satisfied up to the end of the period in which the expenditure is incurred.

6.34.1   UK Oil Taxation

6.34.1 Claims for Abortive Exploration Expenditure

Abortive exploration expenditure incurred by a participator or an associated company before 16 March 1983 may be claimed by the participator against any field in which it has an interest (see 6.21). There is now no time limit for such a claim, and no rules as to the period for which a claim is to be made. The provisions relating to claims for exploration and appraisal expenditure, incurred after 15 March 1983, apply also to claims for abortive exploration expenditure (Sched 7).

6.34.2 Claims For Research Expenditure

The procedure for claims for exploration and appraisal expenditure applies also to claims for research expenditure, incurred after 16 March 1987, not related to a field. The claim cannot be made until three years have elapsed from the date on which the expenditure was incurred (see 6.22).

6.34.3 Elections for Cross-Field Allowance

Relief under the cross-field allowance provisions is triggered by an election, the timing and conditions of which are indicated in paragraph 6.23. The election is required to specify the expenditure in respect of which it is made and the amount, up to 10%, to be allowed in the receiving field, and the relative notice of decision, agreement or determination of the underlying claim.

6.35 PRT Assessment

Each participator is assessed separately in respect of its profit derived from the field. A participator having interests in more than one field is assessed separately in respect of each field.

If the Board considers that an assessable profit or an allowable loss has accrued in a chargeable period, it has to make an assessment to tax or a determination of loss as appropriate. If it considers that neither an assessable profit nor allowable loss has accrued, a notice of determination to that effect is made. The Board has six years from the end of the chargeable period within which to make the assessment or determina-

Petroleum Revenue Tax 6.35.1

tion (TMA 1970 s34). That time limit does not apply to assessments to make good loss of tax due to neglect, wilful default or fraud, which may be made at any time. The Keith Committee on Enforcement Powers recommended in 1983 that in these circumstances there should be a 20 year time limit extended only if the participator carries back losses for a longer period (Sched 2 (10)).

If the Board is satisfied with the participator's return for the period, the assessment or determination is to be made in accordance with the return. If the Board is not so satisfied, or if a return has not been made, the Board has to assess or determine to the best of its judgment: in other words, to estimate the profit or loss (Sched 2 (11)).

The Board has powers, somewhat broader than the discovery provisions applying to CT, to make such adjustments to assessments or determinations as seem to it to be necessary. If it considers that the amount of profit or loss is incorrectly stated in an assessment or determination, it may make such assessments or determinations or amendments as are required to rectify the error, including any consequential revisions for other chargeable periods. The time limit for such action is not specified but is assumed to be six years from the end of the chargeable period for which the revision is made: the Keith Committee recommended that the rules should be amended so as to apply specifically a six year time limit. If an under-assessment is due to allowance of an excessive loss of a later period, the time limit is extended so that a further assessment may be made not more than six years after the end of the period of loss (Sched 2 (12)).

Assessments which carry a tax charge are normally made not later that five months after the end of the chargeable period, the tax, so far as not paid on account, being payable six months after the end of the period. Determinations of loss or assessments on which no tax is payable are sometimes made outside that time-scale, particularly for the early chargeable periods of a field.

6.35.1 Payment of Assessed PRT

The tax formally assessed for the period is due and payable six months after the end of the period or 30 days after the date of the assessment if later (Sched 2 (13)). If an appeal is made against the assessment, the participator may be entitled to withhold payment of some of the tax (see 6.35.4). The PRT liability for a period, to the extent that it is not satisfied by APRT paid for that or earlier periods, is, however, payable wholly or partly under the instalment and payment on account arrangements, not later than two months after the end of the period (see 6.37).

6.35.2 Interest on Assessed PRT

PRT payable for a chargeable period carries interest from two months after the end of the period until payment, even though any balance of tax not accounted for under the instalment and payment on account arrangements is not due, at the earliest, until six months after the end of the period. Interest runs regardless of when the assessment is made and whether the tax is charged in a first or a further assessment or an amended assessment. Interest on unpaid tax is not an allowable deduction for PRT or CT or income tax purposes.

Separate interest provisions attach to unpaid instalments and PRT payments on account (see 6.37.3).

6.35.3 Interest on PRT Repayments

Repayments of assessed PRT carry interest from two months after the end of the chargeable period to which the tax relates, or from the date on which the tax was paid if later, until the repayment is made. Interest received on repayments is not chargeable to PRT, CT or income tax.

There are separate provisions relating to interest on repayments of APRT, instalments and PRT payments on account (see 6.37.3) (Sched 2 (15)).

6.35.4 Appeals Against PRT Assessments

A participator may appeal to the Special Commissioners against an assessment or determination or an amended assessment or determination, within thirty days of issue of the notice. If an appeal is made then, provided that a return for the period has been made, the participator may withhold payment until the appeal is determined of the smaller of:
(*a*) the amount of the tax charged; and
(*b*) tax on the difference between the value returned for production including stock and the amount included in the assessment in respect of that production and stock.

If the market value returned for oil to which the market value rules apply (non-arm's length sales, appropriations and stock) is less than a yardstick value, the latter value is substituted for the returned value for this purpose. The yardstick value is the average price of all arm's length sales made by participators in all UK fields as shown by returns for the previous chargeable period. That price is not of course within the knowledge of the participator itself, and if the amount of tax to be withheld is subject to this restriction, the OTO needs to inform the participator of the amount of the restriction. The rationale of the limitation is presumably that the participator could otherwise withhold an excessive amount of tax as a result of returning artificially low oil values. In an era of falling oil prices, however, the formula can set an unreasonably high yardstick value.

An appeal may be abandoned at any time, if the Board agrees. Otherwise, the appeal may be settled by agreement or by the Commissioners, the assessment or determination or amendment being varied according (Sched 2 (14)).

6.36 Advance Petroleum Revenue Tax

APRT was introduced with effect from 1 January 1983, combined with an increase in the PRT rate to 75%. It was to apply, at a rate of 20%, to the first chargeable period ending after 31 December 1982 in which a gross profit arose to the participator and to each one of the succeeding nine periods in which there was a gross profit. As part of the relaxation of the fiscal regime effected by the 1983 Finance Act, APRT was phased out, ceasing to apply to any chargeable period ending after 31 December 1986. The rate was successively reduced as follows:

15% for chargeable periods ending on 31 December 1983, 30 June 1984 and 31 December 1984;
10% for chargeable periods ending on 30 June and 31 December 1985;
5% for chargeable periods ending on 30 June and 31 December 1986.

APRT was charged on the gross profit, as computed for PRT purposes (6.7), but increased so as to bring royalty in kind oil within the charge. It was not charged on exempt gas, nor on tariff or disposal receipts.

The gross profit was reduced by an exempt allowance of 500,000 tonnes of oil for each chargeable period, divided between the participators in proportion to their shares of oil won and saved in the period. This allowance was similar in concept to the PRT oil allowance, but it was available for every period and not subject to a cumulative limit (FA 1982 ss139–141 and Sched 19).

6.36.1 Credit of APRT against PRT

APRT paid for a period, together with any earlier excess APRT not used in set-off against PRT, is set against the PRT liability for the period and discharges a corresponding amount of that liability. The set-off is made first against the PRT payment on account due two months

6.36.1   UK Oil Taxation

after the end of the period. If the total of available APRT, the APRT credit, exceeds the PRT liability for the period, the excess is carried forward for offset in subsequent periods or, in the case of an excess subsisting at 31 December 1986, for repayment (see 6.36.2).

APRT is not allowed in its own right as a deduction for CT purposes, but PRT which is satisfied by APRT credit is specifically allowed as a CT deduction (FA 1982 s 142).

6.36.2 Repayment of APRT

APRT paid in excess of the APRT liability for a period is repayable, carrying interest from two months after the end of the period, or, if later, from the date on which it was paid.

APRT which, together with any brought forward excess APRT credit, exceeds the PRT liability for the period is carried forward for credit against later PRT liabilities. If there is such an excess at the end of the last chargeable period for which APRT can apply, 31 December 1986 it is repayable, but without interest.

In a case where PRT liabilities up to 31 December 1986 are insufficient to absorb APRT payments, because field expenditure and other allowances delay the onset of those liabilities, APRT is in essence an interest-free loan to the government. Generally, the excess credit is not repayable earlier than two months after the end of the ninth chargeable period following the first for which APRT was payable for the field: this sets the earliest repayment date at 29 February 1988. In response to the industry's needs for cash-flow assistance, however, the Government brought forward the repayment date in some circumstances. A participator who had an excess credit at 31 December 1986, after covering the PRT due for the period ended on that date as shown in his payment on account return, was entitled to repayment of the excess up to £15m for each relevant field. This facility did not apply if the participator had reached 'payback' in any period up to 30 June 1986: for this purpose, certain modifications were made in making the payback calculation. Claims were required not later than 28 February 1987 (APRT Act 1987).

6.37 Schedule of Payments of APRT and PRT

The general scheme is that the PRT for a chargeable period is accounted for by a system of instalments commencing in the period and a payment on account two months after the end of the period, any balance then remaining being payable six months after the end of the period. APRT, allowed as a credit against PRT liability, was satisfied in the first instance by the instalment payments, any balance becoming payable two months after the end of the period.

6.37.1 Instalment Payments

Chargeable periods ending after 31 December 1984
A system of payment in advance applies to APRT and PRT liabilities. In respect of each chargeable period, six monthly instalments are required, beginning two months into the period itself. Each instalment is calculated as;
⅛th × the amount of PRT shown as payable on account for the preceding chargeable period *before* any reduction for APRT credit.

The PRT payment on account is due two months after the end of the chargeable period to which it relates, so that the instalments for the next chargeable period, based on that payment on account, begin on the same day. The total amount payable by way of instalments is normally 75% of the PRT payment on account for the preceding period. There is, however, a right not to pay an instalment in certain circumstances. If the participator in any month makes no delivery of oil and no relevant appropriation, the instalment otherwise due at the end of the following month may be withheld. The rationale for this facility is the avoidance of a tax impost in advance of the relative cash flow. In order to take advantage of it, the participator must give notice of its intention not later than the date on which the instalment would be due. The Board is entitled to seek supporting information or accounts and to charge penalties for an incorrect notice as though it were an incorrect return (see 6.31.2). It is assumed that, if the notice proved to be incorrect, the instalment in question would become payable, carrying interest from the date on which it should have been paid. By concession, the right to withhold instalments extends to circumstances in which production is halted by major loss or damage to facilities, such as the Piper Field disaster in July 1988.
The aggregate of instalments paid for a period is applied;
(*a*) in satisfying the APRT liability (for periods up to 31 December 1986) and, if there is an excess over that liability;
(*b*) in satisfying the PRT payment on account liability for the period (that is, the net payment on account after the offset of any APRT credit);
if a balance still remains, it is repayable.

It will be seen that, because of the base used in calculating the instalments, a participator which has no PRT liabilities, perhaps in the

6.37.1 UK Oil Taxation

early stages of the field's life, does not need to make instalment payments. (FA 1982 Sched 19 (2)).

Periods up to 31 December 1984
For chargeable periods ending on 31 December 1984 or earlier, instalments were calculated as:
$\frac{1}{8} \times$ the aggregate of:
(*a*) APRT shown as payable for the preceding period; and
(*b*) the amount of PRT shown as payable on account for the preceding period, net of any APRT credit.

6.37.2 Payment on Account

Although assessed PRT is due not earlier than six months after the end of the chargeable period to which it relates, a payment on account in respect of it is required two months after the end of the period; and any amount of the tax which is not so paid carries interest from that time. A statement is called for two months after the end of the period, showing how much, if any, PRT is payable for the period. The penalty provisions relating to participators' returns apply also in relation to the payment on account statement. At the same time, the amount of PRT shown, less any APRT credit set against it, has to be paid. That amount constitutes a payment on account of the tax to be charged in the assessment. If the payment on account exceeds the assessed tax, net of APRT credited in the assessment, the excess is repayable, carrying interest from two months after the end of the period or, if later, from the date on which it is paid. If an appeal is made against the assessment, the repayment is limited to the excess of the payment on account over that amount of the assessed tax which the participator is not entitled to withhold.

Calculation of payment on account
The calculation of the amount payable on account is made in accordance with general PRT provisions, subject to the following particular rules and modifications:
(1) The figures for price or market value of sales, appropriations and stock, any excess of nominated proceeds, and for royalties and other licence payments and repayments in the period, are derived from the participator's return;
(2) No provisional expenditure deduction is allowed, and no addition is made in respect of the provisional expenditure deduction allowed in the last but one chargeable period;
(3) Credit is taken for expenditure and supplement which has been agreed by the Board so far as it has not been taken into account in an earlier assessment or determination. Expenditure and supplement which has been claimed, whether by the responsible

Petroleum Revenue Tax 6.37.3

person or by the participator, but in respect of which the Board has not made a decision, may be treated as though it had been agreed by the Board. In the case of a claim by the responsible person, the participator's share of the allowances is taken to be the share allocated to the participator in the claim;

(4) Any unrelievable field loss which has been claimed but not determined may be allowed in the calculation;

(5) Expenditure or loss as in (3) or (4) above cannot be taken into account in the payment on account calculation for more than one chargeable period;

(6) An agreed loss of an earlier chargeable period may be deducted from the assessable profit;

(7) Any balance of assessable profit is to be reduced by the participator's share of oil allowance for the period;

(8) The tax payable is subject to the safeguard limitation if appropriate. For this purpose, expenditure claimed to qualify for supplement, which has been taken into account under (3) above in the absence of the Board's decision on the claim, is assumed to have qualified; it is therefore added back in arriving at the safeguard adjusted profit and increases the accumulated capital expenditure.

Bearing in mind that the assessed tax which has not been satisfied by the payment on account carries interest from the date on which the payment on account is due, a participator will normally wish to pay on account the best estimate of the final liability for the period. If it was obligatory to take credit for all expenditure and supplement claimed, some of which might in due course prove not to be allowable, the payment on account might fall short. The provisions therefore allow the participator to choose how much credit, if any, is taken for expenditure and supplement on which the Board has not made a decision. Similarly, the participator may take credit for a brought forward field loss, or an unrelievable field loss claimed but not yet determined, but is not obliged to do so (PRTA 1980).

6.37.3 Interest on Unpaid APRT and PRT

Instalments (see 6.37.1) which are unpaid carry interest from the date on which they are due until payment, or until two months after the end of the chargeable period to which they relate if earlier. From the latter date, the general provisions concerning interest on unpaid APRT and PRT take over. If part or all of an instalment payment is repaid, the repayment carries interest from two months after the end of the chargeable period or from the date on which it is paid if later.

Interest does not attach to a late paid or unpaid PRT payment on

6.37.3 UK Oil Taxation

account as such. Instead, interest runs on assessed tax from the date on which the payment on account was due, that is, two months after the end of the chargeable period. If a payment on account exceeds assessed tax, the repayment carries interest from the due date for the payment on account or the date on which it is paid if later.

APRT unpaid carries interest from two months after the end of the chargeable period until payment. Repaid APRT carries interest from two months after the end of the period or from the date on which it is paid if later: but repayment of excess APRT credit does not carry interest.

Interest paid in respect of unpaid tax is not allowable as a deduction for the purposes of PRT, CT or income tax. Correspondingly, interest received on repayment of tax is not income for PRT, CT or income tax purposes.

Certificates of Tax Deposit may be used to satisfy payment of instalments, APRT, PRT payments on account and assessed PRT. (FA 1982 Sched 19 (10).

6.37.4 Schedule of Payments

The following example shows the timing of payments in respect of instalments (6.37.1) and PRT payment on account (6.37.2).

Date	Nature of payment	Amount payable £m		In respect of chargeable period
28/02/1988	(b) Payment on account	80		31/12/1987
	(c) Satisfied by instalments	52.5	27.5	
28/02/1988	Instalment ⅛ × 80		10	30/06/1988
31/03/1988	Instalment ⅛ × 80		10	30/06/1988
30/04/1988	Instalment ⅛ × 80		10	30/06/1988
31/05/1988	Instalment ⅛ × 80		10	30/06/1988
30/06/1988	Instalment ⅛ × 80		10	30/06/1988
31/07/1988	Instalment ⅛ × 80		10	30/06/1988
31/08/1988	(b) Payment by account	85	25	
	Satisfied by instalments	60	25	
31/08/1988	Instalment ⅛ × 85		10.6	31/12/1988
31/08/1988 et seq.	Instalment ⅛ × 85		10.6	31/12/1988

Notes
(*a*) The legislation provides that payments are due on the last day of the months referred to.
(*b*) It is assumed in the example that the PRT payment on account exactly matches the assessed PRT for the period.
(*c*) Instalments paid in respect of the chargeable period to 31.12.1987 are assumed to be

6 × (1/8 × payment on account due 31.8.1987, 70) = £52.5m

6.38 Double Taxation Relief for PRT

Companies not resident in the UK may be within the charge to both PRT and to tax in their state of residence in respect of UK oil production profits or related tariff or disposal receipts. This is commonly the case where the beneficial interest in a UK licence is held by a non-UK resident company under an Illustrative Agreement arrangement (see 8.11). Similarly, a company which is resident both in the UK and in a foreign state is within the taxing jurisdiction of each state. Licensees in non-UK fields may also find themselves liable to PRT on receipts derived from assets situated in the UK or the UKCS (see 6.11). Relief from double taxation has then to be considered.

Whether an overseas tax qualifies for tax credit relief in a particular state depends firstly on the domestic law of that state and secondly on the terms of the relevant double taxation agreement. In the UK, credit is allowed for overseas taxes which are covered by a particular double taxation agreement; alternatively, the treaty may authorise exemption from UK tax of certain foreign source income or profits. If no relevant treaty exists, credit may nevertheless be allowed for taxes which correspond to the UK taxes on the income or profits which are dually charged.

The Revenue has expressed the view that PRT, were it to be a tax levied by a foreign state, would be allowable for credit against UK tax as a tax on income corresponding to income tax or corporation tax. However, some states do not regard PRT as a creditable profits tax in its own right: partly, this is because it is field-based rather than company-based and makes no distinction between revenue and capital expenditure. Relief for PRT may then depend on its inclusion among the taxes which are specifically covered under a particular double taxation treaty. A number of treaties negotiated by the UK do make specific provision for credit for PRT, including those with Norway, Canada and the USA. In the case of the 1980 treaty with the USA, the credit against US tax is limited to the excess of the maximum US applicable tax rate over other

6.38 UK Oil Taxation

UK tax (that is, CT) charged on the relative income: unrelieved PRT not exceeding 2% of the taxable income of the years in question may be carried back for two years or forward for five years, for relief in those years within the limit referred to above.

6.39 Supplementary Petroleum Duty

For the four chargeable periods from 1 January 1981 to 31 December 1982 only, a separate production levy was imposed. SPD, as a mechanism for raising front-end government revenue, was then replaced by APRT. It was charged at the rate of 20% on gross profit, calculated as for PRT but grossed up so that the charge also fell on any oil taken by the Secretary of State as royalty in kind, and after deduction of an exempt allowance for each field of 500,000 metric tonnes per chargeable period.

SPD was allowed as a deduction in computing PRT and CT. Payment representing the correct liability for each period was not repayable, unless at the end of field life an unrelievable field loss had accrued: it was then repayable up to the amount of that loss, and the loss available for relief against another field was reduced by the amount repaid. SPD repaid under this provision was treated as income for CT purposes.

Since SPD was more akin to a royalty than a tax on profits, it was not a creditable tax for the purposes of double taxation relief. (FA 1981 s122–8 and Sched 16).

6.40 Obsolete Payment Provisions

Prior to the introduction of the instalment system, a measure of the PRT liability for a period had to be paid in advance. For chargeable periods ending 30 June 1981 to 30 June 1983 only, payment was required two months after the commencement of the period of 15% of the greater of the PRT payment on account for the previous period and the tax assessed, less any withheld on appeal, for the last but one preceding period. Tax so paid went to satisfy part of the PRT payment on account for the period. As part of the arrangements involved in the transition from SPD to APRT and the introduction of instalments, the payment in advance for the chargeable period to 30 June 1983 was treated as payment towards the APRT and PRT payment on account liabilities.

Five monthly payments beginning at the end of March 1983 were required, each 1/5 of the amount of SPD payable for the chargeable period to 31 December 1982. These payments were treated as though they were instalment payments under the new provisions, for offset against the APRT and PRT payment on account liabilities for the period to 30 June 1983.

For the period to 30 June 1983 only, the PRT payment on account was payable in five equal monthly instalments beginning at the end of August 1983. (FA 1982 Sched 19 (11) to (13)).

Chapter 7
Corporation Tax

7.1 Introduction

Profits and gains which a company derives from UK oil or gas production are chargeable to corporation tax (CT). The assessment of those profits and gains is founded in general CT rules, subject to certain modifications and additions. CT was introduced in 1964 as the sole tax on the profits of corporate bodies, replacing the previous combination of income tax and profits tax. The rate of tax remained constant from 1 April 1972 to 31 March 1983 at 52%, but was reduced to 50%, 45%, 40% and 35% for the years to 31 March 1984, 1985, 1986 and 1987 respectively. For the year to 31 March 1988, the rate is 35%, while the rate applying to certain companies with small profits is 25%. Profits for CT purposes include capital gains now chargeable at the same rate as income. CT is normally payable nine months after the end of the accounting period.

The charge to CT falls on companies and unincorporated associations, not including partnerships as such, though a corporate member of a partnership is within the charge. A company which is resident in the UK is liable to CT in respect of its total profits whether arising in the UK or elsewhere. A company not resident in the UK is chargeable on profits attributable to a branch or agency in the UK including, in the case of oil and gas operations, profits derived from UK onshore and offshore fields.

CT profit is, broadly, the commercial profit of the company to which certain adjustments are made. In particular, no capital expenditure may be charged against profits, but much capital outlay qualifies for relief under the capital allowances codes. Interest payments are normally allowable. Losses may be carried forward for relief against future profits of the same trade, offset against other income of the same period or, in limited circumstances, carried back. There is no equivalent in the UK to a consolidated return by a group of companies, but within a group of UK resident companies under common 75% control the loss of one company may be set against the profit of another in the corresponding period.

Since 1973, distributed profits have been dealt with under the imputation system. On payment of a dividend, a UK resident company is required to account for Advance Corporation Tax (ACT), currently at the rate of 25/27 of the dividend. The ACT is available to the company for credit against its mainstream CT, and the recipient of the dividend is treated as receiving an equivalent amount of tax credit. In the case of an individual recipient, the tax credit satisfies the basic rate income tax, on the gross distribution, that is, the dividend plus the tax credit. Under the terms of certain double taxation treaties, such as the UK Treaty with the USA, a recipient who is a resident of the other state may be entitled to a refund of all or part of the tax credit. UK dividends received by companies are treated as franked investment income not chargeable to CT, but available to frank a distribution which the receiving company may make. Subject to election, dividends may be paid between companies within a UK group under common 51% control without the need to account for ACT; the receipt is then group income, not liable to CT in the hands of the recipient and not available to frank distributions by the receiving company.

The 1975 Oil Taxation Act introduced CT rules applying specifically to profits derived from UK oil and gas operations. A ring fence is erected around the UK exploration and production activities of a company, separating them for tax purposes from any other parts of the company's business, so that losses incurred outside the ring fence may not be utilised to reduce the Exchequer's share of oil production profits. The measure of income from production leaving the ring fence is generally the selling price or, for non arm's length disposals and appropriations to refining, market value. Restrictions are imposed on the amount of interest which can be charged against ring fence profits, particularly where the lender is an associated company, and other rules restrict the offset of ACT against ring fence CT. The 1984 Finance Act extended the ring fence concept to certain capital gains.

The provision which imposes a market value standard on transactions with associated companies was extended in 1975 in its application to petroleum companies. The rules for those companies apply whether or not the other party to a transaction is resident in the UK, and in certain circumstances bring in companies which are not under common control.

7.2 Scope of CT Charge

7.2.1 Companies Resident in the UK

A company resident in the UK is chargeable to CT on its profits wherever arising.

A fundamental change was made in 1988 in the concept of company

7.2.1 UK Oil Taxation

residence for UK tax purposes. A company incorporated in the UK is now automatically treated as resident in the UK, subject to a period of grace ending in March 1993 during which existing companies may continue to be resident outside the UK (FA 1988 s66). Other companies continue to be resident in the UK if central management and control are situated in the UK. The Revenue issued on 27 July 1983 a Statement of Practice reaffirming this test. The Statement quotes Lord Loreburn in *De Beers Consolidated Mines* v *Howe* [1906] 5 TC:- 'a company resides, for the purposes of income tax, where its real business is carried on . . . I regard that as the true rule; and the real business is carried on where the central management and control actually abides.' After referring to the endorsement of that finding by Lord Radcliffe in *Bullock* v *Unit Construction Company* (1958) 38 TC 712 the Statement goes on: 'Nothing which has happened since has in any way altered this basic principle; under current UK case law a company is regarded as resident for tax purposes where central management and control is to be found.' This dictum has to be read now in the light of the change relating to UK incorporated companies referred to above.

A UK resident company may also be subject to tax in a foreign country by reason of domicile or incorporation there, or on passive income having a source in that country. It may also be liable if it carries on business in that country. Whether it is so liable depends firstly on the company carrying on trade within that country through a branch or agency; and whether this is deemed to be the case is a question for determination according to the law of the particular country. In general, liability will not arise unless the company has a presence in the other country, and is trading 'within', not merely 'with', that country. Important factors are the site of negotiation and making of contracts, the place of delivery of goods and the frequency of the transactions. If the UK has a Double Taxation Agreement with the other country, liability does not normally arise on trading profits unless the business is carried on in the other country through a permanent establishment. The definition of permanent establishment varies from treaty to treaty. For the purposes of the OECD Model Convention, the term means a fixed place of business in which the business or the enterprise is wholly or partly carried on; it includes a place of management, branch, office, factory, workshop, mine, quarry or other place of extraction of natural resources, and a building site or construction or assembly project which exists for more than twelve months. Transaction of business through an independent agent does not constitute the carrying on of business through a permanent establishment.

If foreign tax is paid, relief for that tax may be available by credit against CT or, by election, as a deduction in calculating CT profits.

7.2.2 Companies not Resident in the UK

A company which is not resident in the UK is not chargeable to CT unless it carries on a trade in the UK through a branch or agency. If it does so, it is chargeable on:
(*a*) trading income arising directly or indirectly through the branch or agency, and income from property or rights associated with the branch or agency; and
(*b*) certain chargeable gains (see 7.26.1)(ICTA 1988 s11)

Whether a company is carrying on a trade in the UK is a question of fact. As a general but not infallible rule, a trade is carried on where contracts are made, though the site of negotiation may in some cases be of more importance than the place of signature. The making of a contract by an independent agent or broker in the UK does not normally mean that a company is trading in the UK, nor does the mere presence of a representative office. If a company is resident in a country which has a Double Taxation Agreement with the UK, it may be protected from liability to UK tax. Such a company is not chargeable to CT unless it carries on business in the UK through a permanent establishment (see 7.2.1).

In order to counter the avoidance of UK tax by use of tax havens, legislation was enacted in 1984 which empowers the Revenue to attribute all or part of the profits of a company not resident in the UK to a UK resident company. The provisions apply to controlled foreign companies, which are defined as companies resident outside the UK, controlled by persons resident in the UK, and subject to a 'lower level of taxation' in the territory of residence. They do not apply if the company in question pursues an acceptable distributions policy (generally, 50% of profits); and exemption is provided in respect of certain bona fide activities not including investment business. A company is considered to be subject to a lower level of taxation if it is resident in a territory where the tax paid on the profits is less than one half of the corresponding UK tax. (ICTA 1988 ss 747-756 and Scheds 24-26.)

A company which holds a UK exploration or production licence is normally required to be managed and controlled in the UK and is therefore resident in the UK. Under an Illustrative Agreement (see 8.11), the beneficial holder of a licence interest may be a company not resident in the UK which, in accordance with the terms of the Agreement, carries on business in the UK through a permanent establishment. Many other non-UK resident companies are active in supplying and servicing the UK oil production industry. Profits derived from such activities are within the scope of UK tax, subject to any exemption or relief provided by Double Taxation Agreements (see 7.2.3).

7.2.3 UK Oil Taxation

7.2.3 UK Oil Extraction Activities

The UK's taxing jurisdiction was extended in 1973 in respect of profits and gains derived from offshore oil rights and activities. The territorial sea, that area of sea extending to twelve miles from the shore, is deemed to be part of the UK for tax purposes (ICTA 1988 s830(1)). Secondly, although designated areas of the UK sector of the continental shelf are not part of nor deemed to be part of the UK, certain profits or gains arising in those areas are specifically brought within the scope of UK tax.

'Any profits or gains from exploration or exploitation activities carried on in a designated area or from exploration or exploitation rights shall be treated for the purposes of income tax or corporation tax as profits or gains from activities or property in the UK; and any gains accruing on the disposal of such rights shall be treated for the purposes of the Capital Gains Tax Act 1979 as gains accruing on the disposal of assets situated in the UK'

Such profits or gains which arise to a company not resident in the UK from activities carried on in the UK (that is, onshore or in the territorial sea) or in a designated area, and gains arising on disposal of exploration or exploitation rights, are treated as profits of a trade or gains on disposal of assets used for the purpose of a trade carried on in the UK through a branch or agency, and consequently within the general charge to CT (ICTA 1988 s830(4)). Exploration or exploitation activities are defined as activities carried on in connection with the exploration or exploitation of so much of the seabed and subsoil and their natural resources as is situated in the UK or a designated area. Exploration or exploitation rights means rights to assets to be produced by exploration or exploitation activities or to interests in or to the benefit of such assets. Capital gains derived by persons not resident in the UK from disposals of unquoted shares deriving the greater part of their value from such rights are also brought within the charge to tax (see 7.26.1).

A lacuna in the 1973 provisions was remedied in 1984. The charge to UK tax is now extended to include gains by non- residents on disposal of exploration or exploitation assets situated in a designated area and of unquoted shares deriving their value or the greater part of their value directly or indirectly from exploration or exploitation assets situated in the UK or a designated area, or from such assets and from exploration and exploitation rights together. Exploration or exploitation assets are either non-mobile assets which are used, or have been used in the two years preceding disposal, in connection with oil exploration or exploitation in the UK or a designated area or mobile assets which have been so used in the two years preceding disposal and are dedicated to a UK oil field in which the disposer or a connected person is or has been a participator. These provisions apply to disposals on or after 13 March 1984. They may be of application, for example, to the disposal by a non-resident company, such as a company having the benefit of an Illustrative Agreement, of an interest in an offshore production platform or pipeline system (FA 1984 s81).

It is normally a defacto condition of the grant of a licence that the licensee company is controlled and managed in the UK, and therefore tax resident in the UK. A company not resident in the UK may hold the beneficial interest in a licence under an Illustrative Agreement (see 8.11), but since, under the terms of that arrangement, its UK licence operations are conducted through a UK branch it is likely to be chargeable to CT under normal rules apart from the territorial extension of taxing rights. The extension may be significant where a company not resident in the UK derives income from an indirect or passive interest in UK production within the definition of exploration or exploitation rights. That income is brought into charge as though it arose from a trade carried on through a branch or agency in the UK (FA 1973 s38(4)). If the company is a resident of a state which has a double taxation treaty with the UK, however, it may not be liable to CT unless it has a permanent establishment in the UK to which the income is attributable. In more recent treaties, the definition of the UK includes the UKCS.

7.2.4 Contractors not Resident in the UK

The main practical impact of the 1973 territorial extension falls not on production profits but on the profits of companies not resident in the UK which provide services to the offshore oil industry. It brings within the charge to CT profits from activities carried on in the UK or in a designated area in connection with oil exploration or exploitation. The charge depends on performance of activities – something more than passive receipt of income – and performance in the UK or in a designated area. Whether lessors of equipment such as drilling rigs satisfy these conditions depends on the particular arrangements. The Revenue issued the following Statement of Practice relating to non-resident lessors:

'Where mobile drilling rigs, vessels or equipment leased by a non-resident lessor are used in connection with exploration or exploitation activities carried on in the UK or in a designated area, the question of whether the profits or gains arising from the lease constitute income from such activities depends on the facts and circumstances of each particular case. However, the practice of the Inland Revene is not to seek to charge such profits or gains to tax under FA 1973 s38 if all the

7.2.4 UK Oil Taxation

following conditions are satisfied:
(1) the contract is concluded outside the UK and the designated areas;
(2) the lessor's obligations are limited to the provision of the asset, eg, a rig on 'bareboat' terms, that is to say, if the lessor has not undertaken to provide any facilities, services or personnel;
(3) the lessee takes delivery of the asset outside the designated areas and is responsible for moving it to the place where it is used, and is not restricted to using it solely in the UK or a designated area;
(4) the lessee and lessor are not connected persons, and no facilities, services or personnel related to the operation of the asset are provided by any person connected with the lessor' (SP6/84).

The charge to UK tax may be overridden by the terms of a double taxation treaty. A resident of a treaty state who is not also resident in the UK is, in general, not liable to UK tax unless he carries on business in the UK through a permanent establishment. A number of more recent treaties, however, including those between the UK and Norway, USA and Canada, contain offshore activities Articles which provide that residents of those states who carry on exploration or exploitation activities on the UKCS are deemed to have a UK permanent establishment.

The Revenue has powers to recover from licence holders certain unpaid tax and interest liabilities of non-resident persons relating to profits or gains from exploration or exploitation activities, rights and assets connected with the licence in question (FA 1973 Sched 15). Technical deficiencies which had rendered the provisions largely inoperable were remedied in 1984 (FA 1984 s124). The oil industry, while acknowledging the Revenue's need for some form of security for tax chargeable on non residents, has frequently voiced its dislike of the recovery powers, which expose licensees to indeterminate and uncertain liabilities. The OTO gives warning of impending notices of charge, so that the licensees may, for example, seek to persuade a defaulting contractor to co-operate with the Revenue, and within the constraints of its duty to keep confidential the affairs of taxpayers – or non taxpayers in this case – it provides basic details of the unpaid assessment. But the licensees are unable properly to verify the underlying charge or to ensure that the contractor's claims and appeal rights have been exercised. A tax withholding scheme has sometimes been mooted as a more acceptable though considerably more cumbersome alternative. The building industry tax deduction scheme is not regarded by the Revenue as applicable to offshore oil operations. A payment which a licensee is required to make in respect of tax unpaid by a non-resident is the more injurious because it is specifically disallowed as a deduction in calculating the licensee's profits.

Licensees are normally able to obtain some form of protection against such liabilities. A contractor who is able to satisfy the Revenue that he will comply with his UK tax obligations may obtain a certificate which exempts relevant licensees from the recovery powers. Alternatively, indemnities may be provided by the contractor or by a third party.

7.3 The Ring Fence

The central purpose of the ring fence is to prevent dilution of the tax payable on the exploitation of UK oil and gas. It does not extend the scope of the UK tax charge. Rather, it specifies the manner in which production and related profits are to be assessed and modifies the general rules governing the measurement of those profits. The ring fence encircles the whole of a company's UK onshore and offshore oil exploration and production operations, segregating them from any other activities and profits which the company may have; but it does not mirror the PRT field-based concept. Capital gains in respect of disposals after 12 March 1984 of licence interests and certain assets used in connection with oil fields are also segregated from other gains or losses (see 7.26.2).

Included within the ring fence are:
(1) oil extraction activities and
(2) activities consisting in the acquisition, enjoyment or exploitation of oil rights.

Where those activities are carried on within a trade, they are treated for all purposes of CT as a separate trade, distinct from all other activities carried on by the company as part of the actual trade (ICTA 1988 s492).

Oil extraction activities means any activities:
(a) in searching for oil in the UK or a designated area or causing such search to be carried out; or
(b) in extracting or causing to be extracted oil in the UK or a designated area under a licence held by the company or by an associated company; or
(c) in transporting or causing to be transported to land in the UK oil extracted offshore under a licence held as in (b); or
(d) in effecting or causing to be effected the initial treatment or initial storage of oil won from a field under a licence held as in (b).

It might be thought that category (a) is wide enough to include the activities of a contractor who carries out exploration for a licensee. The OTO has not taken that view. Bearing in mind the broad purpose of the ring fence and the ambit of the other defined activities, it is likely that a person is searching in this context only if he is searching for oil in which he would have an interest.

Oil rights means rights to oil to be extracted at any place in the UK or

7.3 UK Oil Taxation

a designated area, or to interests in or to the benefit of such oil (ICTA 1988 s502).

A company associated with a licensee may also find itself chargeable under the ring fence rules. The extraction of oil under a licence held by its associated licensee company, transportation of such oil from an offshore field to the UK and initial treatment or storage of it are all ring fence activities. For these purposes, two companies are associated if one is a 51% subsidiary of the other or both are 51% subsidiaries of a third company. Two companies are also associated if one of them is owned by a consortium of which the other is a member: a company owned by a consortium is one in which 75% or more of the ordinary share capital is owned by up to 20 companies each of which owns not less that 5% (ICTA 1988 s502). The definition of association was further extended, with effect from 19 March 1986, to include control by one company of the other or control of both companies by another person or persons: control in this context is construed in accordance with the definition in ICTA 1988, s416 which is a wider concept than ownership of the majority of ordinary share capital on which the subsidiary company test relies. The amendment was intended to cater for situations in which relationships existed which conveyed majority economic interest, perhaps by virtue of issue of preference shares, without coming within the subsidiaries or consortium definitions (ICTA 1988 s502).

The position of the ring fence boundary is discussed in paragraph 7.6.

7.4 CT Profits

'CT shall be charged on profits of companies' ICTA 1988 s6.

CT profit is the aggregate of each category of income which falls to be computed under the separate Schedules and Cases laid down in the Taxes Act, to which are added capital gains. In summary, the Schedules and Cases are:

Schedule A – rental income
Schedule C – certain government securities
Schedule D – Case I trades
                II professions
                III interest
                IV foreign securities
                V foreign possessions
                VI miscellaneous profits not falling in other Cases
Schedule E – employments (not relevant to companies)
Schedule F – distributions by UK resident companies.

Corporation Tax 7.4.2

The charge to tax is levied on total profits after deduction of relief for interest payments and losses. An example of a CT computation is given at 7.4.1.

The calculation of income under each Schedule and Case follows the rules applicable to income tax except where specific CT rules are provided. Tax is charged by reference to a financial year beginning 1 April. Where a company's accounting period, usually twelve months, does not coincide with a financial year, it is apportioned on a time basis to the relevant financial years for the purpose of the tax charge.

7.4.1 CT Computation

			£m
Year to 31.12.1988			
Trade profit		25	
Less Loss brought forward		10	15.0
Annual interest – from UK bank			0.5
from UK company 30.9.1988			1.0
(income tax suffered 0.25)			
Chargeable gain			3.0
Total profits			19.5
Less Annual interest paid to UK company			4.5
Chargeable			15.0
Corporation Tax —			
Financial year to 31.3.99 – ¼ × 15.0 = 3.75			
Financial year to 31.3.89 – ¾ × 15.0 = 11.25	at 35%		5.25
Less ACT, limited to 27% × 3.75 = 1.0125			
25% × 11.25 = 2.8125			3.825
			1.425
Less Income tax suffered on interest received			0.250
Net tax payable			1.175

7.4.2 Payment of Tax

Tax is payable nine months after the end of an accounting period or, if later, thirty days after the making of an assessment. In making an

7.4.2 UK Oil Taxation

appeal against an assessment, a company may also apply to postpone payment of tax to the extent that it is likely to exceed the true liability.

Finance (No 2) Act 1987 gave early warning of fundamental changes affecting the making of returns and payment of tax. These 'pay and file' provisions do not enter into force until they are activated by a Treasury order, which cannot have an effective date earlier than 31 March 1992. Returns, including supporting accounts, will be required not later than twelve months after the end of an accounting period: late filing will render the company liable to penalties. Tax will be payable on the normal due date, nine months after the end of the period, in accordance with the company's estimate of liability and without the need for issue of an assessment. Interest will run on unpaid tax and on tax overpaid.

7.5 Trading

To state the obvious, the rules relating to trade income and expenditure have no application to a company which is not carrying on a trade. A company may be extremely active in exploring and appraising likely sources of oil and yet not be regarded for tax purposes as trading. Such a company will normally wish to commence a trade at the earliest date. In the pre-trading period, a company is liable to tax on any income or gains arising in the UK, but is unable to obtain any relief for expenditure which would be deductible if a trade were carried on: exceptionally, a company not resident in the UK may be able to take advantage of the terms of a double taxation treaty in offsetting certain expenses against interest income. In some cases, trade losses once established may simply be carried forward for relief against future trade income, but in others the loss may be offset against current income or be surrendered to an associated company under the group relief provisions.

In the normal way, a company does not commence a trade until it is in a position to contract for sale of goods or provision of services (*Birmingham and District Cattle By-Products Co Limited* v *CIR* (1912) 12 TC 92). In the case of activities consisting in exploitation of oil or other mineral resources, the Revenue has agreed somewhat more liberal guidelines for identification of a point in the life of a company at which trading begins. The signal is normally taken to coincide with the end of Stage 3 in the progression of activities set out in an Appendix to a joint Memorandum agreed between the Revenue and the UKOITC in February 1967. The Memorandum is given in full at Appendix 3. The end of Stage 3 comes with the decision 'in the event that commercial production is considered worthwhile' to proceed with Stage 4, that is, the drilling of development wells. In the context of UK oil fields, there has not normally been much doubt as to whether or not a company or a consortium has taken a decision to proceed to commercial production, though the precise date of the decision may be less clear. The formal submission to the Secretary of State of the development plan Annex B has often been adopted as the trigger event. This rule of thumb may not give a satisfactory answer in every case. Particular difficulties occur in onshore areas where the appraisal of relatively small sources is inclined to pursue a desultory progress through the labyrinth of planning and other permissions. Both onshore and offshore, there is an increasing trend towards the use of extended production tests prior to the Secretary of State reaching a decision on whether and how a field should be developed. Documentation of a company's relevant decisions is all the more important in these circumstances.

A company involved in UK oil activities may already carry on a trade overseas, or begin to do so. Whether the UK activities then constitute a part of that trade is a question of fact for determination in the light of the particular circumstances, but there is a strong presumption that a company carrying on in different parts of the world the business of exploring for and producing oil carries on only one trade. Some companies have found it more practicable and economic to commence an oil trade by acquiring an interest in a source of overseas production, perhaps in the USA or Canada, thereby triggering relief for exploration expenditure in the UK and elsewhere relating to the world-wide trade. In deciding whether overseas activities amount to trading the same criteria apply as in the case of UK interests. In either case, however, the true nature of the company's involvement needs to be considered. Mere investment in a project in the expectation of more or less certain income return with little if any active participation on the part of the investor is unlikely to be seen by the Revenue as a badge of trade. The scale of the involvement may also be an important factor: the acquisition of a right to a trickle of production does not of itself endorse the trading status of a substantial company.

A company can carry on more than one trade. Relief for expenditure on oil exploration is not available unless the company not only has a trade but also has a trade to which the exploration effort is related: it needs to be a *petroliferous* trade. This is especially relevant to claims to scientific research allowance (see 7.13). Efforts to persuade the Revenue that exploration by a company in prosecuting its licence interests in itself signifies trading have always been unsuccessful, though specialist companies can and do trade by providing exploration services.

The ring fence is superimposed on companies' activities as they exist. It cannot confer trading status on a company which is not otherwise trading, nor can it exclude from trading status activities which are part of a trade. It may be that if the UK ring fence oil activities of a

7.5 UK Oil Taxation

company, consisting only in exploration, were considered separately they would not amount to trading: but if the company is trading by virtue of production in Canada, for example, and the ring fence activities are part of that trade, the ring fence expenditure qualifies for relief, albeit calculated separately.

7.6 Trade Profit or Loss

7.6.1 General Rules

CT is a profits tax, chargeable on the annual profits or gains of a company. The Taxes Acts say very little about the calculation of annual profits or gains. The general rule, founded more in case law than statute, is that trade profits are arrived at by taking the commercial profit according to UK accounting conventions and making such adjustments as the Taxes Acts or case law require. Expenditure which would be deducted in calculating the commercial profits is allowable for CT purposes unless it is specifically prohibited. The full earnings of the year should be credited. The profit calculation is to be made on an accruals not a cash basis, and expenditure is to be matched as far as possible with the income to which it relates. The matching appropriate for tax purposes may not always coincide with the chosen accounting treatment in areas such as long-term contracts and stocks.

7.6.2 Ring Fence Profits

Profits derived from activities or rights which are within the ring fence (see 7.5) are calculated separately. The general corporation tax rules apply subject to certain modifications which are found chiefly in ICTA 1988 s492-502.

The precise position of the ring fence boundary is not always clear. The definitions seem at first sight not to leave much scope for doubt, but difficulties emerge in the translation of the activities referred to into the 'separate trade'. In particular, the definitions make no reference to disposal or sale of oil: viewed in isolation, the defined activities carried on by an oil company would give rise to an accumulation of expenditure but apparently no income. In order to complete the circle, or the ring fence, it seems to be necessary to make the assumption that the profit or loss of the separate trade will be calculated by reference to normal accounting principles, presupposing that the notional separate trade is an actual trade and bringing in income generated by the collection of defined activities.

7.7 Oil Trading Income

The measure of production income in the CT ring fence profit calculation coincides in general terms with the values adopted for PRT purposes or, in the case of excluded oil (see 6.8.1), the values which would have been so adopted if that production had not been PRT exempt. There are, however, differences in details both in timing and in absolute terms.

7.7.1 Sales at Arm's Length

In the case of sales at arm's length, the sale price should be brought in. In deciding whether a sale is at arm's length, the same tests are effectively applied as for PRT (see 6.7): if the sale does not satisfy those tests, particular rules dictate the measure of CT income (see 7.7.2). In most cases, sales are made on free on board (fob) terms at a UK onshore delivery point, but if arm's length sales are made fob an offshore field, the selling price is again the measure of ring fence income.

Where oil is sold at arm's length on a cif (cost insurance and freight) or c & f basis for delivery outside the UK, the full selling price including the freight element is normally chargeable to PRT. If, in performance of the contract, the oil is transported to a non-UK port, it might be argued that the freight element in the price together with the relative freight costs are outside the ring fence because the definition of oil extraction activities does not include transportation beyond the UK. In practice, unless export freight forms a very substantial part of the company's operation, it is likely to be regarded as an incident within the ring fence separate trade.

An exception is made to the general PRT rule in the case of arm's length sales of gas for export. In that case, PRT is charged on a notional UK landed value (see 6.7.7). For CT, the actual sale price including the freight element is brought into charge, again raising the question referred to above whether the freight income and expenditure belong to the ring fence trade.

Disposals to the Oil and Pipelines Agency under participation rights inherited from BNOC are normally accepted for PRT purposes as sales at arm's length. It follows that the selling price is brought in as a receipt of the ring fence trade. The oil may be bought back from the Agency at the same price: that purchase is part of the company's trade outside the ring fence.

7.7.2 UK Oil Taxation

7.7.2 Sales not at Arm's Length

If oil is disposed of in a sale which fails to satisfy PRT arm's length test (see 6.7), the sale price is disregarded for CT purposes. Instead, the oil is deemed to have been sold in the course of the ring fence trade at the market value established for PRT assessment. Furthermore, the purchaser of the oil is deemed, for the purpose of its CT liability, to have acquired it at that same value. The second leg of this provision suggests that the purchaser needs to be privy to the PRT return by the seller and to the value which the seller and the OTO agree upon. If the purchaser is a company associated with the seller, this should not present a problem, but if the two parties are unconnected, an exchange of information confidential to the seller may be required. The market value for these purposes is the value appropriate to a notional contract which requires the oil to be initially treated and, in the case of offshore oil, to be delivered at the nearest reasonable UK port.

The same principles apply to non-arm's length sales of excluded oil, that is, chiefly exempt gas. In that case, the CT value is the PRT value which would have applied if that production had been within the PRT charge. Again, the purchaser is deemed to have acquired it at that value.

If a company sells otherwise than at arm's length oil which it acquires in the course of its oil extraction activities or by virtue of oil rights, the sale, if not otherwise brought in at the PRT market value under the provisions referred to above, is deemed to take place at market value. This may apply, for example. where a company which is not a participator in the field is entitled to oil by virtue of a royalty or other subordinated interest, and disposes of it on terms which do not satisfy the PRT arm's length test. Oil won in the course of a production test before determination of a field in the relevant area is also within the scope of this provision. In arriving at market value, the PRT rules generally apply (ICTA 1988 s493).

The Revenue has power to call for particulars of transactions not only by the ring fence company but also by associated companies for the purpose of determining whether a sale is at arm's length and, if not, what is the market value of the oil (FA 1975 s17 and FA 1984 s115).

7.7.3 Appropriation of Oil

Oil produced from UK areas which crosses the ring fence boundary without being sold also does so at market value. Oil which is 'relevantly appropriated', that is, appropriated to refining or to any other use except field production, is brought into the PRT computation at market value. For CT it is treated as having been sold in the course of the separate ring fence trade at a price equal to the PRT value, and as having been acquired at that price in the course of a trade outside the ring fence. In the case of 'excluded oil' the same principles apply, with the substitution of the PRT value which would have applied had the production not been PRT exempt (ICTA 1988 s493).

Similarly, oil which is appropriated, having been acquired by a company in the course of ring fence activities or by virtue of oil rights which is not itself charged to PRT in respect of the oil, is deemed to leave the ring fence at market value.

7.7.4 Oil Stocks

The PRT treatment of oil stocks – inclusion of one half of the market value of closing stocks and deduction of one half of the market value of opening stocks – has no relevance to CT. The general CT rule, emerging from case law rather than statute, is that in the calculation of profit or loss of the accounting period, stock in trade should be credited to profit and loss account at the lower of cost or market value. The purpose of this adjustment is effectively to carry forward the costs attributable to bringing the stock to the state and condition obtaining at the accounting date, limited if appropriate to the amount likely to be recovered on ultimate sale of the stock. The oil stocks in question are those in transit or storage pending sale or appropriation: oil not yet won is not recognised as stock, and indeed rests in the Crown until it is won.

In an oil production trade, the market value of stocks will normally be higher than cost, however ascertained, so that the stocks come in at cost. A LIFO method of identification is not normally acceptable for UK tax purposes. There is no single accounting convention for the establishment of the cost or value of oil stocks, and practice varies from company to company. In most cases, cost is taken as the aggregate of attributable operating costs, royalties and depreciation of tangible assets, the latter calculated by reference to depletion of reserves or the proportion of revenues earned to date. Some companies may also include an attribution of PRT. Doubts arise particularly as to whether it is proper or necessary to include in cost an element of asset depreciation, and whether its inclusion for accounting purposes commits the company to the same treatment for tax purposes. Case law offers little guidance. In *Ostime* v *Duple Motor Bodies Limited* (1961) 39 TC 537, a case concerning work in progress rather than stock, it was decided that the company was entitled to bring in work in progress at direct cost without addition for oncost, that is, indirect and overhead expenditure. The analogy between motor vehicle manufacture and production of oil

7.7.4 UK Oil Taxation

is not close enough, however, to suggest that the decision has particular relevance in this area. Whichever cost standard is adopted, it is important that it is applied consistently from year to year. The choice is unlikely to affect significantly the tax liability over the life of a field though it may influence the timing of it. The adoption of a standard producing a higher figure of cost may advance the point of liability; on the other hand, it might have given rise to rather more stock appreciation relief, a relief which is not available for accounting periods beginning after 12 March 1984.

The OTO expects to see reflected in the CT computation, if not in the accounts, the company's entitlement to oil in transit from the field, either as stock or work in progress. Its concern here, as with stocks generally, is that expenditure should be matched as far as possible with relative earnings, matching which requires that costs relating to production and transport of the oil in transit should be carried forward. The identification of cost raises issues similar to those applying to other oil stocks.

7.7.5 Underlifting and Overlifting

Most UK oil fields are owned not by single companies but by consortia. In jointly-owned fields, the participators will rarely sell or appropriate production concurrently in precise ratio to their equity entitlement: at any time some may have 'overlifted' and others 'underlifted'.

A participator may report for accounting and CT purposes the sales and appropriations made in the accounting period including those representing overlift. This is the normal and acceptable standard for CT purposes. So far as non-arm's length sales and appropriations are concerned, it is in any case required in consequence of attribution of market values for PRT purposes (see 7.7.2 and 7.7.3).

7.7.6 Ballast Recovery Oil

Income derived from ballast recovery oil is not chargeable to PRT since it is not or may not be oil won from the particular field. There remains the question of whether that income, and related deballasting expenditure, are within the CT ring fence. Deballasting is specifically excluded from the definitions of initial treatment and initial storage for the purposes of PRT and ring fence CT, and is not part of oil extraction activities as defined (ICTA 1988 s502). The OTO usually argues for inclusion within the ring fence on the grounds that the income and expenditure are incidental to the general ring fence activities and would form part of the results of the separate ring fence trade if those results were calculated by reference to general commercial and tax principles applying to trades.

7.8 Tariff etc Receipts

Licensees frequently derive tariff and other income from the hire or lease of field assets for use in connection with other UK or foreign fields, or from services provided in association with such use. That type of income is brought specifically into the CT ring fence if it does not otherwise fall within it (OTA 1983 s11). This provision applies only to income which is within the charge to PRT. It does not include that which derives from assets which are not for PRT purposes 'qualifying assets' (qualifying assets are, broadly, field assets which are not mobile or, if mobile, are dedicated to the field, excluding those used for deballasting (OTA 1983 s8)): on which side of the ring fence that income falls is an issue to be resolved in the light of the particular circumstances.

The PRT anti-avoidance provisions relating to tariffs have CT consequences. If tariff receipts of a company associated with or connected with a field participator are attributed to the participator for PRT purposes, they are then treated as ring fence income of the recipient company (OTA 1983 s11(3)).

7.9 Income from Oil Rights

The ring fence segregates not only income from oil extraction activities but also income from oil rights. Included in the separate ring fence deemed trade are activities consisting in 'the acquisition, enjoyment or exploitation of oil rights'. Income arising from such activities, carried on as part of an actual trade, would ordinarily assume the character of trade income. The restriction on utilisation of non-ring fence losses, however, is not applied specifically and exclusively to trading income: arguably, it may affect also income from oil rights which is assessable to CT under other heads of charge (see 7.3). In many cases that income is received by a company which does not have a direct interest in a licence but rather, in terms of the definition of oil rights, rights to interests in or to the benefit of oil to be extracted in the UK or a designated area.

Income which derives from a subordinated licence interest such as a royalty or net production interest may itself have the character of trading income if it accrues to a company such as a bank. More commonly, it arises as income assessable under the Case III or Case VI

7.9 UK Oil Taxation

heads of Sched D. If it is pure income profit in the hands of the company which receives it, it may take the form of an annual payment from which income tax is normally deductible by the payer.

7.10 Interest Income

Companies generally prefer income to be outside the ring fence, not subject to the bar to relief by non ring fence losses. There are particular difficulties in knowing where the ring fence falls in relation to the range of interest income which arises in connection with, or in consequence of, oil operations. The key questions are whether the meaning of oil rights is wide enough to encompass rights under Joint Operation Agreements or unit agreements, and whether income from oil extraction activities includes income such as interest which arises indirectly as a result of those activities. In practice, most companies accept that the ring fence restriction applies, for example, to relatively small amounts of interest which arise on surplus cash funds held by an operator on behalf of a consortium. On the other hand, the link between interest arising on investment of the proceeds of oil sales and oil rights or oil extraction activities is probably too tenuous to warrant ring fencing of the interest. A more difficult subject is interest which arises under unitisation agreements on the re-determination of the shares of the licensee groups in oil reserves and relative expenditure. The issue is brought into sharper focus because the payers of the interest are normally entitled to deduct it as a ring fence charge. It is very doubtful whether the restriction on the use of non ring fence losses is intended to apply to such interest.

7.11 Expenditure

7.11.1 Capital or Revenue

One of the longest-established tenets of UK income taxation is that no deduction is allowable for capital expenditure in calculating the profit of a trade. Among deductions specifically prohibited are:
  'any loss not connected with or arising out of the trade, profession or vocation';
  'any capital withdrawn from, or any sum employed or intended to be employed as capital in, the trade, profession or vocation';
  'any capital employed in improvements of premises occupied for the purposes of the trade, profession or vocation' (ICTA 1988 s74).
  The courts from the 19th century to the present day have often had to

consider the dividing line between revenue and capital. A central theme emerging from these cases is that expenditure incurred once and for all in order to bring about an enduring benefit to the trade is likely to be capital. The practical significance of the distinction to some extent diminished in the period up to 1984 in which expenditure on plant qualified for 100% capital allowances relief. But by no means all capital expenditure is relievable, and the abolition of first year allowances has again reinforced the need to distinguish capital expenditure.

The commercial profit is the starting point of the tax computation. The courts have attached increased importance in recent years to accountancy evidence as an indication of the proper distinction between capital and revenue. However, the accounting treatment of particular items cannot of itself dictate their quality for tax purposes. Some companies capitalise all exploration expenditure under the full cost method of accounting, while others, using the successful efforts method, expense the cost of unsuccessful exploration: whichever method is used, most such expenditure is likely to be regarded as capital for tax purposes. On the other hand, almost all companies capitalise intangible development or production drilling costs, costs which have been accepted by the Revenue to be allowable as revenue expenditure (see 7.15). Strictly, support costs and overheads which are in essence part of the cost of some larger project should be categorised in the same way as other expenditure on that project.

The prohibition on capital deductions in calculating profit embraces not only the expenditure incurred on the capital project but also all amounts written off such expenditure, whether as depreciation or losses on disposal.

While expenditure incurred in acquiring an asset is invariably capital, the expense of preserving or maintaining the asset is likely to be revenue. Included in the latter category is expenditure on repairs, though in strictness that part of the cost attributable to improvement of the asset is capital. The cost of replacing an asset is also capital. Smaller items of plant or utensils are sometimes dealt with on what is known as the replacement basis under which the original purchase is capitalised, no capital allowance being claimed, but the cost of replacement is allowed as a trade expense as incurred.

7.11.2 Distribution of Profit

Distinction has also to be made between payments incurred in earning the profits of the trade and payments in the nature of appropriation or distribution of the profits. No deduction is allowable for dividends or for the variety of other payments which are defined as distributions

7.11.2 UK Oil Taxation

(ICTA 1988 s209). These include payment out of the assets of a company in respect of securities issued to an associated company not resident in the UK and certain securities convertible into shares, though categorisation as distributions may be overridden by other provisions, in the first case by a double taxation agreement and in the second by domestic law (ICTA 1988 s212).

Apart from distributions in this technical sense, there may be other payments which are not deductible for tax purposes because they represent appropriation out of profits rather than a trade expense. The most common is CT itself, though particular provision is made for allowance of PRT as an expense in arriving at CT profit.

The dividing line between appropriation and trading expense is sometimes difficult to discern in the area of subordinated interests in the benefit of a licence. A royalty or similar payment, whether in oil or cash, which is paid out of production or gross sales proceeds in consideration for services or for the acquisition of the licence interest is likely to be an allowable trade expense. On the other hand, a production interest payable out of proceeds net of expenses including PRT may be an annual payment rather than an expense (see 7.11.3). It is important to have regard to the substance of the payment; it does not qualify as a trade expense simply because it is described and presented as, say, a royalty.

7.11.3 Annual Payments

Some subordinated interest payments may be neither trade expenses nor distributions but annual payments. An annual payment is one which is inherently capable of recurrence and is payable for valuable consideration, and is pure income profit in the hands of the recipient. The final condition in particular presents problems of interpretation because the payer may not be in a position to make the judgment and may in any case take a view different from that of the recipient. If the payment is an annual payment, the paying company is obliged to deduct income tax and account for it to the Revenue. Annual payments are not allowable as trade expenses, but may be allowed as a charge against total CT profits.

An anti-avoidance provision prevents deduction as a charge, and removes the obligation to deduct income tax, where the payment is made under a liability incurred for consideration which was not liable to income tax or CT in the hands of the company making the payment (ICTA 1988 s125). Its effect is to render the payment liable to tax in the hands of both payer and recipient. It catches, albeit by accident, cash payments under interests such as net production interests which represent pure income profit of the recipient. In order to avoid this result, it may be necessary to satisfy the liability in oil, the disposal of which becomes the responsibility of the recipient.

Annual payments not consisting of interest which are paid to an associated company are not allowable as a charge against ring fence profits (ICTA 1988 s494).

7.11.4 Pre-Trading Expenditure

Expenditure incurred before the commencement of a trade cannot under general rules qualify as a trade expense. However, expenditure which would have been allowable if incurred after commencement of trade is treated as allowable on the day on which trade does commence, provided that it is incurred within three years of commencement of the trade (ICTA 1988 s401). Licence rentals, for example, incurred in the qualifying period are allowable under this rule.

Capital allowances in respect of expenditure incurred for the purposes of the trade before the trade begins are calculated as though the expenditure was incurred on the first day of trading.

7.11.5 Financing Costs

Costs attaching to the raising of loan finance are allowable as a trading expense. Qualifying costs include legal expenses, commitment and guarantee fees and other expenses related to security, but do not include losses on exchange or the cost of protecting against such losses, or costs of repayment of the borrowings at a premium to the issue price (ICTA 1988 s77).

Interest
The PRT provisions specifically debar relief for interest. The CT rules in contrast allow interest relief, though the route is strewn with obstacles. Notional interest or interest on capital is not allowable (ICTA 1988 s74). The general rule is that no deduction is allowed for yearly interest in computing trade profits (ICTA 1988 s237). Deduction is due for interest payments as charges against total CT profits provided that they satisfy certain conditions (ICTA 1988 s338-9). If the interest is paid to a UK resident, the relevant conditions are that:
(1) the interest is yearly interest, that is, it accrues or is capable of accruing over a period of at least a year;
(2) it is paid for valuable consideration;
(3) it is paid wholly and exclusively for the purpose of the company's

7.11.5 UK Oil Taxation

trade, which, in the case of a company not resident in the UK, must be the trade carried on by it through the UK branch or agency. Capitalisation of interest does not now debar relief.

Short interest, that is, interest which is not annual, is allowable as a trade expense provided that it is incurred for the purpose of earning the profits of the trade.

Particular rules apply to interest paid to a bank in the UK, including a UK branch of an overseas bank. In that case relief is available as a trade expense rather than as a charge against total profits whether the interest is annual or short. Such bank interest is payable in full without the obligation to deduct and account for income tax.

Special rules also apply where interest is paid to a person not resident in the UK. In order to qualify as a charge against CT profits, that interest must either:

(*a*) be paid under deduction of income tax. For this purpose, it is sufficient that tax would have been deducted and accounted for were it not for an authority given to pay in full in pursuance of a claim to exemption under the terms of a double taxation treaty; and interest on certain quoted Eurobonds may be paid in full (ICTA 1988 s124); or

(*b*) be payable out of income charged under Schedule D Case IV or V; or

(*c*) meet certain other criteria (ICTA 1988 s340). These are:
   (1) the interest is payable and is in fact paid outside the UK and
   (2) either:
      (*a*) the liability to pay the interest was incurred wholly or mainly for the purposes of activities of the company's trade carried on outside the UK; or
      (*b*) the interest is payable in a currency other than sterling, and the liability to pay was incurred wholly or mainly for the purposes of activities of that trade wherever carried on. This avenue is not available if, broadly, the payer and recipient of the interest are under common control.

As regards (*a*), questions may arise as to whether borrowing to finance UK offshore exploration and production operations is obtained for the purposes of activities of the company's trade carried on outside the UK. Although profits or gains derived from those activities are treated as profits or gains of a UK branch operation (see 7.2.3), the UKCS is not part of the UK, and the Revenue will normally accept that the borrowing passes this test.

The s340 route may be of importance to non-UK resident companies operating on the UKCS. The Taxes Acts do not provide for any relief for yearly interest paid by one non-resident to another, but relief may be afforded under the non-discrimination clause of the double taxation treaty between the UK and the payer's country of residence. The payer will then need to show that had it paid the interest as a UK resident it would have been entitled to relief.

Interest paid to associated companies is subject to additional restrictions. The market value rules relating to transactions between associated companies, which are extended as they apply to oil companies, effectively limit the rate of interest allowable to that which might have obtained between third parties. Interest paid by a UK resident company to a non-UK resident associated company on a secured loan is treated as a distribution, for which no relief is available to the payer. This treatment may be overridden by the terms of a double taxation agreement, though not in respect of any part of the interest in excess of a notional third party amount. In determining the availability or extent of treaty exemption, the UK Revenue may have regard to a number of factors, including the capacity to have borrowed from a third party, the ratio of debt to equity and the ratio of likely profits to the interest payable on the loan. Treatment of an excess as a distribution may not necessarily be disadvantageous; the payer has to account for ACT, but the particular treaty, for example that between the UK and the USA, may entitle the recipient to a partial refund of the amount of ACT.

In December 1987, the Government indicated that it was concerned about the drain on the Exchequer of the use of loans as a substitute for equity capital in the financing of UK subsidiaries of foreign companies. It asked for comments on a report by OECD on 'thin capitalisation', presumably as a prelude to possible legislation.

Special rules provide for allowance as a charge of certain discount accrued on deep discount securities (ICTA 1988 s57 and Sched 4).

Ring fence restrictions on interest
Interest which is allowable as a charge against total CT profits under the general rules has to clear additional hurdles if it is to be allowed against ring fence profits. Those restrictions do not apply to short interest or bank interest allowed as a trade expense, but ring fence relief still depends on that interest having been incurred for the purposes of the ring fence activities.

The borrowing must be shown to have been used to meet expenditure incurred by the company in carrying on oil extraction activities, or in acquiring oil rights other than from a connected person, or to have been appropriated to meet expenditure to be so incurred by the company (ICTA 1988 s494).

In the normal course, a company which borrows to finance its UK exploration and production operations will have little difficulty in

7.11.5 UK Oil Taxation

satisfying this condition. It cannot, however, expect ring fence relief for the whole interest burden where the borrowing exceeds UK needs and is partly utilised to meet expenditure in, say, the Irish or Norwegian sectors. On the other hand, deposit at interest of temporary or short term surplus is not likely to prejudice allowance of interest paid as a ring fence charge. Arguably, the raising of loans specifically for the purpose of repaying other loans might not represent borrowing within the qualifying categories, but the OTO has normally accepted interest on replacement borrowing as a ring fence charge if the interest on the original borrowing so qualified, provided that the arrangements generally are regarded as satisfactory. Interest on borrowing to finance the acquisition of oil rights from an associated company cannot qualify as a charge against ring fence profits, though this prohibition does not extend to the acquisition from associates of other assets such as plant; similarly, debt service on the purchase price of shares does not qualify.

In the case of interest paid to an associated company, the amount allowable as a charge against ring fence profits cannot exceed the rate which, 'having regard to all the terms on which the money was borrowed and the standing of the borrower, was a reasonable commercial rate'. For this purpose, two companies are associated if one is a 51% subsidiary of the other or each is a 51% subsidiary of a third company, or one is owned by a consortium of twenty or fewer companies including the other company in question: or one has control of the other or both are under common control (see 7.3). A good deal of controversy has surrounded this provision, the Revenue generally applying a wider interpretation than the industry considers warranted. In order to understand the origins and development of the arguments, it is necessary to know something of the background to the present law.

The Government was concerned to ensure that ring fence profits could not be depleted by excessive interest charges, particularly interest payable to associated companies. The clause in the 1974 Oil Taxation Bill dealing with interest paid to an associated company provided that it was not to be allowed as a charge against ring fence profits unless it was in the nature of reimbursement of interest on money borrowed by the associated company from a third party for the specific purpose of financing the ring fence activities or acquiring oil rights. The Government concluded that this formula was too restrictive. Introducing the amendment which is now incorporated in ICTA 1988 s494, a Treasury Minister said:

'In all the circumstances, we have decided that the only practicable course is to accept that the interest paid by a North Sea company to an associate should be treated under the ring fence, as regards both payer and recipient, in the same way as interest paid to a non-associate, so far as it is paid at a reasonable commercial rate.

The Minister went on to say that the Government would keep under review the capitalisation of North Sea companies, recognising that a parent company could fund the ring fence operations of a subsidiary by minimum share capital and maximum loans, taking out profits in the form of deductible interest payments.

The Revenue argues that the provision requires not simply a review of the rate of interest *per se* but also consideration of the rate in the light of the nature of the funding to which it relates. If part of the funding by the associated company fulfils the role which equity capital might have been expected to play, no interest should attach to that part, and the interest rate applying then to the balance of the funding would be seen to be excessive. The provision is regarded by the Revenue as countering the thin capitalisation of companies operating in the UK or the UKCS by disallowing as ring fence charges that part of intra-group interest which relates to notional equity. The impact of this approach varies from case to case and is dependent on the stage which the company has reached in its exploration and production programmes. The Revenue has generally looked for provision of equity or interest-free borrowing of at least 20% of total funding. The oil industry is less than convinced that the Revenue's interpretation is justified, though companies generally take some account of it in their funding policies.

The associated lending company may be acting simply as a conduit for funds which have been raised from outside sources wholly or partly for the UK exploration and production operations. In these circumstances, the Revenue's concern is with the differential between the rate of interest paid by the associated company and the rate paid by the ring fence company, accepting that a small turn may in some instances be justified. Since the funding of the UK operations is in essence provided by third parties, further restriction of interest payable by the UK borrower on thin capitalisation grounds is not normally sought.

Interest which is not allowed as a charge against ring fence profits solely because it fails the additional ring fence tests is still allowable as a charge against non-ring fence profits and gains. If the disallowed interest is paid to the parent company or to a non-UK resident associated company, however, it may in strictness be a distribution. Interest which is not allowed against ring fence profits could fail to attract any relief if there are insufficient profits or gains outside the ring fence. Interest charges excluded from the ring fence can only be carried forward if there is a non-ring fence trade, for the purpose of which the interest was incurred. The balance may, however, be surrendered to an associated company within a UK group under the group loss relief provisions (ICTA 1988 s494).

7.11.6 UK Oil Taxation

7.11.6 Royalties and Other Licence Payments

Deduction for royalties
Royalties and annual rentals payable to the Secretary of State under the terms of an exploration or production licence are allowable on general principles as trade expenditure. Repayments of royalty or other licence payments are chargeable to CT either as an offset against relative expenditure or as income. This does not apply to royalties repaid at the discretion of the Secretary of State under PSPA 1975 s41(3) to aid continued production from a field; such repayments are specifically exempt from the charge to CT and PRT.

Royalties in kind
Oil taken by the Secretary of State as royalty in kind does not form part of the company's income for CT purposes.

Where royalty liabilities under licences issued in the first four offshore licensing Rounds are satisfied in kind, the Secretary of State makes payments to the licensees equal to the costs of conveying and treating the oil taken by him. Those payments are specifically brought into charge to PRT (see 6.12), but there are no corresponding CT provisions. The relative costs incurred by the company are likely to be allowable for CT, in the case of capital costs under the capital allowances codes and in the case of operating costs as trade expenditure. In practice, the contributions from the Secretary of State are normally brought into charge as additions to CT profits.

7.11.7 Currency Exchange Gains and Losses

Profits chargeable to UK tax are calculated in sterling. In general terms, currency exchange differences which relate to transactions on revenue account are included in the calculation of trading profit or loss while differences on capital account are excluded. The uncertainties which cloud the taxation treatment concern particularly the distinction between revenue and capital and the time at which differences are recognised.

The Revenue issued a Statement of Practice in February 1987 as a guide to the treatment of exchange gains and losses in the computations of trading taxpayers (SP 1/87). It does not have statutory force and does not prejudice the right of taxpayers to argue for different bases. At the same time, the Revenue indicated that legislation might be brought forward if a better solution to the problems could be found. The practice is to bring in for tax purposes exchange differences on an accruals or translation basis, not confining recognition to differences arising on actual conversion of foreign currency to sterling. 'In general, the Revenue view is that if the accounts of a business have been compiled in accordance with Companies Act and generally accepted accountancy principles and have taken account of translation profits and losses, then those profits and losses should normally also be taken into account for tax purposes unless there are particular reasons relevant to the case in question, including whether they are in respect of capital items, for taking a different view.' In determining what adjustments are required, the matching concept applies, authority for which is derived from *Pattison* v *Marine Midland Ltd* [1984] AC 362. To the extent that currency liabilities are matched by monetary assets in the same currency, the matching translation differences are not distinguished or adjusted in the tax computation, even though the liabilities may be part of fixed capital and the assets current assets.

The net exchange difference debited or credited to profit and loss account is adjusted in the tax computation in so far as it relates to capital items on unmatched currency assets or liabilities. Capital liabilities are matched primarily with capital assets in the same currency. Any capital liabilities not matched by capital assets in the same currency are regarded as matched by current assets in the same currency only to the extent that the current assets exceed the current liabilities in that currency. The distinction between capital and revenue items, which is central to the operation of the practice as it is to other facets of the calculation of profits, is derived from case law. As it relates to loans, it is essentially a distinction between loans providing temporary finance on the one hand and loans which add to the fixed capital of the business on the other.

The practice has no relevance to the calculation of capital gains (see 7.26).

7.11.8 Deduction for PRT

PRT is deductible in arriving at CT profits. Arguably, it would be deductible as a trade expense on general principles, but whether that is so or not, particular rules provide both the principle and timing of deduction. PRT paid for a six month chargeable period is deducted in the calculation of ring fence profits for the relevant accounting period, that is, the accounting period in which, or at the end of which, the chargeable period ends. Thus in the case of a company having an accounting period ending 31 December, PRT paid for the two chargeable periods ending 30 June 1988 and 31 December 1988 is deducted in arriving at the ring fence CT profits for the accounting period to 31 December 1988. If the company had a 30 September accounting

7.11.8 UK Oil Taxation

period, PRT for the chargeable period to 30 June 1988 would be deducted in the accounting period to 30 September 1988, that for the chargeable period to 31 December 1988 in the accounting period to 30 September 1989. The PRT for which allowance is given must be paid, though payment need not be made within the accounting period. PRT which is repaid is brought into account for the accounting period in which the payment was deducted, and any necessary re-opening of CT assessments may be effected within six years of the end of the accounting period in which the repayment is made.

Similar rules applied to the deduction for SPD which was payable for the four chargeable periods beginning 1 January 1981 and ending 31 December 1982 only.

APRT as such was not deductible for CT. Instead, allowance was given for an amount paid as APRT which was credited in discharging a corresponding liability to PRT (ICTA 1988 s500).

7.11.9 Abandonment Costs

The fiscal regime relating to abandonment costs may be altered in response to developments in international and domestic law governing abandonment requirements, including security arrangements. As matters stand, there are no CT rules dealing specifically with oil field abandonment, and relief depends on the application of general rules including the capital allowances codes.

The first question for determination is whether the costs of abandoning a field are revenue or capital; and the second, what is the timing of reliefs. In *RTZ Oil and Gas Limited* v *Elliss* [1987] STC 512, the company claimed to deduct in the calculation of profit or loss a provision for the future costs related to closing down the Argyll field. The cost provided for covered mainly the reconversion of the leased semi-submersible production rig and shuttle tankers, removal of subsea well-heads, loading buoy and flow lines and the capping of wells. Vinelott J was in no doubt that all of the expenditure in question would be capital: in consequence, even though the provision was established according to accepted accounting principles, it was not allowable for tax purposes. He reasoned that, since the cost of installing or converting facilities in the first instance was capital outlay, the cost of removal or reconversion must also be capital. It may be deduced from this precedent that the costs of abandoning other fields, and in particular the removal of fixed platforms and pipelines, will be regarded as capital. Relief then depends on the application of the capital allowances provisions.

Most of the infrastructure of oil field facilities is plant or machinery, including production platforms, pipelines and much of the apparatus at onshore terminals. Under the plant and machinery capital allowances code, the cost of demolition, less any salvage proceeds, is treated as an addition to the cost of replacement items or, if the items are not replaced, added to the pool of expenditure on which 25% writing down allowance is given (FA 1971 Sched 8(14)). Under the mineral extraction code, the net cost of demolition of an asset is added to the unrelieved residue of expenditure on which writing down allowance is given (FA 1986 Sched 13(14)). In relation to buildings which have qualified for industrial buildings allowance, demolition costs are added to the residue by reference to which a balancing adjustment is calculated; but no balancing allowance or charge is made if the triggering event occurs more than 25 years after the building's first use (CAA 1968 s4).

Relief for removal or demolition costs by phased allowance after the relevant asset ceases to belong to the taxpayer is an unsatisfactory tax concept which is inconsistent with commercial reality. That apart, these provisions leave in some doubt costs which are incurred after the trade has ceased. There may also be doubt in the context of oil field abandonment about the time at which the trade does cease: the OTO has indicated that it would not interpret the circumstances of closing down in a narrow or restrictive way such as would, in itself, deny relief for abandonment costs related to the trade.

The Petroleum Act 1987 envisages that a licensee may be required to maintain offshore installations and pipelines which are left in place or which are not completely removed, having regard particularly to safety and prevention of pollution, and to provide for inspection. If the licensee has a continuing oil production trade, it is likely that the costs entailed in meeting these responsibilities will be revenue costs of the trade.

7.12 Relief for Exploration and Development Expenditure

Most of the expenditure incurred by a company in exploring for UK oil and in appraisal and development of oil resources qualifies for relief under the capital allowances provisions. If the expenditure is revenue and incurred for the purpose of earning the profit, it is allowed as a trade expense; this may include the intangible costs of drilling development wells. Whether expenditure is revenue or capital is determined on general tax principles. (see 7.11.1). The date on which expenditure is taken to be incurred for capital allowances purposes is generally the date on which the obligation to pay becomes unconditional.

7.12 UK Oil Taxation

The capital allowances relevant to an oil production company which are discussed in the following sections are allowed as though they were trade expenses. Any balancing charge arising on a disposal of an asset on which allowances have been given is treated as though it were a trade receipt.

The 1984 Finance Act effected major changes in the capital allowances codes. The 100% first year allowance for plant and machinery and the initial allowance of industrial buildings were reduced and, subject to transitional provisions, ceased to be available at all for expenditure incurred after 31 March 1986. These changes were associated with the phased reduction in the CT rate from 52% to 35%.

Rates of allowance

Allowance	Rate	Qualifying Expenditure	Main Reference
Scientific research	100%	Exploration and appraisal	CAA 1986 Part II
Mineral extraction	25% writing down (reducing balance)	Exploration and access	FA 1986 Sched 13
	10% writing down (reducing balance)	Mineral assets	
Plant and machinery	25% writing down (reducing balance)	Plant and machinery	FA 1971 Part III
Industrial buildings	4% writing down (straight line)	Industrial buildings and structures	CAA 1968 Part I
New Brunswick	100% revenue deduction	Intangible development drilling costs	

7.13 Scientific Research

Expenditure incurred on UK exploration qualifies for allowance under the scientific research provisions. The expenditure may be capital for tax purposes even though it is written off to profit and loss account. The Revenue's acceptance that the expenditure falls within the requisite scientific research definition is embodied in a Memorandum issued jointly by the Revenue and UKOITC in 1967 (Appendix 3).

Scientific research is defined as any activities in the field of natural or applied science for the extension of knowledge. Expenditure qualifies for allowance if it is incurred by a trader on scientific research related to the trade and directly undertaken by the trader or on his behalf. Alternatively a person is entitled to allowance if he incurs expenditure on scientific research directly undertaken by him or on his behalf and thereafter sets up and commences a trade connected with that research. The qualifying expenditure does not include the acquisition of rights in or arising out of scientific research. References to scientific research related to a trade include any scientific research which may lead to or facilitate an extension of the trade. The final arbiter of what constitutes scientific research is the Secretary of State for Industry (CAA 1968 ss92- 95).

A claimant company needs to demonstrate not only that the research undertaken is of a qualifying kind but also that it is related to the trade carried on or about to be carried on. In connection with oil exploration, the Revenue's guidelines concerning the relationship of the trade to the exploration are contained in the second paragraph of the 1967 Memorandum and indicate that the trade in question needs to be a petroliferous trade. Assuming that the necessary relationship exists, expenditure on exploration undertaken by a licensee directly or by an operator on his behalf should then qualify for allowance. The meaning of 'on his behalf' was considered in *Gaspet Ltd* v *Elliss* [1987] STC 362. The company claimed scientific research allowances for exploration costs borne by it in pursuance of an Illustrative Agreement with an Irish company. In view of the fact that the licence operators invoiced the Irish company and were unaware of the Illustrative Agreement, the court found that the operators undertook the exploration on behalf of the Irish company and not on behalf of Gaspet Ltd.

Expenditure on the acquisition of second hand exploration data is not expenditure on primary research which the provision requires, and relief may in any event be precluded because the expenditure is incurred in acquiring rights in the scientific research. Thus the reimbursement by a farmer-in of the farmer- out's scientific research costs cannot qualify for scientific research allowance. In these circumstances a measure of relief may be available under the mineral extraction provisions. Instead of commissioning research, a licensee may purchase data, particularly seismic surveys, from a contractor. The data is then analysed and used in the course of exploration effort. This type of off-the-peg purchase may be accepted by the OTO as scientific research expenditure it if is a mere incident in a larger research project.

The allowance covers not only the intangible costs of exploring or appraising but also the cost of assets provided for the prosecution of such works. Well hardware, for example, utilised in this context should qualify for scientific research allowance.

7.13 UK Oil Taxation

Expenditure incurred by a UK company on non-UK exploration presents particular problems. Since the expenditure is outside the ring fence, relief for it can only be taken against income which is also outside the ring fence. But within that limitation, it may mitigate or delay liability on non-ring fence profits, while in some cases offering no prospect of later recoupment of UK tax on the overseas project should it prove profitable because that tax would be negated by credit relief for overseas taxes. Another factor of concern to the Government was the much increased use in the late 1970's and early 1980's of limited partnership drilling funds, giving the prospect of UK tax reliefs on overseas investment for offset by individual partners against UK tax. Against this background, the Revenue is inclined to resist claims to scientific research allowance in respect of much overseas exploration, in particular in what may be regarded as 'mature oil provinces' such as parts of Texas, though leaving the door open to claims which satisfy a more critical assessment of what constitutes scientific research.

The criteria of scientific research which are considered appropriate may be discerned from the Revenue's record of a 1949 ruling in which the Privy Council held that unsuccessful oil exploration expenditure incurred in the UK qualified as scientific research. Part of the record reads:

> The facts in the case in which this decision was given were in some respects special. It was claimed on behalf of the company that little was known about the geology and formation of substrata in this country when it commenced its study of the matter, and that, to a large extent, the company's exploration activities (which consisted in general of the survey of given areas by geological and seismic methods, and, if the existence of possible oil-bearing structures was thus established, the sinking of test wells to take actual samples of the various strata) were identical with those being conducted by national, educational and technical Societies in the same field. It was stated that there was a full exchange of information between the company and these Societies at all times, and that while the company was not successful in finding oil in commercial quantities, a large volume of information was built up in a field hitherto unknown, and made freely available to the Board of Trade (Petroleum Department), the Ministry of Fuel and Power, the National Coal Board, the Department of Scientific and Industrial Research, the Ordnance Survey, Universities and geological and scientific Societies.

The 100% scientific research allowance is given for the accounting period in which the expenditure is incurred or, if the expenditure is incurred before the commencement of the trade, for the accounting period in which the trade is commenced (CAA 1968 s91(2)).

7.13.1 Disposal of Scientific Research Assets

The disposal of a scientific research asset may cause withdrawal or restriction of allowances on the expenditure incurred in acquiring or

establishing the asset. The balancing adjustment is required if:
(a) an asset representing allowable scientific research of a capital nature
(b) incurred by the company carrying on a trade
(c) ceases to belong to the company (CAA 1968 s92).

The adjustment is made by reference to the disposal value of the asset, which depends on the event which triggers the adjustment. In the case of a sale at a price not less than market value, the sale price is brought in; loss or destruction, the salvage or insurance recovery; and any other event, open market value.

If the event takes place in the accounting period for which allowance is given or a later period, the adjustment is treated as a trade receipt, restricted if appropriate to the amount of allowance otherwise due. If the event takes place before the period for which an allowance would otherwise be due, the allowance is not then given, but if the disposal value is less than the expenditure the difference is allowed as a trade deduction for the period in which the event takes place.

These provisions, which are apparently designed to deal with tangible research assets, present difficulties in relation to disposals of interests in oil licences and of oil exploration data. This is particularly so in the case of a farm-out in which the farmer-out retains an interest in the licence and related data. The Revenue is understood to take the view that there is in these circumstances, a part disposal of one asset, namely the licence interest, and that that asset may be an asset representing scientific research for the purpose of calculating an adjustment of scientific research allowances. Drilling or other exploration costs incurred in the licenced area, qualifying for scientific research allowance, have been absorbed by the asset unless the work was abortive: the asset is, therefore, an asset representing, at least in part, scientific research. Then, if a part of the licence interest is disposed of, that part, incorporating the proportionate part of the data, 'ceases to belong' to the farmer-out.

This issue is brought into sharper focus in relation to pre-development farm-outs and exchanges in which part of the consideration consists of a work obligation or an interest in an undeveloped licence (see 8.9.2 and 8.9.3). In those cases, exploration or appraisal costs which have been incurred on the licence which is the subject of the disposal are specifically allowed in the calculation of capital gain or loss on the disposal: but that allowance depends on the disposal constituting an event giving rise to a recapture or adjustment of scientific research allowances on the costs and extends only to the amount of the recapture or adjustment.

The recapture provisions were amended in 1985. Under the old rules,

7.13.1   UK Oil Taxation

a recapture was not triggered unless the asset ceased to be used for scientific research related to the trade and was then or thereafter sold.

7.14 Mineral Extraction Allowances

7.14.1 General

Allowances for certain expenditure incurred in acquiring and working mineral sources are given under the mineral extraction code, introduced in 1986 in place of the mines and oil wells provisions. To a company carrying on UK oil operations, the code is of limited significance since the bulk of its exploration and production capital expenditure is allowable under other provisions. However, it does afford relief, within limitations, for the costs of acquiring a licence and for certain second-hand seismic or well data and drilling costs for which other reliefs are not available.

The rates of allowance are 25% writing down allowance for expenditure on 'exploration and access' and 10% writing down allowance for expenditure on acquiring mineral assets, in each case on the reducing balance basis. The allowances are proportionately reduced if the chargeable period or accounting period is less than a year. Balancing adjustments are made in a number of circumstances, including the closing down of particular workings and cessation of the trade.

A company which carries on a mineral extraction trade is entitled to relief for qualifying expenditure as incurred, not dependent on commencement of production from the source to which the expenditure relates. Certain pre-trading expenditure is relieved as though it were incurred on the date on which the trade begins. There is no pooling: each item of expenditure is treated independently, though the event which triggers a balancing adjustment generally refers to the mineral deposit in question rather than the particular expenditure.

Except in relatively unimportant provisions concerning capital contributions and assumptions to be made about planning consents, and in contrast to the old mines and oil wells rules, the mineral extraction code makes no distinction between UK and overseas mineral assets.

Expenditure on buildings or structures which could qualify for allowance under both mineral extraction and industrial buildings codes is to be relieved only under the mineral extraction code; expenditure on scientific research must take scientific research allowance if available to the exclusion of mineral extraction allowance; and plant and machinery expenditure is relieved under the plant and machinery code to the exclusion of mineral extraction allowance, except for certain items provided before a trade begins (FA 1986 s 55 and Scheds 13 and 14).

7.14.2 Qualifying Expenditure

The main categories of qualifying expenditure are:
(a) expenditure on mineral exploration and access, meaning searching for or discovering and testing the deposits of a source of minerals, or winning access to such deposits. A source includes specifically a mine, an oil well and a source of geothermal energy;
(b) expenditure on the acquisition of a mineral asset, defined as any mineral deposits or land comprising mineral deposits, or any interest in or right over such deposits or land. A UK petroleum licence, whether for an onshore or offshore area, falls within this category, as do most overseas oil exploration or production concessions or permits;
(c) expenditure on the construction of works in connection with the working of a source which are likely to have little or no value (in the case of a foreign concession, no value) to the claimant when the source ceases to be worked.

The cost of pursuing an unsuccessful planning application for exploration or access in relation to a mineral asset falls into the first category. This provision is regarded by the Revenue as covering also the costs of unsuccessful applications for oil licences or permits. Particular rules apply to pre-trading expenditure. The amount of expenditure which qualifies is subject to certain restrictions by reference to a predecessor's costs.

Certain expenditures are excluded from mineral extraction allowance. These are the costs of acquiring the site or an interest in the site of qualifying works; construction of works for processing other than preparation of the minerals for use in their raw or unrefined state; and buildings for use as offices or staff accommodation or welfare. The reference to site acquisition does not debar the cost of land containing the mineral deposits, but the qualifying amount of that cost has its own restrictions. The cost of building roads and other means of access, not including the land, will normally qualify as the carrying out of works. In the case of a mineral extraction trade carried on outside the UK, certain capital contributions to the accommodation or welfare of staff may qualify (FA 1986 Sched 13 (4) and (7)).

7.14.3 Pre-trading Expenditure

Exploration expenditure incurred before the mineral extraction trade begins is treated as allowable, at the 25% rate, on the day on which the trade does begin, provided that the exploration of the source in question has not been abandoned before that time. Abortive explor-

7.14.3 UK Oil Taxation

ation of a source in respect of which the search has been given up before a mineral extraction trade begins also qualifies for relief, in this case as a 100% balancing allowance on the first day of trading; but this applies only if the expenditure is incurred not earlier than six years prior to the commencement of the trade.

In either case, it may be important to establish the boundaries of the source. In the context of pure exploration, this may be a difficult exercise; these is an apparent contradiction in testing the admissibility of searching by reference to a 'source' which is not discovered. The meaning and extent of source for the purposes of the mines and oil wells code was a fertile area of debate, and the mineral extraction code does not attempt precise definition. The Revenue has generally regarded as a separate source each oil field or, at an earlier stage of operations, each licensed area, but a wider interpretation may be tenable.

These provisions do not deal with pre-trading expenditure on the acquisition of a mineral asset. In so far as the asset in question has not been abandoned before trading commences, relief is due under the general rules, the expenditure being treated as incurred on the first day of trading; but if the asset has been given up before trading begins, the expenditure fails to qualify. This is a technical anomaly which is acknowledged by the Revenue.

Expenditure on the provision of plant ordinarily attracts relief under the plant and machinery capital allowances code or, if it is provided for use in scientific research, scientific research allowance, and it is not qualifying expenditure for mineral extraction allowance purposes. However, the net cost may qualify for mineral extraction allowance if it is incurred, and the plant is disposed of or abandoned, before a mineral extraction trade begins, subject to the six year restriction referred to above in respect of abortive expenditure: in these circumstances, it would fail to satisfy the trade purpose test for plant and machinery allowance (FA 1986 s55 and Sched 13(5) and (6)).

7.14.4 Restoration Expenditure

The cost of restoring mining sites while a trade continues is normally allowed as revenue expenditure. Such costs incurred not later than three years after the cessation of the trade which might otherwise fall out of relief are picked up by the mineral extraction code and written off effectively as a balancing allowance on the last day of trading. The scope of this relief is fairly widely drawn, including landscaping and carrying out works required as a condition of the development of the source. Receipts within the three year period which are attributable to the restoration are offset against the qualifying costs.

The net cost of demolition of an asset representing qualifying expenditure is added to the residue of unrelieved expenditure on the asset, then qualifying for balancing allowance. If the demolition takes place after the trade has ceased, the cost does not qualify for relief.

These provisions are of somewhat greater relevance to onshore mining operations than to the oil industry. Nevertheless, they are likely to apply to significant amounts of expenditure on the closing down of onshore oil terminals such as Sullom Voe. The industry's concern about the likely consequences of the three year time limit is a part of its larger concern about the tax regime relating to abandonment costs (FA 1986 Sched 13(8) and (13)).

7.14.5 Land

The amount of expenditure on the acquisition of an interest in land which otherwise qualifies for relief is disregarded to the extent that it represents the 'undeveloped market value' of the land. That value is the estimated open market consideration receivable on a deemed disposal of the interest, on the assumptions that no mineral deposits exist and that no development is carried out other than that lawfully already in train or authorised under a pre-existing general order. For this purpose, further assumptions are made in the case of land outside the UK concerning the relative overseas authorisation for development. The gross amount of the expenditure is in any event treated as reduced by any earlier allowance for deemed rent in respect of a premium on a lease (ICTA 1988 s87). Correspondingly, the amount of any disposal receipt which is taken into account in the calculation of a balancing adjustment excludes the then undeveloped market value of the interest in question (FA 1976 Sched 13(16)–(18)).

7.14.6 Second-hand Acquisitions

Cost limitation
The mineral extraction code inherits from the mines and oil wells code, as it applied to overseas but not to UK onshore mineral rights, the concept of limitation of allowable expenditure on purchase to the seller's qualifying costs. The limitation applies on the acquisition by a person carrying on a mineral extraction trade of an asset either from a person within the charge to UK tax who had acquired the asset, or brought it into use, for a mineral extraction trade, or from a seller who did not satisfy this condition but who had himself acquired the asset from one who did. The rules cover any qualifying asset, but the assets

7.14.6 UK Oil Taxation

most commonly at issue in an oil context are mineral assets such as interests in petroleum licences. The ceiling of allowable expenditure is effectively the lower of the purchase price and the 'previous trader's' qualifying expenditure on the asset.

Because the old mines and oil wells code did not limit in this way qualifying expenditure on the acquisition of UK mineral rights, the new code includes a transitional exemption for expenditure in respect of UK mineral assets. The limitation to 'cost' does not apply where the purchase is under a contract made before 16 July 1985, or the acquisition by an intermediate non-trader from a 'previous trader' occurred before 1 April 1986 (FA 1986 Sched 13 (19)–(20)).

Mineral assets
Expenditure on the acquisition of a mineral asset qualifies for the 10% rate of allowance. However, so much of the purchase price as is reasonably attributable to enhancement in the value of the asset brought about by a previous trader's exploration and access expenditure in relation to the asset, not exceeding that expenditure, is itself treated as exploration and access expenditure incurred by the purchaser, qualifying for 25% allowance. This is so even if the previous trader was entitled to scientific research allowance on his expenditure. The extent to which the purchase price is reasonably attributable to that enhancement in value is a matter of judgment depending on particular circumstances. The Inland Revenue is understood to accept the presumption that if the price exceeds the seller's acquisition costs, the excess is identifiable firstly with the seller's exploration and access expenditure.

The inheritance of the 25% rate for exploration and access expenditure applies also to the acquisition to a mineral asset by a succession of traders. Suppose that £X out of the purchase price paid by B to A reflects A's enhancement expenditure, and B incurs £Y on further exploration costs: if C then purchases the asset from B for a price fully reflecting the increased value represented by the exploration and access expenditure of A and B, C is entitled to relief at 25% on £X + £Y.

Particular rules apply to the acquisition at second hand of an interest in a UK petroleum licence. The allowable cost is limited to the amount paid by the original licensee to the Secretary of State for Energy, or the corresponding Northern Ireland authority, for award of the interest. There can be no step-up in the amount of allowable expenditure on the acquisition of the interest per se: but, as in the case of other mineral assets, that part of the purchase price representing a predecessor's enhancement of its worth not only qualifies for relief, subject to the ceiling of the predecessor's allowable costs, but qualifies at the 25% rate (FA 1986 Sched 13 (21)-(22)).

Corporation Tax 7.14.7

If a person who does not carry on a mineral extraction trade sells to a trader assets representing exploration and access costs, the allowance due on the purchase price is also limited to the amount of those costs. To the extent that the purchase price does reflect the seller's exploration and access costs, the purchaser itself is regarded as incurring exploration and access expenditure qualifying at the 25% rate (FA 1986 Sched 13 (24)).

Intra-group transfers of mineral assets
Allowance is restricted if the selling company controls the purchaser or vice versa or both are under common control. The amount of the purchaser's consideration for the acquisition of a mineral asset is not allowable to the extent that it exceeds the expenditure incurred by the seller in acquiring the asset. If the asset is an interest in land, the undeveloped market value which is left out of account is ascertained as at the time when the interest was first acquired by the group.

These provisions apply only to acquisition of a mineral asset: that part of the consideration given by the transferee which reflects value attributable to the transferor's exploration and access expenditure on the asset is deemed to be exploration and access expenditure incurred by the transferee under the rules described above, subject to the market value restriction which applies to control sales generally (CAA 1968 Sched 7(2)). They do not apply to transfers of interests in a petroleum licence, which have their own restrictions (see Mineral Assets above). Nor do they apply if the parties, both being companies resident in the UK, elect to have the purchase price treated as the lower of open market value and the residue of unallowed expenditure of the seller (CAA 1968 Sched 7(4)).

7.14.7 Balancing Adjustments

The residue of unrelieved expenditure, less any 'disposal receipts' attributable to it, is allowed in full for the chargeable period in which a trigger event occurs. The events are as follows:
(*a*) cessation of the mineral extraction trade;
(*b*) the end of the working of particular deposits: balancing allowances are then available on both the acquisition costs and attributable exploration and access expenditure. The event is not defined by reference to source, but as it applies to oil production it is likely to mean the abandonment of a field. If two or more mineral assets are derived from a single asset, the event is delayed until deposits comprised in all of the assets cease to be worked;

7.14.7 UK Oil Taxation

(c) disposal or cessation of use in the mineral extraction trade of an asset not associated with other events;
(d) abandonment of the exploration or appraisal of deposits which are never developed or worked in a course of the trade. This category caters for allowance of the costs of exploration or access which proves to be abortive. Again, it is not defined by reference to source;
(e) cessation of use for the trade of certain overseas buildings or works;
(f) in respect of an asset representing qualifying expenditure, permanent loss of possession, the asset ceasing to exist whether as a result of destruction, dismantling or otherwise, or commencement of use wholly or partly for purposes other than the mineral extraction trade. This head provides, for example, for a balancing allowance on the cost of an interest in a petroleum licence which expires or which is surrendered or revoked. In combination with the general capital allowances rule that references to an asset include references to a part of an asset, it also authorises a balancing allowance on a proportionate amount of the expenditure in the event of surrender of part of the licenced area, provided that a trade is then being carried on.

If the residue of unallowed expenditure is less than the disposal receipts which are required to be set against it, a balancing charge arises rather than a balancing allowance. The charge cannot exceed the allowances given on the relative expenditure (FA 1986 Sched 13 (11) and (12)).

7.14.8 Disposal Receipts

Apart from other requirements to bring to account certain capital receipts, 'disposal value' comes in when a qualifying asset is disposed of or otherwise permanently ceases to be used in the mineral extraction trade. For this purpose, commencement of use which constitutes development of an asset which is neither development for the purpose of a mineral extraction trade nor authorised under certain pre-existing consents is treated as permanent cessation of use for the purposes of the trade. The amount of the disposal value depends on the triggering event. Broadly, the disposal value is, in the case of a sale, the higher of the sale price and market value; in the case of loss or destruction, the insurance or compensation receipts; and in the case of discontinuance of the trade or any other event, market value. It is limited in any event to the qualifying expenditure incurred on the asset by the person in question (FA 1986 Sched 13 (10) and FA 1971 s44).

7.14.9 Mines and Oil Wells Allowances

The mines and oil wells code was replaced by the mineral extraction code and is not relevant, except in a transitional period, to expenditure incurred after 31 March 1986. The scope of the two systems is broadly similar, with the significant difference that the mines and oil wells code provided no relief for geothermal developments.

Expenditure in relation to overseas mineral rights, which included rights to oil in UK offshore fields since the UKCS outside territorial waters is not part of the UK, qualified for a writing down allowance of the greater of 5% and a fraction corresponding to the amount by which reserves were depleted in the chargeable period; expenditure on the construction of works qualified also for 40% initial allowance; allowance was given for abortive expenditure incurred by a trader; and there were provisions for balancing adjustments. Apart from the abortive expenditure relief, allowances were not available until the source in question began to be developed for commercial production. In the case of certain second-hand acquisitions, allowable expenditure was limited to the amount of a predecessor's costs.

UK mineral rights
The allowances referred to above were available for expenditure on exploration and construction of works relating to UK rights. Separate rules provided relief for the cost of acquiring UK mineral rights; this was given by writing down allowance calculated at a fraction of the 'royalty value' of output from the source in the chargeable period, the fraction reducing from 1/2 for the first ten years to 1/4 for the next ten years and to 1/10 thereafter, and by balancing adjustments. Allowance for a second-hand acquisition of UK rights was not limited to a predecessor's costs unless the vendor and purchaser were under common control (CAA 1968 Chapter III).

7.14.10 Inter-action between Mineral Extraction and Mines and Oil Wells Allowances

An accounting period which straddles 31 March 1986 is treated as two separate chargeable periods, the first ending on 31 March 1986 to which the old code applies and the second beginning on 1 April 1986 to which the new code applies. Any balance of expenditure unrelieved under the old code is then deemed to be new expenditure incurred on 1 April 1986 for the same purposes as the actual expenditure was incurred, qualifying for writing down allowance at 25% or 10% as appropriate.

7.14.10 UK Oil Taxation

Expenditure on exploration and access incurred before 31 March 1986 for which no allowance was given under the old code, either because a mineral extraction trade had not been started or because it related to a source not yet working, may qualify for relief under the new code provided that the search had not been abandoned before that date. The expenditure is treated as new expenditure incurred on 1 April 1986. If a mineral extraction trade was being carried on, not including the working of the source in question, allowances run from 1 April 1986. If a trade is commenced after 31 March 1986 and before the search is abandoned, allowances run from the date on which trading begins. Similarly, expenditure on the construction of works which was not relieved under the old code is deemed to be incurred on 1 April 1986. The rule which provides relief for new pre-trading abortive expenditure incurred within six years of the commencement of trading does not apply to expenditure actually incurred before 1 April 1986 which had become abortive by that date (FA 1986 Sched 14 (5)-(7)).

Expenditure on the acquisition of a mineral asset which had not attracted relief under the old code is also deemed to be incurred on 1 April 1986 so as to be considered under the new code. However, this provision may not give relief for pre-trading expenditure, such as the cost of a petroleum licence which has been surrendered, which had become abortive by 31 March 1986, since that expenditure would probably not be regarded as incurred for the purpose of a trade which is eventually established. The balance of the acquisition cost of an asset comprising an interest in land on which mines and oil wells allowances were running is allowable in full under the new code, without restriction in respect of undeveloped market value: in that case, any disposal receipt to be taken into account is the gross amount without restriction (FA 1986 Sched 14 (6)).

Balancing charges under the new code may arise by reference to disposal receipts after 31 March 1986 derived from expenditure incurred before that date, whether that expenditure was fully relieved under the old code or wholly or partly relieved under the new code. The limitation of charge to the amount of allowances given takes account of allowances under both codes (FA 1986 Sched 14 (4) and (8)).

Transitional provisions
Certain expenditure on the construction of works, which would have attracted a 40% initial allowance under the old code, may be treated, by election, as though the old code still applied to it. The expenditure in question is that incurred by a trader in the year to 31 March 1987 under a contract made before 16 July 1985. If an election is made, the initial allowance and writing down allowance under the mines and oil wells code are available up to 31 March 1987, and the residue of expenditure

is then treated as new expenditure incurred on 1 April 1987 qualifying for mineral extraction allowances (FA 1986 Sched 14 (2)).

7.15 Development Drilling

The drilling of production wells is referred to in this book as development drilling, the term used in the 1987 Memorandum (Appendix 3). Both tangible and intangible costs of development drilling are usually capitalised. For UK tax purposes, however, the normal practice is to treat the intangible costs as revenue. The practice applies also to the intangible costs of water or gas injection wells which are drilled to assist production. This treatment has its origin in an appeal decision by the Special Commissioners in 1920 and is indeed usually described as the 1920 Special Commissioners or New Brunswick practice. Special Commissioners' decisions are not published and have no authority as precedent, but very occasionally, as in this case, they may be adopted as the foundation for development of an accepted practice. The part of the decision which has been published by the Revenue reads:

In our opinion the correct principle is:
  (a) the cost of oil wells sunk to prove the presence of oil or gas in commercial quantities in any area or separate group of sands constitutes capital expenditure. The cost of any additional wells sunk in that area or group of sands after the presence of oil or gas in commercial quantities has been proved is properly chargeable against revenue.
  (b) Any deepening below a proved group of sands so as to tap a separate group at a lower level must be charged against capital until the group at that lower level has been proved to be productive.

The stage in field development at which it becomes appropriate for tax purposes to write off drilling costs to revenue is not always self evident. For example, in some instances wells may be drilled before a decision is made to develop the field, those wells being later adopted as production wells. These doubts are unlikely to be material in relation to UK fields since the costs are normally allowable in full either as scientific research expenditure or under the 1920 Special Commissioners practice. The intangible costs of drilling or adopting the first development well, enabling a field or source to begin to produce, may be regarded by the Revenue as capital, qualifying only for mineral extraction allowance. This distinction is particularly important in relation to operations in foreign onshore regions, such as parts of Texas, in which oil leases tend to cover a number of separate and sometimes widely-scattered areas, albeit within what might be described as an oil province. In considering the status of the second and subsequent wells drilled on the lease as a whole, the Revenue will have regard not only to geological and geographic factors but also to the relationship of the wells to any existing infrastructure. Costs associated with starting up a

7.15 UK Oil Taxation

separate production entity are likely to be regarded as capital, qualifying for mineral extraction allowances.

7.16 Plant and Machinery

Radical changes were made in 1984 to allowances for expenditure on plant and machinery. The former first year allowances were phased out, ceasing to be available for expenditure incurred after 31 March 1986, save for expenditure incurred before 1 April 1987 under a contract made before 13 March 1984. The standard allowance is now writing down allowance at 25%, on the reducing balance basis.

The allowances are given in respect of capital expenditure on the provision of plant or machinery for the purposes of a trade. If the contract is of the hire purchase type providing that the user shall or may become the owner of the asset, that part of payments under the contract which represents the 'cash' price is regarded as capital, qualifying for capital allowances, while the 'interest' element qualifies as a revenue expense. If plant is taken on lease, the lessee is entitled to a revenue deduction for the lease payments: the owner of the plant or machinery may qualify for a capital allowance on the capital cost of providing it.

Except for certain categories, qualifying expenditure is not dealt with asset by asset but is added to a pool of costs, from which is deducted disposal values in the event of disposal or destruction of pool assets. Balancing adjustments do not crystallise until the pool is exhausted or the trade ceases. However, an election may be *made to* to treat 'short life' assets (broadly, assets having an expected life of less than five years) separately outside the pool, so that the net cost can be fully relieved over their lifetime (FA 1985 s57).

The question of what constitues plant has exercised the courts many times but has caused little difficulty in connection with oil exploration and production. Virtually all offshore facilities including platforms are likely to be either plant or machinery. Onshore terminals provide more scope for argument, paritcularly as to where the dividing line falls between plant and buildings (see 7.17).

One of the conditions of allowance is that the plant belongs to the claimant, or may become his property under a contract of the hire-purchase type. Under certain 'production sharing contracts' which oil companies enter into with foreign governments, the companies may incur expenditure on plant which either never belongs to them or title to which passes at some stage to the government. The Revenue does not seek to tax oil produced under the contract, which is effectively recovery of the expenditure on plant, to the extent that the expenditure has not qualified for capital allowances.

7.17 Industrial Buildings and Structures

Relief is given for expenditure on the construction or purchase of industrial buildings by 4% writing down allowance on a straight-line basis. In the case of purchase from a vendor who has been entitled to allowances, the allowance is calculated to write off qualifying expenditure over what remains of the period of 25 years, the qualifying expenditure in that case being restricted to the lesser of the purchase price and the original cost. In the case of buildings constructed before 6 November 1962, the writing down allowance is 2% instead of 4%. Balancing adjustments are made in the event of disposal or destruction within 25 years (50 years for buildings constructed before 6 November 1962) of first use (CAA 1968 ss 2-6).

In order to qualify for allowance, a building has to be used for one of the specified purposes. So far as those purposes may be relevant to an oil exploration or production company, they are (CAA 1968 s7):

(a) carrying on a trade in a mill factory or other similar premises;
(e) carrying on a trade consisting in the manufacture of goods or materials or the subjection of goods or materials to any process;
(f) carrying on a trade consisting in certain storage activities;
(g) carrying on a trade consisting in the working of any mine, oil well or source of mineral deposits.

Dwelling houses, retail shops, showrooms, hotels and offices are specifically excluded, unless they constitute a minor part of a larger whole which otherwise qualifies.

The bulk of capital expenditure incurred by an exploration and production company on offshore and onshore facilities is likely to qualify for relief as plant. Some expenditure at onshore receiving and treatment terminals, however, relates to buildings or structures, including control and administration buildings and buildings which house power and other plant. Roads, fences and jetties rank as structures, while storage tanks are accepted as plant.

The prohibition of relief on offices and other premises (see above) does not apply if the building was constructed in connection with the working of a mine, oil well or other source of minerals, or for the occupation or welfare of persons employed in such works, provided that the building is likely to have little or no value to the company when the works are abandoned. A company may be able to demonstrate that buildings in remote locations satisfy this test. A claim in respect of UK mainland administration offices, however, is likely to be difficult to sustain.

7.18 Capital Contributions and Grants

A company which makes a capital contribution towards an asset acquired by another company is entitled to relief under the capital allowances provisions – relating to buildings and structures, plant or mineral assets as appropriate – if the asset owner could have claimed the allowances had it borne the expenditure. In these circumstances, the owner's title to relief extends only to its net expenditure after offsetting the contribution. These rules do not apply if the companies are associated (CAA 1968 ss84-85).

Grants or subsidies by government or local authorities are also required to be deducted for capital allowances purposes from expenditure to which they relate. Regional development grants under Part I of the 1972 Industry Act or corresponding Northern Ireland provisions were excepted, and continue to be so if the relative expenditure is outside the CT ring fence. Where the grant is required to be offset against expenditure incurred after 9 March 1982 which qualifies for PRT allowance (see 6.27.1), it must also be deducted from expenditure qualifying for capital allowances. Apportionment is to be made if part only of the expenditure qualifies for PRT allowance. If the company purchases or makes use of an asset provided by an associated company in respect of which that company is entitled to capital allowances, the amount of the payment made to the associated company in this connection is treated, for the purpose of calculating the profits of the payer's ring fence trade, as the net amount after setting off the regional development grant received by the associated company (FA 1982 s137).

Adjustment of CT liability may be made in accordance with an alteration in a subsequent period in the amount of PRT allowance. Following the 1983 changes in the PRT rules for relief for expenditure on assets, this provision is likely to have little application (FA 1982 s138).

7.19 Know-How

Capital expenditure on the acquisition of know-how qualifies for a 25% writing down allowance. Know-how is defined as any industrial information and techniques likely to assist in the manufacture or processing of goods or materials, or in the working of a mine, oil well or other source of mineral deposits (including the searching for, discovery, or testing of deposits or the winning of access thereto), or in the carrying out of any agricultural, forestry or fishing operations. Companies have contended that the purchase of exploration data, which may not qualify for scientific research allowances because the research was not undertaken directly by the claimant or on its behalf, comes within the meaning of know-how. The Revenue has resisted these contentions, mainly on the grounds that the data relates to knowledge of the whereabouts of potential deposits rather than advancement of technology for winning access thereto.

Receipts for disposal of know-how are normally brought into the calculation of balancing adjustments. In some circumstances the seller and purchaser may elect that they are treated as capital consideration for goodwill (ICTA 1988 ss530-533).

7.20 Capital Allowances: The Ring Fence

Capital allowances generally fall to be given as a ring fence deduction if the expenditure is incurred for the purposes of the separate ring fence trade. It is not normally difficult to establish whether that is the case, but items of mobile plant may give rise to particular problems. If such an asset is acquired with the intention of use partly within the ring fence and partly not, writing down allowances should be apportioned to reflect the extent of those respective uses. Permanent removal from the ring fence of plant acquired solely as a ring fence asset normally requires market value to be offset against the pool of ring fence expenditure on plant and machinery. The law is less clear in relation to a temporary removal and to commencement by an erstwhile ring fence asset of a dual purpose role, partly ring fence and partly not; but in practice a reallocation of allowances may be called for.

Where a non-UK resident company brings into use in its UK branch an item of plant which was formerly used in its non-UK trade, there is some doubt about the base figure on which UK allowances are calculated. The view shared by the Revenue is that the asset is brought into the pool at the sterling market value. There are also doubts concerning the consequences of removal of an asset from the UK branch. The general view is that removal represents cessation of use for the purpose of the trade, whether the UK trade or the ring fence trade, and market value is offset against the pool.

7.21 Relief for Losses

A trade loss may be carried forward without time limit for relief against future profits of the same trade. Alternatively, it may be relieved against other profits or gains in the year in which the loss is incurred or profits or gains, including any profit of the trade, in the preceding year (ICTA 1988 s393). On cessation of a trade, a trade loss incurred in the

7.21 UK Oil Taxation

final year may be carried back for relief against profits of the trade in the preceding three years (ICTA 1988 s394).

Losses and excess interest charges may be surrendered to other companies in the same group, for relief against profits of those companies in the corresponding accounting period. For this purpose, companies are within a group if there is a 75% shareholding relationship, but companies which are not resident in the UK cannot be group members. There are also provisions for exchange of relief between a company owned by a consortium of 20 or fewer UK resident companies and the members of the consortium, including companies in a group to which a member belongs (ICTA 1988 ss402–413). The group and consortium reliefs are subject to anti-avoidance provisions.

A company cannot surrender group or consortium relief if it is a dual-resident investing company, that is, a company which is resident both in the UK and another state and is neither a trading company nor satisfies certain other conditions. Such a company is also precluded from the benefit of other provisions normally available on a transfer to it of assets or a business within a group of companies: assets which have qualified for capital allowances in the hands of the transferor, which otherwise might carry over at tax written down values, are deemed to be sold to the dual-resident company at market value, so that balancing adjustments arise on the transferor (ICTA 1988 Sched 17).

7.22 Restriction of pre 1973 Losses

Steps were taken in 1975 to limit the amount of trading losses of oil companies which could be carried forward for relief against future profits. The cause for concern was that a number of companies had accumulated very large tax losses as a result in particular of the operation of the posted price system, under which crude oil and products were acquired from associated companies at artificially high values; and those losses threatened to diminish the Exchequer's share of the benefits from UK oil operations.

Accumulated losses at 31 December 1972, other than those incurred in activities which would have been within the ring fence had the ring fence rules then been in force, could be carried forward for future relief only within the following limitations:

(*a*) the losses which could be relieved against future profits of the trade arising outside the ring fence were not to exceed the greater of £50 million and the amount of profits arising from those activities between 1 January 1973 and 11 July 1974 (the effective date of establishment of the ring fence;

(*b*) no part of those losses could be set against profits arising after

1 January 1973 within the ring fence, or which would have been within the ring fence had the ring fence rules applied in the period 1 January 1973 to 11 July 1974.
This restriction complements the ring fence barrier against non-ring fence losses after 11 July 1974 (ICTA 1988 Sched 30).

7.23 Ring Fence Restrictions on Losses

The chief significance of the ring fence lies in the prohibition of use of losses arising outside the ring fence against ring fence profits. The ring fence has been described as a one-way valve; ring fence losses may be relieved against non-ring fence profits, but non-ring fence losses cannot relieve ring fence profits. Under the general rules (see 7.21), a ring fence trade loss may be carried forward indefinitely for relief against profits of the ring fence trade, or relieved against any profits or gains of the company in the same year or in the previous year. It may also be surrendered under the group relief or consortium relief provisions, against either ring fence or non-ring fence profits of the recipient company.

A ring fence trade loss may also be allowed against future profits derived from non-ring fence activities, provided that those activities and the ring fence activities are together included within one actual trade (ICTA 1988 s492).

A loss incurred by the company in trading activities outside the ring fence cannot be relieved against profits of the ring fence trade or other income arising from oil extraction activities. Nor can it be set against income derived from oil rights, such as certain royalties or production payments. Similar restrictions apply to claims under the group or consortium relief provisions. Those losses may be applied against ring fence trade profits or income from oil rights only to the extent that they derive from oil extraction activities or oil rights of the surrendering company (ICTA 1988 s492).

7.24 Advance Corporation Tax (ACT)

When dividends or other distributions are paid by a company resident in the UK, the company is obliged to account to the Revenue for ACT: a company not resident in the UK has no such liability. The rate of ACT (25/75 from April 1988) represents, when added to the payment, a tax credit of the recipient of the gross franked payment, equivalent to the basic rate of income tax. The paying company is required to account for ACT quarterly.

7.24 UK Oil Taxation

In the hands of an individual resident in the UK, the aggregate of the distribution and the tax credit is income chargeable under Schedule F, the tax credit satisfying the basic rate income tax thereon. To a UK resident company, such a distribution together with the tax credit is franked investment income, which is not chargeable to CT. It serves to frank distributions which the receiving company itself may make without the need to account for ACT, and in the normal course any surplus franked investment income is carried forward until it is so utilised. Alternatively, a company may claim to have the surplus treated as though it were chargeable to CT, so that trade losses may be set against it and the tax credit released for repayment (ICTA 1988 s242–243).

Companies within a UK group (for this purpose, where there is a 51% parent/subsidiary relationship) may elect to pay dividends within the group without accounting for ACT. In these circumstances, a group dividend is known as group income, not liable to CT but not available to frank payments of distributions outside the group. Similarly, a company which is owned by a consortium may pay dividends to the consortium members without accounting for ACT (ICTA 1988 s247).

7.24.1 Credit for ACT

ACT for which a company has accounted to the Revenue is available for credit against CT, sometimes called mainstream CT, payable on the company's profits including capital gains. The set-off is limited to a percentage of those profits charged to CT equal to the current basic rate of income tax (25% from April 1988). Any balance of ACT not so utilised is available to be carried forward for credit against mainstream CT on profits of later periods; alternatively, it may be carried back for two years (or, in respect of a surplus for periods ending after 31 March 1984, for a maximum of six years) for credit against the mainstream CT charge for those years. A company may surrender ACT to a 51% subsidiary, which is then treated as having paid the ACT and able to utilise it against current or future mainstream CT (ICTA 1988 s239–240).

For accounting periods ending before 1 April 1984, companies with PRT liabilities were able in some circumstances to claim repayment of ACT. PRT is allowed as a deduction in calculating the CT profits of the ring fence trade. If, because of the PRT deduction, the amount of ACT set off against mainstream CT was less than the amount which could have been set off apart from the PRT deduction, the difference could be repaid. The ACT in question might consist of or include amounts surrendered to the company by its parent, whether it derived from the distribution of ring fence or non-ring fence profits (s17(3)). A similar provision enabled ACT to be repaid where the set-off was restricted because of deduction of SPD in arriving at CT profits. The right to repayment in these circumstances was withdrawn in respect of ACT paid on distributions made in accounting periods ending on or after 1 April 1984.

7.24.2 Ring Fence Restriction of ACT Credit

As part of the defence against diminution of the CT charge on ring fence profits, certain restrictions are placed on the use of ACT paid in respect of distribution of ring fence profits. If ring fence company accounts for ACT on a distribution to an associated company which is resident in the UK, and therefore also within the charge to CT, that ACT cannot be set against mainstream CT of the distributing company on its ring fence profits. The definition of associated companies for ring fence purposes applies (see 7.3). The main purpose of the restriction is to counter the indirect use of non-ring fence losses to offset ring fence profits. The recipient company might otherwise obtain repayment of the tax credit attaching to the franked investment income represented by the distribution by relieving its own non-ring fence losses against that income normally. In view of this restriction, the two companies will normally elect under the group provisions that dividend payments by the ring fence company are made without accounting for ACT.

The restriction is extended to ACT surrendered to a subsidiary. Again, if the ACT relates to a distribution made to an associated UK resident company, the subsidiary to which it is surrendered cannot use it as credit against mainstream CT on its ring fence profits (ICTA 1988 s497).

The general restriction does not affect ACT on dividends paid in respect of shares held by persons who are not associated with the payer, whether resident in the UK or not. Were it not for a further restriction, a company might raise finance for activities outside the ring fence by issuing certain kinds of security to outside shareholders and using the ACT on related distributions to offset mainstream CT on its ring fence profits. This restriction applies to redeemable preference share dividends paid after 16 March 1987 by a company which is under the control of a UK resident company, whether the owner of the shares in question is resident in the UK or not, and prevents offset of the ACT on such dividends against ring fence CT. It does not operate if, or to the extent that, the funds raised by the share issue are used to meet expenditure incurred by the issuer on oil extraction activities or the acquisition of oil rights from a non-connected person, or are appropriated to such purposes. The relevant shares are either shares described as redeem-

7.24.2 UK Oil Taxation

able preference shares or shares which fulfil the following condition (*a*) and one or both of conditions (*b*) and (*c*):
(*a*) they carry a preferential right to dividends or to assets in a winding up;
(*b*) they are liable to be redeemed, cancelled or repaid;
(*c*) there are arrangements under which the holder has a right to require another person to acquire them or is obliged to dispose of them, or another person has a right to acquire or is to obliged to acquire them (ICTA 1988 s497).

7.24.3 Carryback of Surrendered ACT

Because of the ring fence restrictions, a ring fence company owned by a UK resident parent company normally depends on ACT surrendered to it for offset against its mainstream CT. Under general rules, surrendered ACT cannot be carried back against CT on profits of earlier periods, but, in part compensation for the ring fence restrictions, a company with ring fence profits does have a limited carry-back facility. The ACT which may be used in this way is that surrendered to the company in respect of a dividend paid after 16 March 1987 by a parent which is not itself under the control of a UK resident company. If the recipient has a surplus of ACT for an accounting period including the surrendered ACT but excluding any ACT paid which is caught by the ring fence restrictions, it may carry back some or all of the surplus for use in any accounting period beginning in the preceding six years, taking relief for a later in priority to an earlier period. The company must carry on a ring fence trade throughout the period beginning with the earliest accounting period to which the ACT is carried back and ending with the period of surplus.

The total amount of ACT surrendered by a parent company which may be carried back under these provisions is limited to £10 million for each accounting period ending after 16 March 1987 and before 1 April 1989, £15 million for later accounting periods ending before 1 April 1991, and £20 million for accounting periods thereafter: these amounts are reduced proportionately for accounting periods of the surrendering company which are shorter than twelve months.

Surrendered ACT which is carried back cannot give rise to repayment on account of PRT or SPD paid (see 7.2.1)(ICTA 1988 s498).

7.24.4 Surrender of ACT by Consortium Companies

The ring fence restrictions on the use of ACT apply to a company which is owned by a consortium of UK resident member companies as they do other companies. Although such a company is able to pay dividends to its members without accounting for ACT, those members which own less than 51% of the ordinary shares are unable under general rules to surrender ACT to it.

An exception is made in the special case of a consortium company arrangement in which a ring fence company is owned in equal shares by two members only. All of the issued share capital of the consortium company needs to be of the same class and carry the same voting and distribution rights. ACT relating to dividends paid by either member after 16 March 1987 may be surrendered to the consortium company. The mainstream CT offset by ACT surrendered by each member is restricted to that arising on one half of the ring fence profits: a similar restriction applies to surrendered ACT which is carried forward.

These provisions do not enable the surrendered ACT to be carried back, under the rules described in paragraph 7.24.3. Nor do they override the ring fence restrictions: ACT for which the consortium member accounts in respect of a dividend paid to an associated UK resident company may be surrendered to the consortium company, but that company is unable to credit it against CT on ring fence profits (ICTA 1988 s499).

7.24.5 ACT and Double Taxation Agreements

Under some double taxation agreements, a recipient of a UK distribution may be entitled to a refund of part of the tax credit represented by the ACT which has been accounted for on the payment. For example, under the 1980 agreement between the UK and the USA, a US corporation which controls, directly or indirectly, at least 10% of the voting stock of a UK resident company paying a dividend is entitled to a payment of one half of the amount of the ACT on the dividend, subject to deduction of a withholding tax of 5% of the aggregate of the dividend and the amount of that payment. The Revenue's entitlement to withholding tax in these circumstances has been challenged in the courts.

The refund is normally made on a claim by the overseas recipient to the UK Revenue, the payer having accounted in full for the ACT. Alternatively, the payer of the distribution may by special arrangement pay the 'refund' direct to the overseas shareholder when the distribution is made.

The amount of ACT available for credit against the mainstream CT of the payer of the distribution is unaffected by the ability of the recipient to obtain a partial refund.

7.25 UK Oil Taxation

7.25 Transactions Between Associated Companies

The general concept is that if the consideration in a transaction between associated companies does not represent arm's length value, that value is substituted for CT purposes. Two companies are associated if they are under common control, and in judging the power to control there are attributed the rights and powers of nominees and connected persons. The substitution of arm's length value is not automatic, but depends on a direction by the Revenue. The general rules do not apply where both parties to the transaction are resident in the UK and the transaction is in the course of their UK trades.

The provisions apply chiefly to transactions of purchase and sale, but they also apply, with necessary adaptations, to 'lettings and hirings of property, grants and transfers of rights, interests or licences, and the giving of business facilities of whatever kind'. This extension is taken by the Revenue to encompass the provision of funding, permitting an examination of the rate of interest, if any, which may be appropriate to the circumstances. It may, for example, take the view that some or all of the funding by a UK parent company of an overseas subsidiary is in the nature of loan capital which should carry a commercial rate of interest (ICTA 1988 ss770-773).

7.25.1 Petroleum Companies

The general rules are substantially modified and extended in order to safeguard the UK tax charge on profits derived from trading relating to crude and products from both UK and overseas sources and the provision of associated services. Companies subject to the wider rules are petroleum companies, defined as those whose activities include one or more of the following:

(*a*) acquisition or disposal of petroleum or rights to acquire or dispose of petroleum;

(*b*) the import into or export from the UK of petroleum products or the acquisition or disposal of rights to such import or export;

(*c*) the acquisition otherwise than for import into the UK of petroleum products outside the UK or the disposal ouside the UK of petroleum products not exported from the UK by the company making the disposal;

(*d*) refining or processing of crude petroleum;

(*e*) extraction of petroleum.

A company may also be a petroleum company if it is associated with a company which carries on any of the prescribed activities, and the company itself owns, operates or manages ships or pipelines used for

Corporation Tax 7.25.1

conveying petroleum or products.

If either of the parties to a transaction is a petroleum company or both parties are petroleum companies, the arm's length rules may apply even though both parties are resident in the UK. This applies if the transaction is part of or connected with activities of one or both of the companies which are either:

(*a*) activities the profits from which are chargeable at overseas tax which could be allowed as tax credit against UK tax; or

(*b*) activities carried on in connection with exploration for or exploitation of UK offshore oil.

UK production which is disposed of to an associated company in circumstances requiring the market value to be brought into the PRT calculation of the producing company also appears in that company's ring fence CT calculation at market value (see 7.7.2). This extension to the arm's length rules catches any transaction between a UK resident producer and a UK associated company providing services in connection with the UK exploration or production effort.

Where a direction is made in respect of a transaction between two UK resident companies, the adjustment in price may, if the direction so requires, be applied reciprocally in the computations of both companies.

A further modification brings certain transactions within the arm's length test even though the two parties are not under common control, provided that one of the parties is a petroleum company or both are such companies. It is sufficient that the transaction is part of a larger transaction or series of transactions and its terms are affected by the remainder, as would be the case in a swap deal. Alternatively, if the transaction is a sale of petroleum extracted under rights exercisable by a company other than the buyer, but not less than 20% of the ordinary share capital of that company is owned by the buyer or its associated companies, it is also caught.

For petroleum companies, as under the general rules, the arm's length price is that which the property might have been expected to fetch had the parties been independent persons acting at arm's length. For the purposes of the extended rules, further detailed guidance is provided as to the assumptions to be adopted. These are:

(*a*) the terms of the transaction would have been such as might have been expected to secure both to the buyer and to the seller a reasonable profit from transactions of the same kind carried out on similar terms over a reasonable period;

(*b*) the seller would not have been compelled by law or by government action to demand a price fixed by law or such action or a price not less than one so fixed;

(*c*) if the transaction were part of a transaction or series of transactions,

7.25.1 UK Oil Taxation

its terms would not have been affected by those of the remainder;
(*d*) where the whole of the property sold is not delivered by the seller within twelve months from the date of the sale, the different parts of the property sold are considered saparately (ICTA 1988 s771).

7.26 Capital Gains

Capital gains of companies are chargeable to CT at the same rate as income. All forms of property come within the scope of the charge, subject to certain exemptions. The exemptions include gains realised on disposal of a debt, other than a debt on a security, by the original creditor; but exchange gains realised in transactions on foreign currency bank accounts are not exempt unless they are chargeable as income.

In broad terms, a capital gain is calculated as the difference between the expenditure incurred on the asset and the consideration received for its disposal. The allowable cost consists in expenditure on acquiring or providing the asset, enhancement costs and incidental expenses, not including expenditure allowed as an income deduction. In the case of a wasting asset (an asset having a predictable life not exceeding 50 years), the allowable cost is restricted to the proportion appropriate to the remaining life of the asset. Gains accruing up to 31 March 1982 are effectively exempt. Assets acquired before 1 April 1982 which are disposed of after 5 April 1988 are rebased: the market value at 31 March 1982 is generally substituted as the cost of acquisition. If the substitution would result in a gain instead of a loss by reference to actual costs, or a loss instead of an actual gain, there is deemed to be neither gain nor loss: if the gain or loss by reference to market values at 31 March 1982 is greater than the actual gain or loss since acquisition, only the smaller gain or loss is recognised. In some circumstances, an election may be made to adopt the 31 March 1982 value where the foregoing restrictions otherwise exclude it: but the election does not apply to disposals of oil licences, plant or machinery, or other assets of a mineral extraction trade which qualify for capital allowances (FA 1988 s96 and Sched 8). In relation to disposals after 1 April 1982 an indexation adjustment is allowed as an addition to the allowable costs. Capital losses are available to carry forward without limit for relief against future gains.

Deferment reliefs are available in respect of disposal of shares in exchange for other shares in the course of a reorganisation, subject to anti-avoidance provisions. Transfers of assets between companies within a UK group (companies of which there is 75% or more common ownership) are deemed to take place for a consideration giving rise to neither gain nor loss; in these circumstances, a gain may crystallise if the receiving company leaves the group within six years. A gain realised on certain categories of asset (chiefly, land or buildings, plant, ships and aircraft and goodwill) may be rolled over against the cost of a replacement asset which also falls within those permitted categories; but if the replacement asset is a depreciating asset, the gain is deferred only for a maximum of ten years.

The statement of practice relating to the treatment of currency exchange differences has no application to the computation of capital gains (see 7.11.7). The cost of an asset and the proceeds of its disposal must be established in sterling terms. The sale of an asset at a price in foreign currency equal to the purchase price may give rise to a chargeable gain or an allowable loss simply because of a movement in the exchange rate (*Bentley* v *Pike* 53 TC 590).

7.26.1 Gains of Companies not Resident in the UK

A company which is not resident in the UK is chargeable to CT on capital gains if at the time of disposal it is carrying on a trade in the UK through a branch or agency. The chargeable gains are those in respect of:
(*a*) assets situated in the UK and used in or for the purposes of the trade at or before the time when the capital gain accrued, or
(*b*) assets situated in the UK and used or held for the purposes of the branch or agency at or before that time, or assets acquired for use by or for the purposes of the branch or agency (CGTA 1979 s12).

In the case of gains related to UK oil rights and related assets, the scope of the charge is extended. Gains on disposal of exploration and exploitation rights and assets are treated as gains arising on disposal of assets situated in the UK. If such gains are realised by a company not resident in the UK, they are treated as arising on disposal of assets used for the purposes of a trade carried on in the UK through a branch or agency (FA 1973 s38) (see 7.2.3.).

A gain realised by a company not resident in the UK on disposal of a direct or indirect interest in a UK onshore licence is within the CT charge under the general rules, while a gain on disposal of a UK offshore licence is caught by the extension. In either case, the liability might be subject to the provisions of a particular double taxation agreement. Most of the current UK agreements allow the UK to charge tax on such gains. Under Article 13 of the 1980 UK agreement with the USA, for example, 'Except as provided in Article 8 (Shipping and air transport) of this Convention, each Contracting State may tax capital gains in accordance with the provisions of its domestic law.'

The 1973 extension, as amended by FA 1984 s81, also broadens the scope of the charge on gains on exploration and exploitation rights and assets to include gains on disposal of shares deriving their value or the

7.26.1 UK Oil Taxation

greater part of their value directly or indirectly from such rights or assets, other than shares quoted on a recognised stock exchange. For this purpose, quotation on the Unlisted Securities Market does not constitute quotation on a recognised stock exchange.

A person resident in the UK is in any case chargeable under the general rules in respect of gains on shares. For persons not resident in the UK, however, whether individuals or companies, the provision is a significant extension of exposure to UK tax. The shareholder may be liable to UK tax on gains which are in part unrelated to UK operations, since the whole of the gain on the shares is chargeable even though a part of the underlying value, albeit less than 50%, may lie outside the UK. Again, the liability may be subject to the terms of a double taxation agreement.

7.26.2. Gains on Disposal of Licence Interests

Measures were introduced in 1984 to counter loss of tax on gains arising on disposal of interests in UK fields. The ring fence concept which already applied to income from oil activities and rights is extended to include those gains. The gains in question are those which arise, after 12 March 1984 and in pursuance of a transfer by a participator in a UK field of the whole or part of its interest in the field, on disposal of that interest or of an asset used in connection with the field. They include a gain deemed to arise to a company leaving a group which previously received the asset, in pursuance of such a transfer, in circumstances in which the group deferment provision applied.

The ring fence gains and ring fence losses in a period are aggregated. If a net gain results, it cannot be relieved by other, non-ring fence, losses of that or an earlier period nor can it be relieved by trading losses or by losses surrendered under the group relief provisions: but it may be relieved by ring fence losses brought forward. If a net ring fence loss results, it is carried forward for relief against later ring fence gains. Alternatively, the company may elect, within two years of the end of the period in which the loss occurs, to treat the loss or part of it as though it were a non-ring fence loss, available to relieve non-ring fence gains of the same or a later period. A ring fence loss arising on a transaction with a connected person is allowable only against gains arising on transactions with the same person (FA 1984 s79).

Gains on disposal of licence interests do not qualify for rollover relief. A petroleum licence is specifically excluded from the classes of assets to which the rollover provisions apply. The legislation so providing, which has retrospective effect, followed a decision by the Special Commissioners understood to uphold a company's claim to roll over a gain on disposal of a licence interest (F(No2)A 1987 s80). It stimulated renewed representations by the industry for more equitable treatment of changes in licence interests, a factor which led the Government to authorise the Revenue to consult with the industry about the capital gains aspects of farm-outs in particular. The outcome of this process found expression in 1988 in the tax-free treatment of certain work obligation farm-outs and licence exchanges.(see 8.9.2).

Certain gains which are now brought within the ring fence may nevertheless arise on related assets such as plant or machinery which are qualifying assets for rollover purposes. In that case, the gain may be rolled over against a qualifying replacement asset, but only if that asset is used for the purposes of the ring fence trade. The replacement asset is presumed to be a depreciating asset, so that deferment of the gain cannot exceed ten years (FA 1984 s80). Other capital gains consequences of changes in licence interests are dealt with in paragraphs 8.9 to 8.9.7.

Chapter 8

Changes in UK Licence Interests

8.1 Introduction

Most UK exploration and production licences are issued to consortia of companies, though in a few cases a licence is held by a single company. Licensees may retain their interests in the original proportions until the licence is surrendered; but it is more likely that during the currency of a licence, particularly a production licence, there will be changes in the identity of the licensees and in proportionate interests. Changes in interests give rise to a wide range of taxation problems. This chapter deals mainly with changes which are effected by farm-in, drawing together the tax consequences of transactions entered into at varying stages in operations under a licence. It also includes consideration of transfers of licence rights and obligations under Illustrative Agreements (see 8.11) and Unitisation Agreements (see 8.12).

All assignments of licence interests require the consent of the Secretary of State for Energy. The suitability of a prospective assignee will generally be judged by reference to the criteria applying in the issue of licences, and the assignee needs to be able to demonstrate ability to satisfy licence obligations. Consent will probably not be given for assignment of an interest in certain licences before the drilling of initial obligation wells has been completed.

In August 1984, the Government indicated that it proposed to limit the scope for changes in licence interests. An Energy Minister, in a letter to representative oil industry bodies, stated that in future interests in a single licence should not be held by more than ten companies, and that a licensee would not be permitted to dispose of a licence interest unless it had contributed significantly to exploration in the licensed area. These moves were believed to stem from concern about the consequences of disposal and fragmentation of interests in producing fields, particularly possible loss of revenue and the administrative complications. The guidelines are applied with some flexibility, in the light of the broad intention to encourage the prospects of successful developments.

8.2 Farm-ins

A farm-in is a concept adopted from US oil and gas practice, denoting in essence acquisition of a licence interest by one party, the farmer-in, in return for provision of some form of consideration to the owner of the interest, the farmer-out. In a true farm-in, the farmer-out retains an interest in the licence, whether a proportionate part of his direct interest or a subordinated or indirect interest in production or net profit relating to his original interest. A purchase of an entire licence interest, however, is sometimes also described as a farm-in.

There are many reasons why licensees seek to add to or reduce their licence interests and obligations. Expectations of future movements in the world oil market and oil price influence the extent of commitment to oil exploration and production. To a multinational company, perception of the relative attraction of the investment climate and exploration prospects in the UK will determine, at least in the longer term, whether the proportion of its efforts channelled to the UK expands or contracts. The influences for change, however, often stem from the manner in which prospects and operations in the licensed area unfold. Smaller companies may find that, faced with an expensive drilling programme or a full-scale development project, they are unable to fund the expected outlay and need in any event to share the risk. Other companies may be happy to meet or to share the costs, in return for acquisition of an interest in the licence. A licensee in a producing field may decide that the balance of its corporate operations would be improved by a reduction in its share of production in order to free resources for other developments. The introduction in 1988 of tax-free treatment of certain work obligation farm-ins and exchanges is likely to encourage an increasing number of such transactions.

In any decision to increase or reduce licence commitments, the tax consequences are likely to play a major role. As in any other aspect of UK oil operations, the high marginal rate of tax requires a very careful assessment of costs and benefits. A key element in company planning is the matching as far as possible of a highly taxed income stream with expenditure allowances and other tax reliefs. A company which has a high exposure to tax, especially PRT, on profits from a field which has exhausted most of its reliefs may look to reduce the exposure and to commute remaining profits, as, for example, BP did in respect of part of its interest in the Forties field in 1983. Another company faced with exploration or development expenditure well in excess of income may acquire an additional income stream, giving the prospect of effective tax relief for its expenditure. Tax efficiency, then, is a concept which is particularly significant in relation to UK oil activities. It is still perhaps slightly surprising to see described as 'tax inefficient' a company

8.2 UK Oil Taxation

possessing a highly profitable field interest but generating little expenditure elsewhere.

The tax consequences of changes in licence interests are often complex, and they vary substantially according to the structure of the transaction. In general, a company disposing of a licence interest aims to minimise the tax charge on the consideration received for the disposal, while the acquiring company aims for maximum tax relief on the consideration which it provides. This is not to suggest that the changes are other than proper commercial rationalisations of exploration and production interests. The transaction may take the form either of disposal of assets or of disposal of shares: which of the routes the parties follow will depend on a variety of commercial and legal factors including assessment by each of the relative tax consequences.

Farm-ins may be characterised as falling into three broad categories, taking place at the (*a*) exploration (*b*) development and (*c*) producing phases of operations under the relative licence. The form of the transaction depends very largely on the stage at which it takes place. The boundaries between the stages are not necessarily sharply defined.

(a) Exploration farm-in

In the most common type of exploration stage farm-in, sometimes called a classical or work obligation farm-in, the consideration given by the farmer-in consists wholly or mainly in his undertaking to bear certain future costs on behalf of the farmer-out. The farmer-in may agree to meet the entire cost, relating to the proportion of the interest in the licence to be retained by the farmer-out as well as the proportion to be acquired by the farmer-in, of a specified work programme represented, for example, by the drilling of the next well under the licence.

Arrangements are not always so straightforward. The farmer-in may also make a cash reimbursement of that part of the cost already incurred by the farmer-out under the licence relating to the proportion of the interest to be acquired by the farmer-in. The farmer-in may grant a subordinated interest out of the licence interest which he is to acquire, which may take the form of a net profit interest, a production interest or an overriding royalty. Agreements commonly include options to re-assign the licence interest or to proceed to assignment of an additional interest in the licence in return for further consideration.

In the case of certain licences, the Secretary of State will not consent to terms such that the farmer-out profits from the transaction. Generally, this means that the farmer-in earns an interest of the same percentage as the percentage of the well costs which he undertakes to bear. In similar circumstances, the transaction may be in essence an 'earn-in', the farmer-in having no interest in the licence until his work obligation has been fulfilled.

(b) Development farm-in
If it is undertaken at a stage at which a field development is in prospect or under way, a farm-in is often a device not only enabling the farmer-out to continue pursuit of an interest in the licence by reducing his commitments to manageable proportions, but also a source of funding of those reduced commitments. Then it is likely that other features appear. The farmer-in may 'carry' the farmer-out, agreeing to meet the development costs otherwise to be incurred by the farmer-out in respect of his retained interest, those costs to be recovered out of the proceeds of production accruing to the farmer-out. Similarly, a non-recourse loan may be provided by the farmer-in, repayable only out of the farmer-out's share of production: the loan may be interest-free or at a commercial rate of interest. In connection with such financing arrangements, the farmer-out may also be required to pay a royalty in cash or oil to the farmer-in or perhaps to a guarantor.

(c) Production farm-in
The owner of an interest in a producing field may dispose of part of that interest. In these circumstances, the object is usually achieved by a relatively straightforward transaction of purchase and sale for cash or shares. More complex arrangements may involve the grant as part of the consideration provided by the farmer-in of a residual or subordinate interest in production relating to the acquired interest, or a consideration package the value of which is wholly or partly dependent on the future performance of the field.

8.3 Tax Consequences: General

There are detailed PRT provisions relating to the transfer between participators of interests in fields, the broad aim of which is to achieve continuity in the treatment of income and expenditure despite the change of ownership (see 8.8). Transfers of interests which take place before any part of the licensed area is determined as a field are not covered by those provisions. Instead, the PRT consequences have to be sifted from the general rules.

The general CT and capital gains rules apply to farm-outs, subject to some important modifications. Two provisions introduced in 1984 extend the ring fence to encompass capital gains arising on the disposal of field interests and limit a transferee's capital allowances. Rollover relief is specifically denied for gains on disposal of UK licence interests. Consideration represented by a work obligation or a licence given in

8.3 UK Oil Taxation

exchange is treated as having no value, for capital gains and capital allowance purposes, in the case of certain pre-development transactions (see 8.9.2 and 8.9.3); and there are particular rules relating to allowable costs for capital gains purposes (see 8.9.5).

Royalties are charged on the holder for the time being of an interest in a licence in respect of his share of production under the licence. Transfers of licence interests cause few royalty problems except in relation to transfers of interests in conveying and treating assets: this aspect is referred to in 5.5.3.

Paragraphs 8.4 to 8.9 deal with direct transfers of licence interests and related assets. Paragraph 8.10 refers to acquisition of interests by share purchase and the main differences in tax consequences which may result from this form of transaction.

8.4 Reimbursement of Expenditure

A farmer-in may pay to the farmer-out, as part of the consideration for acquisition of a licence interest, an amount representing the costs borne by the farmer-out in relation to that part of his interest which is to be transferred. In some instances reimbursement may also be made of the costs incurred by the farmer-out on his entire licence interest including that part which he retains. The reimbursements may cover licence acquisition costs, seismic data and drilling costs.

PRT effects
The general theme of the PRT provisions is that the expenditure incurred by the farmer-out continues to rank for PRT allowance, if it had been incurred for a qualifying purpose. It is unlikely that the 'subsidies' rule applies in these circumstances (under which expenditure met or to be met by another person is disregarded — see 6.27). The farmer-out may retain the right to claim exploration and appraisal relief for the expenditure against any field in which he has an interest. Allowance for expenditure so claimed which gives rise to receipts is reduced by the amount of those receipts: but this does not apply to 'a sum received for the assignment of any of the rights conferred by a licence or of any interest in a licensed area' (s5A(5)(c)). If the expenditure is not allowed to the farmer-out as exploration and appraisal relief, or, in relation to pre-16 March 1983 expenditure, as abortive exploration relief, it may be included in a claim by the responsible person for the field if a field is ever developed in relation to the licensed area. In that case the relief might be apportioned to the farmer-in (see 6.32.1). Even if the expenditure has been allowed to the farmer-out as exploration and appraisal relief, it may become allowable to another person

as field expenditure, though this is not a view shared by the Revenue (see 6.20).

Otherwise, the farmer-in is precluded from making a PRT claim in respect of the reimbursement. Expenditure is not allowable if it is 'any payment made for the purpose of obtaining a direct or indirect interest in oil won or to be won from any area whatsoever, other than a payment to the Secretary of State' (s3(4)(e) applied by s5).

CT effects
Licence acquisition costs

Licence acquisition costs incurred by the farmer-out qualify for writing down allowance under the mineral extraction provisions. If such allowance has been made, the reimbursement occasions a balancing adjustment (see 7.14.7). The reimbursement by the farmer-in is qualifying expenditure for the purposes of those provisions, available for writing down allowance at the 10% rate.

Seismic data and drilling costs

Assuming that the farmer-out is trading, he may be entitled to scientific research allowance for seismic costs and for the costs of exploration and appraisal drilling. A cash reimbursement is likely to occasion a claw-back of those allowances as a trading receipt, subject to the doubts referred to in 7.13. Development drilling costs are normally allowed as revenue expenditure. It is unusual to find in a farm-in at the development or production stage specific reimbursement of those costs by the farmer-in. In any case, the farm-in consideration is likely to be wholly capital, and that element which might be intended to recognise the drilling costs of the farmer-out is not normally separable and chargeable as a revenue receipt.

The expenditure incurred by the farmer-in as direct or indirect reimbursement of the costs of the farmer-out does not entitle the farmer-in to scientific research allowances. This applies whether the seismic and drilling costs of the farmer-out have qualified for scientific research allowances or could have so qualified if the farmer-out had been trading, or have been claimed for mineral extraction allowances by the farmer-out. The condition that the scientific research is undertaken directly by the claimant or on his behalf is not satisfied, and the expenditure of the farmer-in may in any event be excluded as 'expenditure incurred in the acquisition of rights in, or arising out of, scientific research' (CAA 1968 s94). Instead, the expenditure qualifies for mineral extraction allowances as part of the cost of acquiring a mineral asset. To the extent that it is attributable to enhancement in the value of the licence interest resulting from the exploration expenditure of the farmer-out, the rate of allowance is 25% rather than 10%.

8.4 UK Oil Taxation

If the farmer-out has not commenced a trade at the time of the farm-in, he will not of course have qualified for relief on any of his costs. If he subsequently begins a trade in connection with a retained interest in the licence in question or another licence, reimbursements received from the farmer-in may require to be set off against expenditure otherwise qualifying for allowance. In the case of licence acquisition and other costs falling to be considered under the mineral extraction provisions, reimbursements are specifically brought in to reduce qualifying expenditure.

The scientific research provisions are not so explicit. It is fairly clear that the claw-back mechanism does not apply in the case of a seller who has not commenced a trade (CAA 1968 s92). But the Revenue may argue that, to the extent that costs are reimbursed by the farmer-in, they are met by another person and that no relief is due to the farmer-out (CAA 1968 s95(6)); or that the costs are not qualifying scientific research expenditure. In the case of a part disposal of a UK licence before commencement of a trade, which would trigger a recapture of scientific research allowances on the assumption that a trade was carried on, a reimbursement is applied against the relative costs. The costs relating to the entire licence interest up to the amount of the reimbursement or other capital sum received, are treated as allowable in calculating the capital gain or loss on the part disposal. The costs which are so offset are not then available for scientific research allowances on eventual commencement of a trade: but the costs which are not reimbursed or otherwise offset by capital sums received remain potentially allowable (FA 1988 s61).

8.5 Drilling Costs

The most common feature in an exploration stage farm-in is the undertaking by the farmer-in of a work obligation usually involving the drilling of one or more wells. It is assumed that the costs which the farmer-in bears in order to earn an interest in the licence are incurred by him as principal and not as agent for the farmer-out, and that he is not merely discharging liabilities of the farmer-out.

PRT effects
Provided that the expenditure is incurred for a qualifying exploration and appraisal purpose within s5A, the farmer-in is entitled to relief on the full cost borne by him, even though part may relate to the licence interest to be retained by the farmer-out. The Revenue does not take the view that any part of the costs is disqualified as 'any payment made for the purpose of obtaining a direct or indirect interest in oil won or to

be won from the field, other than a payment made to the Secretary of State' (s3(4)(e)). If the costs become allowable as expenditure related to a field, rather than as exploration and appraisal relief, the responsible person may allocate them wholly to the farmer-in.

CT effects
The farmer-in is normally entitled to scientific research allowance on the full amount of exploration and appraisal drilling costs incurred in earning the licence interest, including that part which relates to any retained interest of the farmer-out. On the assumption that the expenditure of the farmer-in is not incurred on behalf of the farmer-out, the farmer-out has no claim for allowance in respect of it. This position applies even if the transaction is one in which the consideration represented by the work obligation is treated as having no value for the purposes of the capital gains calculation and any adjustment of capital allowances of the farmer-out (see 8.9.2).

8.6 Royalty and Other Subordinated Interests

The consideration provided by a farmer-in may include the grant to the farmer-out or to another party of the right to receive a royalty, a net profit interest or similar payment out of production relating to the acquired licence interest.

It is assumed in the following broad summary that the farmer-out disposes of the whole of his direct interest in the licence. The right may entitle the owner of it to an amount of oil as won, but more usually the entitlement is to cash. It is also assumed that the right is granted before any part of the licensed area is determined as a field. The tax consequences in a particular case may depend on the precise rights and obligations of the parties under the agreements, including the Joint Operating Agreement.

PRT effects
The grant of the right has no PRT effect. If a field is subsequently developed and the owner of the right actually takes oil in pursuance of it, liability to PRT in respect of that oil rests with the farmer-in, as the participator possessed of the licence interest which gives rise to the oil. He is treated as having disposed of it to the owner in a sale not at arm's length (Sched 3(6)).

If the right gives rise to cash payments out of the proceeds of the farmer-in's share of production, the farmer-in similarly remains chargeable to PRT in respect of his full share. Deduction of the payments in calculating his PRT liability is likely to be prohibited as 'expenditure

8.6 UK Oil Taxation

wholly or partly depending on or determined by reference to the quantity, value or proceeds of, or the profits from, oil won from the field' (s3(4)(*d*)).

The farmer-out, having disposed of his direct licence interest, is unlikely to be a participator in the relevant period (s12). If, however, the farmer-out were to retain an interest in the licence and to be entitled under the agreement to oil as won, the farmer-out would be chargeable on that oil.

CT effects

No allowance is due for the grant of the right except possibly as part of the consideration for acquisition of the asset for the purposes of calculating a capital gain or loss on disposal. If the right is satisfied by the owner taking oil, the farmer-in and the owner normally each account for the oil which they take. Although for PRT purposes the farmer-out may be treated as having disposed of the oil in question to the owner at market value, the CT consequences which would apply to an actual disposal not at arm's length (s14 — see 6.7.2) do not apply in these circumstances.

Whether the farmer-out is entitled to a deduction in calculating his CT profit for a cash payment depends on the precise nature of the arrangements. If the payment is in the nature of a royalty, it may be allowable as an expense of earning the profit. A net profit or net production payment, however, is more likely to be seen as a distribution or allocation of profit for which allowance is not due. If it is an annual payment, representing pure income profit of the owner, it is likely to be caught by an anti-avoidance provision: the payer is not then entitled to offset the payment against profits even though the owner is chargeable in respect of it. In view of the risk of this unfavourable treatment, the parties will generally avoid this kind of arrangement (ICTA 1988 s125) (see 7.11.2 and 7.11.3).

The owner is liable to CT (or, in the case of an individual, to income tax) on cash receipts. Depending on the recipient's circumstances, they may be either trading income or chargeable under Case III or VI of Schedule D (see 7.3); and they are likely to be regarded as ring fence income.

8.7 Development Carry

A participator may agree to bear some or all of the exploration and development costs of another participator in the field and to recover the costs, perhaps including an addition calculated as interest, out of production relating to the other participator's licence interest. After that recovery is achieved, each participator is then entitled to the benefit of production in accordance with its equity interest in the licence established under the Joint Operating Agreement. This kind of carry arrangement is sometimes adopted as a means of financing development, the participators' equity interests in the licence remaining unchanged: but more usually it is associated with a farm-in in which the farmer-in provides the carry as part of the consideration for the acquisition of an interest in the licence. The tax consequences are dependent on the substance which the arrangements achieve. It is assumed here that the expenditure in question is incurred by the farmer-in as principal and not as agent for the farmer-out, and that the farmer-in is entitled to the oil produced out of which recovery is made rather than to proceeds of disposal of that oil by the farmer-out. It is also assumed that a field is successfully developed and the costs borne by the farmer-in under the carry arrangement are recovered.

PRT effects
That amount of production to which the farmer-in is entitled is usually regarded, in accordance with the Joint Operating Agreement, as oil won and saved by him and is accordingly to be brought into the calculation of his profit or loss. In contrast, it should be noted that if a participator forgoes title to some or all of his share of production in favour of another person who is not a participator — for example, a bank — the participator remains chargeable to PRT in respect of it and is treated as having disposed of it to the other person in a sale not at arm's length (Sched 3(6)). The development expenditure incurred by the farmer-in will in the normal course be included in a claim for the field by the responsible person, and recovery of the costs out of production does not affect the claim. The allowance for expenditure and related supplement is to be allocated between the participators in accordance with their respective interests in the field. The OTO will accept that exploration and appraisal expenditure incurred before production begins may be allocated as the participators agree, in this case presumably to the farmer-in. In the case of development costs, the OTO may need to be convinced that allocation to the farmer-in will not distort the overall field liability (see 6.32.1).

On the assumption that the farmer-in is entitled to the recovery oil as won, it is likely that reversion of entitlement at payout will constitute a transfer of interest to the farmer-out falling within the special rules relating to transfers of field interests (see 8.8.1). One effect of such a transfer is a reallocation of the safeguard base between the two parties.

CT effects
The farmer-in and farmer-out normally account for the proceeds of

8.7 UK Oil Taxation

production to which they are each entitled under the agreement. The farmer-in is entitled to relief for his expenditure, to the extent that it qualifies under the appropriate capital allowances code or, as may be the case for development drilling costs, as revenue expense: the entitlement is not normally prejudiced by the potential or actual 'recovery' of the expenditure out of production. Title to a proportion of the assets corresponding to the carried interest may pass to the farmer-out at payout for nominal consideration. Such a transfer triggers a balancing adjustment in the capital allowances of the farmer-out, although in practice this may be no more than deduction of the consideration from the pool of plant and machinery expenditure.

8.8 Transfer of a Field Interest

The distinction is made here between a transfer of a field interest and transfer of a licence interest where no part of the licensed area lies within a field. The difference is established simply by the question whether the licence covers any part of the area determined as an oil field under the procedure in Schedule 1 (see 6.4). The distinction has important PRT consequences: it also determines whether a capital gain on the transaction is subject to ring fence rules and whether certain capital allowances of the transferee are restricted. A farm-in to a field, particularly a producing field, normally takes the form of a cash transaction, though one or more additional elements of consideration, such as cost reimbursement, development carry or subordinated interest, may also feature in the package. The tax consequences of those elements are discussed in 8.4 to 8.7. It is assumed for the purposes of paragraphs 8.8.1 and 8.8.2 that the field farm-in in question is a straight disposal for cash.

8.8.1 PRT Effects

The Oil Taxation Act 1975 contained no provisions enabling the benefit of unused expenditure or losses relating to an interest in a field to be transferred to a successor to the interest. The omission was rectified by establishment of detailed rules for transfers of field interests, the broad aim of which is to achieve continuity of PRT treatment of income and expenditure despite the change in ownership (FA 1980 Sched 17). The rules apply to all field transfers except
(a) the making of an agreement or arrangement under which the title to oil to be produced under a licence is transferred to an associated company in consideration for that company undertaking the obliga-

Changes in UK Licence Interests 8.8.1

tions under the licence (Illustrative Agreements—see 8.11); and (*b*) redeterminations under a Unitisation Agreement (see 8.12). A unitisation itself, however, effected after determination of the field may involve a transfer of interest within these rules.

There are also other less obvious circumstances in which the transfer rules may apply. Among the variety of 'sole drilling' arrangements in Joint Operating Agreements are some under which a non-consent party may make a relevant transfer to the sole driller; and there may be a transfer in reverse if the non-consent party recovers his original equity interest in the oil to be won. Similarly, a development carry can entail a relevant transfer.

The rules are not restricted to transfers between participators under common control. The transferor and transferee are referred to in the legislation and in the following paragraphs as the old participator (OP) and the new participator (NP) respectively. The application of the transfer provisions is mandatory and not subject to a claim, and they apply both to simple transfers between one OP and one NP and to the splitting of an interest between two or more NPs. They are not to apply, however, if the participators so elect and the Board is satisfied that non-application would not materially affect the overall PRT liability in respect of the field. The election is to be made in the notice of transfer which the participators are required to give within two months of the end of the period in which the transfer takes place (the transfer period).

There are some weaknesses and anomalies in the field transfer rules, particularly relating to terminal losses, which may require amendment.

Expenditure reliefs
The consideration received by the OP for assets disposed of in connection with the transfer of a field interest is not chargeable as a disposal receipt (OTA 1983 Sched 2(6)). The NP is not entitled to allowance on what it pays for the assets. Field expenditure and related supplement which is allowed on a claim by the responsible person and allocated to the OP, and which would accordingly be taken into account in the OP's profit or loss of the transfer period or a later period, is instead transferred for the benefit of the NP. Similarly, field expenditure and related supplement allowed to the OP on a claim by it under the Schedule 6 procedure, which would otherwise be taken into account in the calculation of profit or loss for the transfer period or a later period, is transferred for the benefit of the NP; this only applies, however, if the OP is transferring the whole of its field interest.

The amounts so transferred to the NP are then allowed in calculating the profit or loss of the NP. In the ordinary course, expenditure and supplement which would have been allowed to the OP for the transfer period is allowed in arriving at the NP's profit or loss for that period. It

8.8.1 UK Oil Taxation

is immaterial whether the claims were made or agreed before or after the date of the transfer of the licence interest. One effect of these provisions is that unless the transfer takes place very early in the transfer period, the OP may have income assessable for the transfer period but no expenditure allowance to set against it. In some circumstances a remedy may be available in the carry back of a loss of the NP (see Losses).

Where the OP is transferring only a part of its field interest, the allowances to be transferred to the NP are a 'corresponding part', to be such part as the OP and NP specify and the Board determines. The Board's determination in this respect is subject to rights of appeal.

Exploration and appraisal expenditure
In some circumstances the NP may also inherit the benefit of exploration and appraisal expenditure, and expenditure incurred before 16 March 1983 allowable as abortive exploration expenditure. This provision applies only if neither the OP nor any company associated with it retains an interest in any licence, and the NP is the participator which is party to the final transfer of interest made by the OP. Then the NP may claim the expenditure which was incurred either by the OP or by any company associated with it as though the NP had itself incurred the expenditure, though it may be claimed only against the field in which the interest is transferred. For this purpose, companies are associated if there is a 51% shareholding relationship or each is a 51% subsidiary of a third company which is not itself a 51% subsidiary of another company.

These rules do not override the general ability of a licensee to claim as exploration and appraisal relief expenditure incurred by an associated company. For example, if in a group reorganisation a subsidiary company transfers its field interest to its parent company while other companies in the group retain licence interests, the parent will be able to claim the exploration and appraisal expenditure incurred by the transferor provided that they were associated when that company incurred the expenditure. They do, however, present problems where the transfer follows acquisition of the transferor because the NP itself is a company associated with the OP.

Exploration and appraisal expenditure incurred by the NP prior to the acquisition of an interest in a producing field cannot be relieved against profits derived by the NP from that interest (see. 6.20.1). Similar transfer rules apply to research expenditure incurred by the OP.

Provisional expenditure relief
Apart from the transfer, any provisional expenditure relief (a maximum of 5% of turnover — see 6.24) allowed to the OP in the transfer period and the preceding period would fall to be clawed back in the two

subsequent periods. In order to tidy up the liability of the OP, no provisional allowance is given for the transfer period and the clawback of the provisional allowance given for the preceding period is effected in the transfer period instead of the following period.

Royalty deduction
The PRT deduction for royalty payments is under the general rules calculated on an accruals basis. If the OP transfers the whole of its field interest, any royalty debit or credit which would otherwise fall to be taken into account in periods after the transfer period is in effect rolled into the debit or credit for the transfer period.

Losses
Any unrelieved losses of the OP for the transfer period or earlier periods are transferred to the NP, for use by it against profits of the transfer period or later periods. In the case of a transfer of part only of an interest, a 'corresponding part' of the losses is transferred.

A loss of the NP for the transfer period or a later period which is to any extent attributable to field expenditure incurred by the OP or related supplement and which, because of the transfer of interest, accrues to the benefit of the NP, may be surrendered to the OP. This applies only if the OP retains no interest in the field, and the amount surrendered is restricted to the lesser of the OP's field expenditure allowances so transferred and the OP's profits, net of relief for its losses, up to and including the chargeable period after the transfer period.

Terminal losses
At the end of the life of a field, a participator's terminal loss is required to be relieved against any profits from the field which have accrued to it in earlier periods. If the participator acquired the field interest from another participator in a transaction to which the transfer rules applied, any balance of the loss which cannot be relieved against its own field profits is to be allowed against profits of the OP. Only the residue of loss then remaining qualifies as an unrelievable field loss for use against the profit derived by the NP from another field, or possibly as a loss for use against future tariff income (see 6.29.1).

This provision could give rise to anomalous effects. The terminal loss of the NP may be attributable in part to the NP's extra-field expenditure, such as exploration and appraisal expenditure, for which relief has been taken against the field, the benefit of which may be inherited by the OP for no consideration. Secondly, the profits of the OP against which the NP's loss is required to be set are not apparently restricted to those attributable to the interest transferred to the NP but may include

8.8.1 UK Oil Taxation

those arising in respect of an interest which the OP has retained in the field. There is also a lack of clarity as to how relief is to be apportioned between two or more OPs who may have transferred interests to the same NP at different times. Where there is a succession of transfers of the same interest, a terminal loss of the NP holding the interest at the end of field life is carried back only to the OP from which it acquired the interest.

Oil allowance
If the transfer period is one of the first three chargeable periods for the field, the OP is not entitled to any oil allowance in any of those periods. This is an anti-avoidance provision which prevents acceleration of oil allowance which otherwise might be occasioned by a transfer of interest; it may, however, have the effect of penalising innocent transfers, partly because it denies any oil allowance in the periods concerned even though the OP may retain an interest in the field.

Safeguard
The NP inherits the OP's safeguard base, that is, the amount of its accumulated capital expenditure at the end of the period preceding the transfer period or, in the case of a partial transfer, a 'corresponding part' thereof. It is treated as part of the NP's accumulated capital expenditure for the transfer period and for later periods. For the purposes of calculating safeguard benefit for the transfer period only, a separate formula is required. The accumulated capital expenditure of the OP and NP respectively is the aggregate of:
(a) the fraction, equal to the fraction of the transfer period falling before the date of transfer, of the amount appropriate to each participator assuming no transfer of unused expenditure and no transfer of accumulated capital expenditure; and
(b) the fraction, equal to the fraction of the transfer period falling after the date of transfer, of the amount appropriate to each participator assuming that those transfers are made.

More complex rules apply where there are two or more transfers of interest in the period.

Payback
The net profit period of a participator is the last period for which expenditure may qualify for supplement, and determines the number of periods for which safeguard may apply. In the case of a transfer of a field interest, the net profit period of the NP is the earlier of:
(a) its own net profit period or
(b) (unless the NP, already having an interest in the field, had reached its net profit period before the transfer) the net profit period of the

OP, or if the interest is acquired from two or more OPs, the earliest of the net profit periods.

In arriving at the NP's own net profit period for the purpose of (a), the assessable profits and allowable losses of the OP are treated as having accrued to the NP.

If the OP retains part of its field interest, a just and reasonable proportion of the profits and losses of the OP is treated as having accrued to the NP and the net profit of the OP is recalculated excluding that proportion. APRT paid by the OP or, in the case of a partial transfer, a just and reasonable proportion of it, is also treated as having been paid by the NP (FA 1981 s112).

Exempt gas
In the case of a field producing gas which is exempt under a contract of sale to BGC made before July 1975, the production of other oil is also exempt if the cumulative amount does not exceed 5% of the total cumulative production (s10(1)(b)). In calculating the cumulative production of a NP for this purpose, the amounts of oil won and saved by the OP, or a 'corresponding part' relating to a partial transfer, is treated as though it had been won and saved by the NP.

Transfer of oil
If the OP in pursuance of the transfer of a field interest disposes of its share of oil stocks to the NP, that oil is not charged on the OP but instead is brought into the calculation of the profit or loss of the NP as though it were part of the NP's share of oil won from the field.

Retention of share of oil by OP
Where the OP retains a right to part of the oil won which is attributed to the licence interest transferred, and the NP is responsible for meeting the obligations in connection with the field relating to that part, the oil is deemed to belong to the NP and to be disposed of by it to the OP at market value, so that the NP is assessable to PRT in respect of it.

8.8.2 CT Effects

If a licence interest is disposed of by farm-out for a cash sum, the price paid may need to be allocated between the assets included in the disposal. This is especially so in the case of a transfer of an interest in a field under development or in production, involving not only rights in the licence and related agreements but also items of plant and perhaps buildings. The composite price is to be allocated on the basis of a just and reasonable apportionment between the categories of assets, even

8.8.2 UK Oil Taxation

though the Agreement may specify separate prices attributable to each asset. The prices arrived at in this way are adopted for the purposes of a claim to capital allowances by the farmer-in and the calculation of any restriction or recapture of allowances of the farmer-out (CAA 1968 s77). References in the remainder of this paragraph to expenditure incurred by the farmer-in on particular assets include references to the expenditure attributed to those assets out of a composite price.

The farmer-in is entitled to capital allowances on the expenditure incurred in acquiring plant and machinery. Offshore production platforms and related facilities and pipelines come within this category. In the case of acquisition of a field interest, the amount of expenditure on which the farmer-in is entitled to relief cannot exceed the disposal value taken into account in calculating the balancing adjustment on the farmer-out: the farmer-in's allowance is then effectively limited to the capital expenditure incurred on the asset by the farmer-out (FA 1984 s78).

Allowances may be due on expenditure on industrial buildings used in connection with the field. The buildings concerned are chiefly situated at onshore treatment and storage terminals. The amount on which allowance is due to the farmer-in cannot exceed the cost incurred by the farmer-out.

That part of the price which does not relate to tangible assets such as plant or buildings is generally attributable to the acquisition of rights in the licence and in related agreements including the joint operating agreement and any unitisation agreement. It falls to be considered, under the mineral extraction allowance code, as a cost of a mineral asset. The allowable expenditure is effectively restricted to the qualifying expenditure incurred by the farmer-out. The rate of allowance is generally 10%, except that the amount, if any, which is attributable to enhancement in value effected by the exploration expenditure of the farmer-out qualifies at the 25% rate (see 7.14.6).

8.9 Capital Gains on Transfers of Licence Interests

For several years, the impact of the capital gains rules on farm-ins and similar transactions has been a source of controversy between the industry and the Revenue. Changes in the law in 1988 in relation to certain work obligation farm-ins and licence exchanges have gone some way to resolve the more sensitive issues. Elsewhere, however, a number of difficulties remain, both in the application of the capital gains rules and their interaction with capital allowances provisions.

The capital gains provisions governing disposals of interests in producing fields, bringing gains within the ring fence, are discussed in 7.26.2.

8.9.1 Disposal of an Asset

In a conventional work obligation farm-in, the farmer-out agrees to assign part of his interest in the licence in return for the undertaking by the farmer-in to assume the responsibility for and bear the costs of the drilling of a well or other works in the licensed area. On one analysis, the farmer-out is merely prosecuting his general interest in the licence, making available the necessary funding and arranging for expansion of exploration or appraisal effort in potential enhancement of that interest. This is a view consistent with the way in which a similar farm-in in the USA might be regarded by the Internal Revenue Service. In the early days of farm-ins in the UK, the Revenue was also prepared to accept that transactions of this kind represented utilisation of assets in pursuit of trade. Since the mid 1970s, however, the Revenue has argued that an assignment of an interest in a licence and in related agreements such as the joint operating agreement is a chargeable occasion, representing a disposal of an asset or, as the case may be, a part disposal. Two companies were understood to have appealed successfully to the Special Commissioners in 1980 against assessments made in accordance with this position: the Revenue's appeals against those decisions were settled by agreement, and the issue remained untested in the courts.

The 1988 provisions relating to work obligation farm-ins and licence exchanges proceed on the assumption that such a transaction constitutes a disposal or part disposal of a licence or an interest in a licence. Given the favourable treatment which flows therefrom, that assumption is unlikely to be challenged by the industry in such cases.

If the consideration for an assignment consists of or includes a capital sum, defined as money or money's worth, the transaction may in some circumstances be specifically treated as a disposal or part disposal of an asset (CGTA 1979 s20).

8.9.2 Work Obligation Farm-ins

On the assumption that assignment of an interest in a licence and related agreements constitutes an actual or deemed disposal for the purposes of tax on capital gains, certain work obligation farm-ins qualify for tax-free treatment. In so far as the consideration received by the farmer-out consists in an undertaking by the farmer-in to perform exploration or appraisal work in the area of the licence which is being disposed of, the consideration is treated as having no value. By the

8.9.2 UK Oil Taxation

same token, the farmer-in, in providing the undertaking, incurs no allowable 'cost' for the purpose of any future capital gains disposal by him of the interest which he acquires. The licence must be a UK petroleum licence. Transactions which are not at arm's length, such as those between associated companies, are excluded. The provision applies only if the licence which is farmed out relates to an undeveloped area, that is, a licensed area for no part of which consent for development has been granted nor for which a programme of development has been served or approved by the Secretary of State before the date of disposal. If only a part of the licensed area is assigned, the remainder of the area is disregarded for this purpose. Development has the same meaning as for post 1982 oil allowance entitlement (see 6.28.1) (FA 1988 s62).

A relevant farm-in undertaken solely in consideration for a work obligation cannot give rise to a capital gain. It may, however, result in an allowable capital loss. The amount of any loss depends on the amount of allowable acquisition and enhancement costs and, in relation to a licence acquired before 1 April 1982, the market value at that date (see 7.26). If the consideration includes other elements apart from the work obligation, capital expenditure incurred by the farmer-out on drilling or other exploration or appraisal work in relation to the interest disposed of is treated as allowable enhancement cost; and in the case of a part disposal, the whole of the qualifying cost is treated as relating to the part disposed of. This specific allowance applies only if the expenditure qualifies for scientific research allowance, or would so qualify if the farmer-out were carrying on an oil trade, and the disposal is an event such as would trigger a scientific research allowance balancing adjustment: and the allowance is restricted to the amount of the 'balancing adjustment' (see 8.9.5). Exploration or appraisal expenditure incurred before 31 March 1986 in respect of which the farmer-out chose to claim mines and oil wells allowance instead of scientific research allowance does not qualify as enhancement cost under this provision: whether it does so under general capital gains rules is a matter for debate (FA 1988 s63).

The extent to which acquisition or enhancement costs create or augment a capital loss is in any case subject to limitations. Since a petroleum licence has a life of less than 50 years, the wasting asset rules restrict allowance to that part of the costs which relates to the remaining life, though that restriction is itself overridden if the costs qualify for capital allowances. Secondly, a loss is not allowable to the extent that it is attributable to expenditure on which capital allowances have been or may be given. A loss may be created or augmented by the indexation allowance.

In the case of a 'hybrid' part disposal of an undeveloped licence, involving both a work obligation and other consideration such as cash, the normal rules of computation generally apply by reference to total consideration to which the work obligation contributes no value. However, the allowable costs apportioned to the part disposed of are calculated, not by means of the normal formula, but by reference to A/C, where:

A = the value of the consideration for the disposal, and
C = the sum of 'relevant allowable expenditure' (broadly, allowable capital gains cost) and the indexation allowance on the disposal.

This modified formula obviates the need to value the interest which is retained by the farmer-out. No apportionment of costs is made if the amount of the C factor referred to above, on the assumption that the disposal is of the whole of the licence, is less than the value of the consideration.

The rules relating to work obligation farm-ins were introduced in the 1988 Finance Act but they have effect for transactions both before and after its enactment. A large number of cases which had remained open pending clarification of the taxation consequences come within the ambit of the new rules.

8.9.3 Licence Exchanges: Undeveloped Areas

The rules relating to work obligation farm-ins of undeveloped acreage apply generally to the exchange by unconnected persons of one UK licence, or an interest in a UK licence, for another such licence or interest. The licence or interest which is disposed of must relate to an undeveloped area: but if part only of a licensed area is disposed of, the retained part, which may be subject to development, is disregarded. To the extent that the consideration for the disposal consists of another UK licence or interest in such a licence, which also relates to an undeveloped area, that element of the consideration is treated as having no value, for the purposes of the capital gains liability of the disposer and of any capital allowances balancing adjustment. This may mean, for example, that an unrelieved balance of acquisition cost which qualifies for mineral extraction allowance is released as a balancing allowance. By the same token, the other party incurs no acquisition 'cost' for the purpose of any future capital gains liability on disposal and no expenditure for mineral extraction allowance. The rules have effect for disposals made both before and after enactment of Finance Act 1988 (FA 1988 s62).

8.9.4 UK Oil Taxation

8.9.4 Other Licence Disposals

Outside the relatively narrow areas referred to in 8.9.2 and 8.9.3, the general capital gains rules continue to apply. An exchange of licences involving a UK licensed area under development or an overseas licence, for example, requires valuation of the consideration given by each party. In a hybrid farm-in, the element of consideration other than the work obligation comes into the reckoning, whether or not the work obligation itself qualifies for nil consideration treatment.

Consideration

If a work obligation falls to be valued, the approach favoured by the Revenue is to estimate the enhancement in value of the licence interest retained by the farmer-out in the light of the commitment by the farmer-in to perform the work free of cost to the farmer-out. This would not necessarily apply if the farmer-in relieves the farmer-out of a liability, as may be the case when the work programme undertaken by the farmer-in consists in the drilling of wells which are required as a condition of the licence: in that case, the Revenue might argue that the full amount of the cost to be incurred in pursuance of the undertaking represents consideration.

Other non-cash elements also require to be included in the value of the consideration. The grant of a subordinated interest in the benefit of production from the licence interest assigned to the farmer-in has a capital value, even though the stream of future receipts which may derive from it will be chargeable as income. Its valuation may depend on a complex assessment of risk, oil price, cost escalation and discount factors. Similarly, the value of a non-recourse loan varies according to circumstances. If it is made before any discovery on the licence and is interest free it may have a value not very different from the amount of the cash advance, while a loan at a commercial rate of interest made in circumstances suggesting virtual certainty of repayment will add little to the worth of the consideration received by the farmer-out. Carry arrangements pose the same kind of questions. In all of these matters, it is reasonably clear that there are no rigid yardsticks by which the consideration for tax purposes is to be found. Valuation is not a precise science and it is unlikely that any two experts will arrive at the same answer.

These doubts do indeed raise a question which is very relevant to the capital gains calculation: is the consideration capable of being valued? If an asset is disposed of for consideration which cannot be valued, the disposal is deemed to be for consideration equal to the market value of the asset. In the case of the disposal of part of an interest in a licence for a consideration which cannot be valued, the computation then requires a valuation of that part of the licence disposed of. It is perhaps tempting, in view of the difficulties referred to earlier, to think that this may be the appropriate route to follow, but the difficulties do not necessarily signify impossibility (CGTA 1979 s29A).

8.9.5 Allowable Costs

Expenditure allowable in computing a capital gain or loss is carefully circumscribed. It consists of:
  (a) consideration, in money or money's worth, given wholly and exclusively for the acquisition of the asset or expenditure incurred wholly and exclusively in providing the asset, and incidental costs of acquisition;
  (b) expenditure wholly and exclusively incurred on the asset for the purpose of enhancing the value of the asset, being expenditure reflected in the state or nature of the asset at the time of the disposal, and any expenditure wholly and exclusively incurred in establishing, preserving or defending title to, or a right over, the asset;
  (c) the incidental costs of making the disposal.

Expenditure allowable in computing the profit or loss of the trade is excluded. Thus, development drilling costs which have been allowed as revenue expenditure cannot be allowed for capital gains purposes. Expenditure on which capital allowances have been given is not excluded: the cost of acquiring a licence interest which has qualified for mineral extraction allowance may be included in the calculation of gain or loss on disposal of that interest. A loss is not allowable, however, to the extent that it is attributable to expenditure qualifying for capital allowances.

Drilling Costs

In order to qualify as 'enhancement' of an asset, the expenditure in question must be reflected in the state or nature of the asset at the time of the disposal. Prima facie, expenditure incurred in exploration or appraisal of a licensed area would be expected to satisfy that condition, the more so if it proved successful: the worth of the licence interest is directly related to the sum of knowledge of the area acquired as a result of the expenditure. The Revenue's view, however, is understood to be that such expenditure does not qualify as enhancement cost because the asset disposed of, incorporeal property represented by the licence, is not altered by the expenditure.

The allowance of costs is substantially and specifically modified in relation to certain exploration or appraisal expenditure which is

8.9.5 UK Oil Taxation

incurred on undeveloped UK licence acreage. The new treatment applies only to capital expenditure which qualifies for scientific research allowance or would so qualify if the incurrer were trading: and the disposal of the licence interest is such as to trigger a scientific research allowance balancing adjustment in respect of the costs. The exploration or appraisal expenditure is treated as allowable in the calculation of capital gain or loss, but only to the extent of any capital sum which is brought into the balancing adjustment. The amount of the scientific research allowance recapture is not deducted from the consideration in calculating the capital gain or loss on disposal of the licence interest. If the costs have not attracted allowance because the incurrer has not commenced an oil trade, they are disqualified, up to the amount of the capital sum received, for the purpose of any future scientific research allowance claim. Costs which are allowable for capital gains purposes under these provisions are attributed, in the case of a part disposal, wholly to the part disposed of (FA 1988 s63).

The new rules provide a code of allowance for circumstances within defined limits, while the treatment appropriate to all other circumstances continues to derive from general capital gains provisions. They beg a number of questions. They seem to make the assumption that a disposal or a part disposal of a licence interest in respect of which scientific research expenditure has been incurred is an event which triggers a balancing adjustment of scientific research allowances: as indicated in 7.13, that assumption may not necessarily be valid. In the case of a disposal for no consideration such as a qualifying exchange of licences (see 8.9.3) the rules have no application since there is no capital sum by reference to which scientific research allowances might be recaptured.

The new cost allowance rules encompass a considerably wider range of transactions than those conveying nil consideration treatment (see 8.9.2 and 8.9.3). In particular, they are brought into effect by reference to the circumstances of incurral of the exploration or appraisal expenditure, and they apply whether or not the relative disposal comes within the scope of the nil consideration rules and regardless of the form which the consideration for disposal takes. They apply to disposals both before and after enactment of Finance Act 1988.

8.9.6 Part Disposals

Where a part only of an asset is disposed of, the capital gains tax rules provide a formula for apportioning the allowable costs. The amount of costs appropriate to the part disposed of is a fraction of the costs relating to the asset as a whole, that fraction being

$$\frac{A}{A+B}$$

where A is the consideration for the part disposed of and B is the market value of the part retained.

These rules are modified in the case of certain work obligation farm-ins and licence exchanges (see 8.9.2). Where exploration or appraisal expenditure is specifically treated as allowable for capital gains purposes, it is attributed wholly to the part of the licence interest disposed of (see 8.9.5).

8.9.7 Rollover Relief

A capital gain on disposal of a trade asset may be deferred if the consideration is applied in acquiring a replacement asset, provided that both the old and new assets are within certain specified classes. The disposal is treated as though it were made for consideration yielding neither gain nor loss, and the actual gain is treated as reducing the expenditure on acquiring the replacement asset. If the replacement asset is a depreciating asset such as plant, the period of deferment cannot exceed ten years (CGTA 1979 ss115–119). Gains on the disposal of UK licence interests do not qualify for rollover relief (see 7.26.2).

Rollover relief which would otherwise be available is subject to further conditions if the gain is a ring fence gain, such as a gain on plant sold in connection with the disposal of an interest in a field (see 7.26.2). In that case, the replacement asset in which the disposal proceeds are invested must itself be an asset acquired and used only for the ring fence trade of the company realising the gain, or for the ring fence trade of a company within the same group. For this purpose, all replacement assets are treated as depreciating assets (FA 1984 s80).

8.10 Acquisition of Licence Interest by Share Purchase

The acquisition of a licence interest may be achieved by transfer of the assets comprising the interest. Alternatively, the acquiring company may achieve essentially the same end by purchasing the shares of the company owning the interest. The taxation consequences for both seller and purchaser which flow from an asset purchase are markedly different from those appropriate to a share purchase. For a variety of reasons, the choice between these routes may not be available in the particular circumstances of a prospective deal. For example, a company which is intending to dispose of a part of its interest in a producing field to a number of purchasers is unlikely to find the sale of shares route a

8.10 UK Oil Taxation

practical proposition: on the other hand, purchase of shares may be a means, in some cases, of avoiding the triggering of pre-emption rights under the joint operating agreement. Tax issues must play an important part in the negotiation of price if not in the structure of the transaction.

The analysis in the following paragraphs concentrates on the acquisition by share purchase of an interest in a producing field. Significant differences may also emerge, however, in the tax consequences of an acquisition by asset purchase and by share purchase respectively of a licence interest at the exploration or development stage, affecting particularly the CT position of the purchaser. If the company owning the interest has a CT loss, attributable to allowances for exploration or development expenditure incurred in connection with the licence interest, the company remains entitled to any relief for the loss (subject to anti-avoidance provisions) even though ownership of the shares may change. No relief is available to the purchaser in respect of the price paid for the shares, other than for the purpose of calculating a capital gain or loss on subsequent disposal. On the other hand, a direct sale of the licence interest and related assets would be likely to trigger a recapture of allowances, reducing or eliminating the loss, while the purchaser would be entitled to capital allowances on those parts of the consideration attributable to plant and to the licence interest, restricted in some cases to the cost incurred by the vendor. If the company owning the interest has not commenced a trade, acquisition by share purchase preserves the company's entitlement, under present practice, to scientific research allowances for exploration costs already incurred if and when a trade is commenced.

8.10.1 Share Acquisition: Producing Field

In summary, the direct acquisition of assets comprising a licence interest and related equipment and facilities entitles the purchaser to capital allowances on those elements of the price relating to plant and buildings, limited to the vendor's relative costs, and to relief for the part relating to the licence interest, limited to the vendor's qualifying expenditure. The vendor suffers a recapture of capital allowances and liability on any capital gain. The PRT rules achieve a transfer of unused expenditure and losses, but the purchase price attracts no PRT relief.

These effects may be compared with the consequences of an acquisition by share purchase. In the following analysis of a straightforward transaction at arm's length, it is assumed that the licensee company (Owner) owns a working interest in field A: it is a 100% subsidiary of the selling company (Vendor); and the purchasing company (Purchaser) acquires 100% of the shares in Owner. All companies concerned are assumed to be resident in the UK.

PRT effects
The share purchase has no direct effect on the PRT liability of Owner. By virtue of the purchase, Purchaser and Owner are associated companies: the exploration and appraisal expenditure incurred by either of them after the date of purchase may be claimed against field A or any other field in which either has an interest (see 6.20.1). Similarly, the benefit of an unrelievable field loss and of cross-field allowance for expenditure incurred after that date may be transferred from one to the other. Exploration and appraisal and research expenditure incurred by Owner prior to the acquisition continues to be available for claim against field A. The consideration received by Vendor for sale of the shares is not chargeable to PRT.

CT effects
The consideration given by Purchaser for the shares does not attract any relief except that, on any subsequent disposal or deemed disposal of the shares by Purchaser, it is allowable as the base cost in calculating the capital gain or loss.

The liability of Owner is unaffected by the change in ownership of the shares. Trade losses existing at the time of the change continue to be available for relief against future profits of the company, subject to the proviso that if, within three years before or after the change there is a 'major change in the nature or conduct' of the trade, the loss would cease to be available to carry forward (ICTA 1988 s768).

Vendor is liable to tax on any capital gain on sale of the shares in Owner. If the transaction takes the form of a share exchange, Purchaser issuing shares to Vendor in exchange for the shares in Owner, the gain may be deferred: Vendor's holding of shares in Purchaser is then treated as the same asset as the original holding of shares in Owner, acquired when those shares were acquired (CGTA 1979 s85). The deferment is available only if the transaction is effected for a *bona fide* commercial reason, not wholly or mainly for tax avoidance reasons.

Other aspects
Acquisition of a licence interest by share purchase is not always possible without some preliminary reconstruction. If the interest to be disposed of does not comprise the whole of Owner's business, but is part only of Owner's interest in the field or its total assets, the interest in question may first be transferred to a shell company (Target) within Owner's group, in consideration for issue of shares, or shares and debt, to Owner. The PRT transfer rules apply (see 8.8.1). It is usually accepted that the CT trade succession rules relating to the transfer of a part of a

8.10.1 UK Oil Taxation

trade extend to an intra-group transfer of a part only of a field interest, so that no recapture of capital allowances arise and an appropriate part of any loss is inherited by the successor company (ICTA 1988 s343). No capital gain arises at this stage since the deferment rules for group transfers apply (ICTA 1970 s273).

On the subsequent acquisition by Purchaser of the shares in Target, title to carry forward losses against future profits is preserved, provided that within three years before or after the change in ownership there is no major change in the nature or conduct of the trade of Target (ICTA 1988 s768). Target's leaving the Owner group on acquisition of the shares by Purchaser triggers a capital gains event in Target. The gain or loss is calculated by reference to the difference between the market value of the assets at the time of their transfer from Owner to Target and the allowable costs incurred on those assets by Owner, subject to any indexation allowance (ICTA 1970 s278). Assuming that the purchase of the shares by Purchaser follows quickly on transfer of the asets from Owner to Target, it is likely that little if any gain will arise on sale of the shares or debt. The cost to Owner for capital gains purposes is the market value of the consideration given by Owner, that is, the market value of the assets transferred by Owner to Target.

8.11 Illustrative Agreements

One of the conditions of award of a UK licence up to 1976 was that the licensee company should be registered in the UK. While that condition no longer applies, a licensee company is still required to be managed and controlled in the UK. Where the licensee is owned directly or indirectly by an overseas company, these conditions in some circumstances presented an obstacle to the group in obtaining effective relief for UK expenditure in the calculation of its overall foreign tax liabilities. This has especially been so in the case of US groups, since a UK incorporated and resident member of the group could not be included in the consolidated return for US tax purposes. Agreements, usually called Illustrative Agreements, were adopted in order to circumvent these problems.

The essence of an Illustrative Agreement is the transfer from the licensee company to an associated company, known as the X company, of the beneficial interest in production of oil from the licensed area, in consideration for the undertaking by the X company of the entire burden of cost of prosecuting the operations under the licence which would otherwise fall on the licensee company. The licensee company retains legal title to the licence interest and is ultimately responsible to the Secretary of State for satisfaction of licence obligations. The arrangement requires the sanction of the Secretary of State and in practice, since it has important tax consequences, also of the Revenue. One of the clauses in the model Illustrative Agreement always incorporated in these arrangements provides that the X company will be resident in the UK or will carry on business in the UK through a branch or agency constituting a permanent establishment under the relevant double taxation agreement.

Although Illustrative Agreements are not exclusively employed by US groups, the extent to which they are in vogue is largely dictated by their advantages or disadvantages from a US tax viewpoint. Few new Illustrative Agreements are now made by US groups. Under later licence Rounds a US incorporated company may hold the legal interest in a licence provided that it is managed and controlled in the UK, and the use of a dual resident licensee company became more common. In some instances, the partial tax credit refund available under the double taxation agreements with the USA and certain other states was an advantage stemming from the use of a UK resident company: in others, the transition to profitability of the UK operations removed part of the rationale for continued use of an Illustrative Agreement. In consequence, a number of Illustrative Agreements have been cancelled in the course of group reconstructions. This was not a trend to which the Revenue was likely to take exception, since X companies could in isolated circumstances obtain a UK tax advantage not available to a UK resident company. For example, it was possible under the terms of a double taxation agreement for a company not resident in the UK which had not commenced a trade to offset expenses attributable to the UK permanent establishment against interest income.

The restrictions imposed on 'dual resident investing companies' in 1987 may also affect the choice of corporate vehicle for UK licence operations (see 7.21). Although many existing dual resident licensee companies are not caught by these provisions, some group restructuring may be required, and adoption of a dual resident structure will be less common in future. These developments seem unlikely to stimulate any marked revival in the popularity of Illustrative Agreements.

PRT consequences
The X company is not a licensee within the definition in s12 and is not therefore a participator. It is, however, brought within the charge to PRT by special provision. The X company is treated, as regards any chargeable period during which the Agreement exists, as though it were a participator at all times when the licensee company is a participator. It is accordingly assessable on the share of oil won and saved to which it is entitled and is able to make expenditure claims as a participator.

8.11 UK Oil Taxation

Anything which is done by or in relation to the licensee company in connection with the field or the licence is treated as being done by or in relation to the X company, and all rights, interests or obligations of the licensee in that connection are treated as rights, interests or obligations of the X company (Sched 3(5)).

An Illustrative Agreement is usually made at about the time when a licence is issued and the X company then assumes *ab initio* the role as proxy participator in respect of income and expenditure associated with operations in the licensed area. An Agreement made after determination of a field falling wholly or partly within the licensed area is excluded from the transfer of field interest rules in FA 1980 Sched 17 (see 8.8.1). The application of the general PRT rules and Schedule 3(5) ensure that the X company is assessable in respect of production accruing to it from the date of the Agreement. A difficulty might arise where the licensee company has an unrelieved loss at the time when the Agreement is made. Arguably, the provision that 'all rights interests or obligations of the participator . . . shall be treated as being or having been rights interests or obligations of the other party' permits the X company to inherit the loss, and the OTO may be prepared to apply that interpretation (Sched 3(5)). The specific exclusion from the transfer rules of the making of an Illustrative Agreement does not extend to the cancellation of such an Agreement, nor to assignment of the rights and obligations under the Agreement to an associated company.

CT consequences
The Revenue accepts that the transactions of the X company in prosecuting its interests and obligations under an Illustrative Agreement in standard form are undertaken as principal and not as agent for the licensee company, and the Agreement is not seen as mere financing of the operations of the licensee. The X company is assessable under normal CT rules in respect of profit derived from operations under the licence subject to the Agreement. Title to capital allowances also follows normal rules. If the company is not resident in the UK, the taxable profits are those attributable to the UK branch. For the purposes of capital gains tax, the making of an Illustrative Agreement constitutes a disposal of assets by the licensee company, and cancellation of an Agreement a disposal of assets by the X company. Any gain emerging in the second of these events is normally deferred under the provisions relating to transfer of assets within a group of companies. Those provisions are extended in the case of transfers of exploration or exploitation rights and related assets from a company resident overseas to a UK resident company, or between two companies which are both resident in the same overseas territory (FA 1973 s38(5)). Transfers from UK resident companies to companies resident overseas are not simi-

larly protected, but the making of an Illustrative Agreement at an early stage in the currency of a licence may not in practice be regarded as giving rise to a gain.

Illustrative Agreements are occasionally adopted in contexts other than UK licence operations. In *Gaspet Ltd v Elliss* [1987] STC 362 a UK resident company (under its former name Saga Petroleum UK Ltd) entered into such an agreement with its associated company Saga Ireland Ltd, under which Gaspet undertook to bear all costs of exploration relative to Saga Ireland's licence interests, in return for ownership of any petroleum won to which Saga Ireland might become entitled under the licences. The Court of Appeal refused Gaspet's claim to scientific research allowances on the exploration costs, finding that the exploration was not 'directly undertaken by him or on his behalf' (CAA 1968 s91). Although there was no doubt that Gaspet bore the burden of the expenditure, the licence operators transacted with Saga Ireland and were apparently unaware of the existence of the Illustrative Agreement. In the absence of a relationship, akin to agency but not necessarily contractual, between the operators and Gaspet which the court indicated was required by the expression 'on behalf of', the expenditure incurred by Gaspet was regarded as mere financing of the exploration carried out by Saga Ireland.

8.12 Unitisation

Where a source of production is thought to lie partly within an area under licence to one licensee group and partly in one or more other such areas held by different licensee groups, the Secretary of State may require that the field be developed as one unit by all licensees having an interest in it. The Secretary of State will be concerned to see that the field is developed in a manner which best suits the national interest, and in particular avoids wasteful duplication of facilities and competitive drilling. He has reserve powers to dictate the development programme if the licensee groups fail to produce a programme satisfactory to him. The rights and obligations of the licensees and their relations with each other are formalised in what is usually a highly complex Unitisation Agreement. The broad purpose of the Agreement is to provide for the ascertainment of the share of oil to be won to which each group is entitled, including periodic redetermination of those shares, and to bring the sharing of expenditure into line with the entitlement to oil. The Agreement also serves as an operating agreement in respect of the unit area, overriding to that extent the provisions of the Joint Operating Agreements of each of the licensee groups, which, however, remain in full effect in relation to those parts of the licensed areas not included in

8.12 UK Oil Taxation

the unit area.

Unitisation also applies to fields which straddle the median line between the UK sector and another sector of the continental shelf. The legal framework lies in treaty arrangements between UK and the other country concerned. The UK and Norway concluded a treaty in 1965 which defines the median line between the two sectors. It provides that if any petroleum or other mineral source extends across that line, and the part lying on one side of the line is exploitable from the other side, the countries in consultation with the licensees are to seek to agree how the source should be developed and how the production should be apportioned. Under this aegis, the Frigg Field Treaty was signed in 1976, followed by the Murchison and Statfjord Treaties in 1979. The treaties safeguard the taxing rights of each state in relation to the share of production apportioned to its licensees.

Apart from a PRT provision relating to transmedian line fields, the tax codes make no attempt to prescribe rules to cope with the peculiarities of unitisation. It is not surprising that the transactions flowing from a Unitisation Agreement do not fit neatly into the general rules. The difficulties which arise are very largely concerned with payments made between licensees in balancing up liabilities for expenditure, both on the setting up of a unit and on subsequent redeterminations. The precise nature of these payments varies from Agreement to Agreement. In some cases they may represent simply the equalisation of liabilities for costs: in others they also signify disposal and acquisition of an interest in the relevant assets. The following analysis proceeds on the assumption that the Agreement in question is of this second type.

For the purposes of conveying and treating relief for royalty, the general practice is to reflect redetermination payments back to the period when the original expenditure was incurred. In some cases, the consequential adjustment of reliefs between licensees may be waived.

PRT consequences

Each participator accounts for the sales or appropriations which it makes in a chargeable period, adjusted for its share of opening and closing stocks. A participator which becomes entitled on a redetermination on an increased share of oil brings the catch-up oil to account as it becomes available to it, and the accumulated 'underlift' is not brought in until that happens.

Unitisation usually occurs at a relatively early stage. If a unitisation were to take place when production from the field was well under way, the allocation of reliefs between the licensee groups would, arguably, be made under the transfer of interest rules (see 8.8.1). Those rules do not apply to unitisation redeterminations (FA 1980 Sched 17(1)). Instead, a practice evolved in applying the expenditure relief rules which, although intended to result in a fair allocation, may be of doubtful statutory authority. Under the old rules governing, broadly, expenditure on assets incurred before 1 July 1982, the OTO took the view that the participator which paid an amount to other participators in recognition of an increase in oil entitlement was not entitled to relief on that expenditure per se, because the expenditure in acquiring or enhancing the asset in question had been allowed to the participator which originally incurred it (Sched 4 (1)). It was, however, prepared to allow the field expenditure and supplement, disregarding the redetermination adjustments, incurred in the period in which the adjustments took place to be allocated between participators in such a way as to bring the cumulative allocation into line with the redetermined liabilities. Claims for earlier periods were not adjusted. This worked well enough if the redetermination took place before the participators reached the point of liability, but if it occurred in a period in which some or all of the participators were liable to PRT limited by safeguard, serious inequities emerged. These are not wholly removed by the facility in making a claim to allocate supplement to some but not all of the participators (see 6.32.1).

Expenditure on long-term assets incurred after 1 July 1982 falls to be considered under the new relief rules (see 6.17). The restriction in Schedule 4(1) referred to above does not apply to any expenditure which:

'(a) consists of a payment made to a participator or a person connected with him; and
(b) constitutes a tariff receipt or disposal receipt of the participator' (OTA 1983 s5(4)).

Assuming that under the Unitisation Agreement the redetermination adjustment is made in consideration for disposal of an interest in a qualifying asset, it appears that it is chargeable as a disposal receipt, and that the payer is entitled to relief on what it pays. Once again, the impact of safeguard may reduce the value of the relief. If the redetermination takes place before the payer has reached payback, there is then the question whether the payer is entitled to supplement. The test of most common application in this context is whether the expenditure is incurred for the purpose of 'improving the rate at which oil can be won or transported to the UK from the field'. Although, in considering whether the expenditure is incurred for a qualifying purpose, the relevant purpose is that of the payer, not that of the licensee group or the unit, the OTO may argue that the redetermination adjustment contributes nothing to the volume or rate of production from the field as a whole. The recipient nevertheless may suffer a restriction of supplement to which it would otherwise be entitled in respect of current field expenditure (see 6.19.7).

8.12 UK Oil Taxation

In the case of a transmedian field, the share of oil of UK participators is determined as if the amount of oil won from the UK part of the field is that amount won from the unit area as a whole which is apportioned to the UK participators under the relevant Treaty (FA 1980 s107). On a transmedian field redetermination, a UK participator which receives a repayment, credit or set-off in respect of expenditure on a qualifying asset is specifically treated as disposing of an interest in the asset and chargeable on the receipt as a disposal receipt. This provision says nothing about the treatment of redetermination adjustments paid by UK participators, but it seems reasonable to assume that they qualify for relief under normal rules (OTA 1983 s7(3)).

CT consequences

The Revenue normally accepts that a conventional Unitisation effected at an early stage does not constitute a disposal of rights giving rise to a capital gain or loss. It may be regarded as the pooling by each licensee in its group of rights and obligations in the unit area, without the acquisition of entitlement to oil which it did not already hold. A Unitisation at a later stage in field life may contain terms as to recognition and compensation for rights and obligations which would not be consistent with that perspective. Whether a redetermination involves a transfer of entitlement to oil, rather than adjustment of pre-existing rights, is debatable: since the redetermination payments are related to the balancing of expenditure, the question is normally academic. Payments made in consideration for disposal of an interest in related assets, particularly plant, may, however, give rise to a gain if the capital element exceeds the relative costs borne by the disposer. That excess may be attributable to provision in the Agreement that adjustment payments are indexed for inflation or provide other compensation to the recipient, or to movements in exchange rates.

The measurement of income derived from a unitised field and the treatment of expenditure follow normal principles. Problems commonly arise which relate to the payments made between licensees in adjusting liabilities for costs. Most Unitisation Agreements provide that the adjusting payments carry an addition for interest, running from the time when the expenditure which is to be adjusted was originally incurred. Those provisions apply to redetermination adjustments and may also apply to the initial equalisation of liabilities when the Agreement is made. Whether these additions are interest *per se* or simply part of the capital consideration depends on the precise terms of the Agreement. Under the Ninian Unitisation Agreement, interest factors were included in the adjusting payments required on redetermination. The court decided that these elements were actually interest, even though some of the expenditure to which they attached pre-dated the

Agreement (*Chevron Petroleum (UK) Ltd and Others v BP Petroleum Development Ltd and Others* [1981] STC 689).

The issue may have a material effect on tax liabilities. If the payment is annual interest, the payer is entitled to deduct income tax (which is then accounted for to the Revenue) and to allowance of the interest as a charge in calculating CT profits: the recipient is chargeable on the income. If the payment is capital, the payer may be entitled to allowance but only by gradual write-off under the capital allowances rules: to the extent that the recipient recovers costs, he is chargeable on allowances recaptured, while any excess over recovery of costs is chargeable only under the capital gains rules. Adjusting payments are made in respect of a number of categories of cost which have been borne by the recipient. Under Agreements made at a relatively early stage in the history of the field, the payments required in balancing up initial unit obligations are largely related to exploration and appraisal costs. Redetermination payments, on the other hand, may cover exploration and appraisal, development drilling and operating costs and, most importantly, the costs of the field's production and transportation systems. The effects on tax allowances of each of these elements needs to be considered separately.

The recipient is likely to have received scientific research allowances on the exploration and appraisal costs. In practice, allowances are withdrawn of an amount equal to that part of its costs which are recovered: as indicated in 7.13, the legal basis for withdrawal in circumstances in which the scientific data is effectively retained is not beyond doubt. The adjusting payment cannot strictly be said to be expenditure incurred by the payer or on its behalf on scientific research, and the payer is not entitled to scientific research allowances. It may claim writing-down allowance under the mineral extraction provisions on so much of the payment as does not exceed the relevant costs incurred by the recipient. Payments in respect of expenditure for which the recipient has had mineral extraction allowances are brought in as disposal receipts, reducing the residue of expenditure available for future allowance or giving rise to a balancing charge: the payer is entitled to mineral extraction allowances, restricted to the recipient's costs.

Recovery of development drilling costs is considered by the OTO to be a revenue receipt. As a corollary, the OTO may agree that the payment is also allowable as revenue expense. Similarly, recovery of operating costs represents a revenue receipt, and again the OTO may allow a revenue deduction to the payer.

Assuming, in relation to adjustment of plant costs, that the recipient is disposing of an interest in the assets, the receipt, not exceeding costs incurred by the recipient, is brought into the capital allowance compu-

8.12 UK Oil Taxation

tation as disposal value, reducing the pool of unallowed costs or triggering a balancing charge as appropriate. Any excess of the recovery over cost is chargeable under the capital gains rules. The payer is entitled to allowances on the amount of the payment, not limited to the cost incurred by the recipient unless the two parties are connected persons. If the Agreement is such that the adjustment reallocates the burden of expenditure without affecting title to the assets, the capital allowances consequences are less clear, though the end result may be the same. The recipient may be required to bring in the payment as disposal value, the assets beginning to be used in part, not for the purposes of his trade, but for the trade of the payer; alternatively, the payment may be treated as a contribution to his expenditure which is reduced accordingly. The payer should be entitled to allowances on the payment.

Appendix 1
Offshore Licences

Round	No. of blocks on offer	No. of applications	No. of companies in consortia	No. of blocks applied for
First (1964)	960	31	61	394
Second (1965)	1102	21	54	127
Third (1970)	157	34	54	117
Fourth (1971/ 1972)	421 discretionary	92	228	271 ⎫
	15 for cash tender	31	73	15 ⎭
Fifth (1976/1977)	71	53	133	51
Sixth (1978/1979)	46	55	94	46
Seventh (1980/ 1981)	Specified area of Northern North Sea; 80 elsewhere	125	204	97
Eighth (1982/ 1983)	169 discretionary	40	94	76 ⎫
	15 cash tender	20	47	8 ⎭
Ninth (1984/1985)	180 discretionary	117	107	134 ⎫
	15 cash tender	32	13	52 ⎭
Tenth (1986/ 1987)	127	75	61	84

Source – Department of Energy 'Brown Book' 1988

Round	Licences		
	No. of blocks	No. awarded	No. of companies
First (1964)	348	53	51
Second (1965)	127	37	44
Third (1970)	106	37	61
Fourth (1971/1972)	282	118	213
Fifth (1976/1977)	44	28	64
Sixth (1978/1979)	42	26	59
Seventh (1980/1981)	90	90	157
Eighth (1982/1983)	70	55	81
Ninth (1984/1985)	89	93	103
Tenth (1986/1987)	51	51	60

Appendix 2
Examples of Calculation of Cash Equivalent of Tariff Receipts Allowance (TRA)–s9 and Sched 3, OTA 1983

Example 1

This example illustrates the calculation required by Sched 3 para 2, in a straightforward case where all qualifying tariff receipts derive from a contract made after 7 May 1982.

Ruby Field is owned 60% by participator L
                      40% by participator M

L and M enter into an agreement on 1 January 1984 with the participators in Sapphire Field, under which production of oil from Sapphire will be transported to the UK through the pipeline system owned by L and M and used by them in connection with Ruby Field.

Tariff payable to L and M	– £1 per barrel of Sapphire throughput
Sapphire Field throughput	– 50,000 barrels per day (constant)
Sapphire Field production begins	– 1 May 1986
One tonne	= 7 barrels

The cash equivalent of L's TRA for the chargeable period to 31 December 1986 in respect of the Sapphire Field tariff is:

$$A \times \frac{B}{C}$$

where:

A   represents L's share of Sapphire tariffs;
B   represents the field TRA, in tonnes; and
C   represents the total Sapphire throughput, in tonnes.

$$= £5,460,000 \times \frac{250,000}{1,300,000}$$

$$= £1,050,000$$

Example 2

This example illustrates the calculation required by Sched 3 para 3, where the qualifying tariff receipts derive partly from a pre-8 May 1982 contract and partly from a later contract, not relating to the same oil.

Ruby Field is owned 60% by participator L
40% by participator M

(a) On 1 January 1982, L and M entered into an agreement with the participators in Diamond Field, under which production of oil from the D structure of the Diamond Field would be transported to the UK through the pipeline system owned by L and M and used by them in connection with Ruby Field.

Tariff payable to L and M	– £1 per barrel
Throughput from D structure	– 50,000 barrels per day (constant)
Diamond field production from D begins	– 1 January 1984
One tonne	= 7 barrels

(b) On 1 May 1984 L and M enter into a further agreement with the Diamond Field participators, under which production of oil from the E structure of the Diamond Field will be transported to the UK through the same pipeline system.

Tariff payable to L and M	– £1.25 per barrel
Throughput from E structure	– 20,000 barrels per day (constant)
E structure begins to produce	– 1 October 1985
One tonne	= 7 barrels

The cash equivalent of L's TRA for the chargeable period to 31 December 1986 in respect of the Diamond Field tariff is:

Stage 1 (in respect of 1 January 1982 agreement)

$$A_1 \ (\pounds 5{,}460{,}000) \times \frac{B_1 \ (375{,}000)}{C_1 \ (1{,}300{,}000)}$$
$$= \pounds 1{,}575{,}000$$

Stage 2 (in respect of 1 May 1984 agreement)

$$A_2 \ (\pounds 2{,}730{,}000) \times \frac{B_2 \ (250{,}000)}{C_2 \ (520{,}000)}$$
$$= \pounds 1{,}312{,}500$$

Stage 3
(i) The Stage 1 sum is reduced:

$$£1{,}575{,}000 \times \frac{C_1\ (1{,}300{,}000)}{C_1\ (1{,}300{,}000) + C_2\ (520{,}000)}$$
$$= £1{,}125{,}000$$

(ii) The Stage 2 sum is reduced:

$$£1{,}312{,}500 \times \frac{C_2\ (520{,}000)}{C_1\ (1{,}300{,}000) + C_2\ (520{,}000)}$$
$$= £375{,}000$$

The cash equivalent of L's TRA is the total of the sums as reduced in Stage 3 (i) and (ii), £1,500,000.

Appendix 3

Joint Revenue and UKOITC Memorandum Expenditure on Exploration for and Development of Oil and Natural Gas Resources

1 Introduction

This memorandum, which has been agreed between the Board of Inland Revenue and representatives of the Oil Industry, deals with certain special questions of tax law which arise in connection with petroleum exploration. It must, however, be stressed that the final determination of tax liabilities under Schedule D is the responsibility of the appropriate body of Commissioners, subject to the right of appeal to the courts.

In this memorandum and its appendix the expressions 'petroleum' and 'oil' are used to cover all naturally occurring hydrocarbons including natural gas, and the expressions 'petroleum exploration' and 'petroliferous trade' are used in a similar sense.

2 Scientific Research Allowances

(a) The cost of searching for, discovering and testing new petroleum deposits is generally regarded as expenditure on scientific research qualifying for relief under Part XI ITA 1952. In any particular field these allowances will be available to an operator in respect of expenditure in that field up to the end of Stage III of the Appendix to this memorandum describing the sequence of petroleum exploration activities. Once it is established that two or more concessionnaires are operating in the same field in which the existence of petroleum in commercial quantities has been proved by any one of them scientific research allowances will terminate for each operator as regards that field from the date when it is so established for each such operator.

(b) Scientific Research Allowances are granted to a trader under ss335 and 336 only on research related to his trade which by virtue of s340 includes research which may lead to, or facilitate, an extension of that trade (see Note). A trade is normally regarded as related to petroleum exploration in this sense if it includes some aspect of the oil trade, or mining. A trader who does not carry on such a related trade at the time the expenditure is incurred but who thereafter sets up and commences a petroliferous trade would be entitled to relief under s336. The date on which trading commences is one for determination by reference to the facts of the particular case.

(c) Normally, if a company's activities consist of exploration which is regarded as scientific research, its expenditure on exploration cannot be scientific research expenditure related to a trade — because the trade itself is scientific research — and would not qualify for Part XI allowances. Where, however, a subsidiary company is formed for the purpose of carrying out research related to the parent company's trade or to the trade of a group of associated companies, it will be treated as carrying on a trade and entitled to Part XI allowances. It would therefore be assessed under Case I on any excess of the receipts from its parent or associates over the revenue expenditure incurred on research work and research allowances made to it in respect of any capital expenditure. Payments by the parent or associates to the subsidiary are allowable as deductions in computing the profits of those companies.

Note: ITA 1952 ss335, 336 and 340 — now CAA 1968 ss90, 91 and 94.

Appendix to Joint Statement

The Successive Stages of Work Involved in Oil Exploration and Development Referred to in Paragraph 2 of the Joint Statement

Stage 1

1 Study of all available literature on the geology of the region in question.
2 Concession acquisition (in the case of marine areas this step is often delayed until after (3) below).
3 Reconnaissance geological and/or geophysical surveys over the region in order to select the most attractive areas. Geophysical surveys may be aeromagnetic, gravity or seismic surveys.
4 Detailed geological and/or geophysical surveys over the most attractive (concession) areas in order to select the best locations for drilling. Geophysical surveys may be gravity and/or seismic, most usually the latter.
5 In certain marine areas sea-bed sampling might be undertaken to increase geological knowledge. On land in some cases shallow holes may be drilled for the same purpose.

Stage 2

1 Drilling of exploration wells. In certain cases in marine operations sea-bed bearing capacity investigations may be required prior to commencement of drilling.
   During the drilling of an exploration well the obtaining of maximum information of the geological section penetrated by:
   a Taking samples of cuttings at regular intervals.
   b Cutting solid cores at selected depths (either full hole or side wall).
   c Running electrical and other surveys in the hole.
   d Testing prospective intervals.
2 Either:
   a If no oil shows are found or shows do not imply commercial

quantities, abandonment of the exploration hole.
Or
b If the oil shows are sufficiently promising, the exploration well might be either:
   i Abandoned immediately or after prolonged testing — if production from such an isolated well is considered inadvisable.
   ii Completed as a test well and/or potential producing well.

Stage 3

1 Drilling of additional test holes, normally referred to as appraisal wells, to help determine whether the accumulation is large enough and suitable to commercial production.
The number of appraisal wells necessary for this purpose can vary considerably: at times as few as three might be sufficient, at others more than ten wells may be required. Some of the appraisal wells may be dry holes while others may be suitable for completion as producing wells.
2 Either:—
   a In the event that commercial production is not established, abandonment of all wells.
   Or
   b In the event that commercial production is considered worthwhile, then commencement of Stage 4.

Stage 4

1 Drilling of development wells.
2 Installation and erection of production and storage facilities.
3 Installation of offtake facilities including pipelines, storage and pumping facilities, and tanker loading facilities.

Stage 5

Production operations.

7 February 1967

Index

Abandonment of offshore installations, 4.5
Accountant —
  Report from independent, 5.5.4, 5.5.5
Administration —
  Government Departments, 3.1
Advance petroleum revenue tax —
  charge, 2.1, 6.36
  credit against PRT, 6.36.1
  instalments, 2.1
  interest, 6.37.3
  payment, 6.37
  phasing out, 2.1, 6.36
  repayment, 6.36.2
Assets —
  disposal, *see* Disposal receipts
  expenditure —
    acquisition from fellow participator, 6.17.1
    apportionment, 6.17.1
    associated assets, 6.17.1
      remote, 6.17.1
    background, 6.16
    brought-in assets, 6.17.1
    cessation of use, 6.17.1
    dedicated mobile assets, 6.17.1
    enhancement, 6.17.1
    mobile assets, 6.17.1
    new rules, 6.17
    non-dedicated mobile assets, 6.17.2
    non-mobile assets, 6.17.1
    old rules, 6.16.1
    transitional provisions, 6.18
    use for —
      deballasting, 6.17.1
      exempt gas, 6.17.1
      several —
        fields, 6.17.1
        purposes, 6.17.1
  hiring, supplement, 6.19.6
  mobile, 6.10.2
  use, *see* Tariff receipts
Association of British Independent Oil Exploration Companies, 3.1

British National Oil Corporation, 4.6
Britoil Plc, 4.6
Butane —
  nomination scheme, exemption, 6.7.3

Butane—*cont*
  valuation, 6.7.2

Capital gains —
  generally, 7.26
  illustrative agreements, 8.11
  licence interests —
    consideration, 8.9.4
    valuation, 8.9.4
    costs —
      allowable, 8.9.5
      enhancement, 8.9.5
      undeveloped acreage, 8.9.5
    disposal, 7.26.2, 8.9.1, 8.9.4
    exchanges, undeveloped areas, 8.9.3
    generally, 8.9
    losses, 8.9.2
    non-recourse loans, 8.9.4
    part disposals, 8.9.6
    rollover relief, 8.9.7
    work obligation farm-ins, 8.9.1–8.9.2
  non-UK resident companies, 7.26.1
Claims —
  abortive exploration expenditure, 6.34.1.
  appeals, 6.32.2
  by —
    participators, 6.33
    responsible person, 6.32
  decisions, 6.32.1
    variation, 6.32.3
  disallowance, 6.32.1
  division between participators, 6.32.1
  exploration and appraisal expenditure, 6.34
  research expenditure, 6.34.2
  secrecy, trade, 6.33
  supplement, 6.32
Corporation tax —
  abandonment costs, 7.11.9
  advance —
    credit for, 7.24.1
      ring fence restriction, 7.24.1
    double taxation agreements, 7.24.5
    generally, 7.1, 7.24
    group companies, 7.24
    repayment, 7.24.1
    ring fence profits, 7.24.2
    set-off, 7.24.1
      ring fence restriction, 7.24.1

Corporation tax—*cont*
  surrender —
    by consortium companies, 7.24.4
    carry-back, 7.24.3
    to subsidiary, 7.24.2–7.24.3
  advance petroleum revenue tax as deduction, 6.36.1
  allowances —
    assets, pool, 7.16
    capital, 7.18, 7.20
    changes, 712
    drilling, development, 7.15
    exploration and development, 7.12, 7.13
    grants, 7.18
    hire purchases, 7.16
    industrial buildings and structures, 7.17
    know-how, acquisition, 7.19
    mineral extraction, *see* Mineral extraction allowances
    offices, 7.17
    plant and machinery, 7.16
    scientific research, 7.13
      disposal of assets, 7.13.1
  anti-avoidance provisions, receipts, 6.10.9
  appeal, 7.4.2
  associated companies, transactions between, 7.25
    petroleum companies, 7.25.1
  background, pp 1–2, 7.1
  capital gains, *see* Capital gains
  changes —
    background, 2.1
    recent, 2.1
  computation, example, 7.4.1
  currency exchange differences, 7.11.7
  deballasting, 7.7.6
  demolition costs, 7.11.9
  depreciation, asset, 7.7.4
  expenditure —
    annual payments, 7.11.3
    capital, 7.11.1
    distribution of profit, 7.11.2
    financing costs, 7.11.5
    generally, 7.6.1
    interest, 7.11.5
      non-UK resident companies, 7.11.5
    licences, 7.11.6
    pre-trading, 7.11.4
    redundancy payments, 6.15.6
    revenue, 7.11.1
    royalties, 7.11.2, 7.11.6
    written off, 7.11.1
  field interest transfer, 8.8.2, 8.9
  gas —
    banking schemes, 6.9
    sales, 6.7.7, 7.7.1, 7.7.2
  generally, 7.1
  illustrative agreements, 8.11

Corporation tax—*cont*
  know-how, 7.19
  licence farm-ins —
    annual payments, 8.6
    development carry, 8.7
    drilling costs, 8.5
    generally, 8.3
    reimbursement of expenditure, 8.4
    royalties, 8.6
  licence interests, share purchase, 8.10, 8.10.1
  losses, relief —
    generally, 7.21
    group companies, 7.21
    pre-1973 losses, 7.22
    ring fence restrictions, 7.23
  market value, 6.7.2
  oil —
    appropriation, 7.7.3
    ballast recovery, 7.7.6
    overlifting, 7.7.5
    rights, 7.9
    stocks, 7.7.4
    not won, 7.7.4
    trading —
      generally, 7.7
      sales —
        arm's length, 7.7.1
        not at arm's length, 7.7.2
        Oil and Pipelines Agency, 7.7.1
        transportation beyond UK, 7.7.1
    transit, in, 7.7.4
    underlifting, 7.7.5
  payment, 7.4.2
  petroleum revenue tax as deduction, 2.2, 7.11.8
  profit, 7.1, 7.4, 7.6.1
    distribution, 7.11.2
  rate, 2.2, 7.1
  removal costs, 7.11.9
  returns, 7.4.2
  ring fence —
    associated licensee, 7.3
    background, 2.1, 7.1
    capital allowances, 7.20
    generally, 7.3
    income, 7.10
    interest, restrictions, 7.11.5
      associated companies, 7.11.5
    losses, use, 7.23
    profits, 7.6.2
    trading status, relationship with, 7.5
  rollover relief, 8.9.7
  scope —
    contractors, non-UK resident, 7.2.4
    oil extraction, UK, 7.2.3
    residence —
      in UK, 7.2.1

Corporation tax—*cont*
    not in UK, 7.2.2
    tariff receipts, 7.8
    trading —
        commencement, 7.5
        exploration, 7.5
        generally, 7.5
        pre-trading period, 7.5
        world-wide, 7.5
    unitisation agreements, 8.12
Costs —
    abandoned installations, 4.5
    allowance, 5.4.1
Cross-field allowance —
    effect in receiving field, 6.23
    elections, 6.23, 6.34.3
    generally, 6.4, 6.23
    interaction with safeguard, 6.30.2
    qualifying expenditure, 6.23
Crude oil —
    sales, 2.1

Department of Energy, 3.2
Development of oil —
    abandonment of fields, p 2
    history, p 1
    new fields, p 2
Disposal receipts —
    anti-avoidance provisions, 6.10.9
    brought-in assets, 6.10.7
    charge to PRT, 6.10.6
    enhancing value of disposable asset, 6.17.1
    generally, 6.10.1
    insurance receipts as, 6.10.7
    meaning, 6.10.6
    mineral extraction, asset, 7.14.8
    non-arm's length receipts, 6.10.8
    particular disposals, 6.10.7
    qualifying assets, 6.10.2
    supplement, connection with, 6.19.7
Disuse of Offshore installations, 4.5

Enterprise Oil Plc, 4.6
Ethane —
    component, valuation, 6.7.6
    election, pricing formula, 6.7.5
    nomination scheme, exemption, 6.7.3
    petrochemical purposes, use for, 6.7.5
    valuation, 6.7.5
Exploration and appraisal expenditure —
    abortive exploration expenditure, 6.21
    assets, 6.20
    associated —
        companies, 6.20
        receipts, 6.20
    claims, 6.34
    double allowance, prevention, 6.20
    generally 6.20

Exploration and appraisal expenditure—*cont*
    interaction with safeguard, 6.30.2
    oil won, 6.20
    onshore works, exclusion, 6.20
    restriction on relief, 6.20.1
    set-off, associated receipts, 6.20
    territorial sea, 6.20
    transfer of field interest, 6.20.1
Field —
    cross-field allowance, *see* Cross-field allowance
    determination of, 6.4
    ending, 6.5
    expenditure —
        abandonment of facilities, 6.15.6
        allowable, 6.15.6
        apportionment, 6.15.3, 6.15.5
        appraisal works, 6.15.6
        assets, long term, 6.15.3
        before determination, 6.4
        buildings, 6.15.5
        claim periods, 6.15.1
            liability, relationship with, 6.15.1
        closing down field, 6.15.6
        contractors' tax, 6.15.5
        credit, obtaining of, 6.15.5
        deballasting, 6.15.6
        disposing of oil, 6.15.6
        double allowance, prevention, 6.15.5
        excluded oil, 6.15.5
        gas, exempt, 6.15.5
        indirect, 6.15.4
        initial —
            storage, 6.15.6
            treatment of oil, 6.15.6
        installations, 6.15.5
        insuring production facilities, 6.15.6
        interest, 6.15.5
        land, acquisition, 6.15.5
        licence —
            acquisition costs, 6.15.5
            payments to Secretary of State, 6.15.6
        metering, 6.15.6
        not allowable, 6.15.5
        payments pro rata to production, 6.15.5
        purpose test, 6.15.3
        redundancy payments, 6.15.6
        removal of buildings, 6.15.6
        responsible person, 6.15.2
            appointment , 6.15.2
        sale costs, 6.15.6
        searching for oil, 6.15.6
        supplement, *see* Supplement
        transportation of oil, 6.15.6
            notional landing in UK, 6.15.6
        uplift, *see* Supplement
        winning of oil, 6.15.6

Field—*cont*
  foreign, *see* Foreign field
  production before determination, 6.4
  redetermination, 6.4
  self-sufficient, 6.4
  separate, 6.4
  transfer of interest —
    abortive exploration expenditure, 8.8.1
    anti-avoidance, 8.8.1
    exempt gas, 8.8.1
    expenditure reliefs, 8.8.1
      provisional, 8.8.1
    exploration and appraisal expenditure, 8.8.1
    generally, 8.8–8.8.1
    losses, 8.8.1
      terminal, 8.8.1
    oil —
      allowance, 8.8.1
      retention of share, 8.8.1
      transfer of stocks, 8.8.1
    payback, 8.8.1
    research expenditure, 8.8.1
    royalty deductions, 8.8.1
    safeguard, 8.8.1
    supplement, 8.8.1
Foreign field —
  assets, receipts, from —
    charge to PRT, 6.11.2
  definitions, 6.11.1
  double taxation relief, 6.11.3
  generally, 6.11.1
  returns, 6.11.2
  meaning, 6.11.1
  tariff receipts allowance, 6.10.5

Gas —
  associated, 6.9
  banking schemes, 6.9
  fractions —
    application of PRT to, 6.1
    valuation, 6.7.4
  initial treatment, 6.7.4
  levy, 6.8.1
  light, alternative valuation, 6.7.6
  natural, 6.1, 6.2, 6.7.7
  oil allowance, calculation, 6.28
  sales —
    cost insurance & freight terms, 6.7.7
    to British Gas Corporation, 6.7.4, 6.8.1
      price revision clauses, 6.8.1
  valuation, 6.7.4, 6.7.6

Illustrative agreements —
  generally, 6.3, 8.11
  non-UK resident companies, 7.2.2, 7.2.3, 8.11
Income tax —

Income Tax—*cont*
  annual payments, 7.11.3
  gas banking schemes, 6.9
  rights in oil, 7.9
Insurance —
  allowance for premiums, 5.5.3
  expenditure from recoveries, 6.27
  facilities for production, 6.15.6
  receipts —
    as disposal receipts, 6.10.7
    exempt gas fields, 6.10.2
    transit, cargoes in, 6.15.6

Joint operating agreements, 8.7

Licences —
  abandonment of offshore installations, 4.5
  assignment, consent, Secretary of State's, 8.1
  changes in interests, 8.1
  corporation tax, 7.11.6, 7.26.2, 8.3, 8.9
  Department of Energy, 3.2
  disposal, gains, 7.26.2, 8.9.1
  entitlement to benefit, 6.3
  farmer-out, 8.2
  farm-ins —
    development, 8.2
    carry, 8.7
    drilling costs, 8.5
    exploration, 8.2, 8.5
    generally, 8.2
    loan, non-recourse, 8.2
    production, 8.2
    reimbursement of expenditure, 8.4
    work obligation, 8.2
  generally, 4.1
  illustrative agreements, 6.3, 8.11
  issue —
    criteria, 4.1
    Regulations, 4.1
  Model Clauses, 4.2, 4.5
  offshore —
    designated areas, 4.3
    issue —
      method, 4.3
      original, 2.1
    types, 4.3
  onshore —
    issue —
      existent, 4.3
      initial, 2.1
    types, 4.3
  part interest, disposal, 7.13.1
  payments —
    relating to, 6.12, 6.20
    relief, 6.13, 6.15.6
    under, 4.4
  second-hand acquisition, 7.14.6

Licences—*cont*
  share purchase for acquisition, 8.10, 8.10.1
    assets transfer contrasted, 8.10, 8.10.1
  surrender, 7.14.7
  transfer of interests —
    corporation tax, 8.3
    field interest transfer distinguished, 8.8
    PRT, 8.3
    tax consequences, 8.3
  unitisation, 8.12

Market value —
  appeals, 6.7.2
  application, 6.7.2
  average price for month, 6.7.2
  Brent prices, 6.7.2
  butane, 6.7.2
  evidential base —
    extended, 6.7.2
    primary, 6.7.2
  information —
    Revenue's rights, 6.7.2
    sources, 6.7.2
  notional contract, 6.7.2
  propane, 6.7.2
  rules, valuation, 6.7.2
    application, 6.7.2
Methane —
  component, valuation, 6.7.6
  nomination scheme, exemption, 6.7.3
Mineral extraction allowances —
  balancing adjustments, 7.14.7
  buildings, 7.14.1
  cost limitation, 7.14.6
  demolition, 7.14.4
  disposal receipts, 7.14.8
  enhancement part, purchase price, 7.14.6
  expenditure —
    excluded, 7.14.2
    exploration and access, 7.14.6
    pre-trading, 7.14.3
    qualifying, 7.14.2
    restoration, 7.14.4
    unrelieved, 7.14.7
  generally, 7.14.1
  group transfers, l7.14.6
  land, 7.14.5
  mines and oil wells allowance, 7.14.9
    interaction of allowances, 7.14.10
  plant, provision, 7.14.3
  rates, 7.14.1
  second-hand acquisitions 7.14.6
Mines and oil wells code, 7.14.9–7.14.10

Nomination scheme —
  aim, 6.7.3
  amendment, 6.7.3
  background, 6.7.3

Nomination scheme—*cont*
  blended oil, 6.7.3
  composite nominations, 6.7.3
  effective volume, 6.7.3
  exemptions, 6.7.3
  failure to fulfil transaction, 6.7.3
  format of nominations, 6.7.3
  invalidation of nomination, 6.7.3
  lapse of nomination, 6.7.3
  making of nominations, 6.7.3
  period, 6.7.3
  price, 6.7.3
    foreign currency, 6.7.3
  profit chargeable, effect on, 6.7.3
  reconciliation, 6.7.3
  regulations, 6.7.3
  revisions, 6.7.3
  scope, 6.7.3
  surcharge, 6.7.3
  time limit, 6.7.3
  timing, 6.7.3
  transaction base date, 6.7.3
  transactions, nominated, 6.7.3
  volume, nominal, 6.7.3
  withdrawal, 6.7.3

Oil allowance —
  adjustment, final periods, 6.28
  anti-avoidance, 6.28.3
  division between participators, 6.28
  gas, alternative calculation, 6.28
  generally, 6.28
  increased, new fields, 5.2, 6.28.1
  interaction with —
    expenditure relief, 6.28.3
    loss relief, 6.29.1
    safeguard, 6.30.2
  reduced, new fields, 6.28.2
Oil and Pipelines Agency, 4.6, 5.5.2, 7.7.1

Petroleum revenue tax —
  acceleration devices, 2.1
  advance, *see* Advance petroleum revenue tax
  allowance, 6.1
  assessment —
    appeals, 6.35.4
    generally, 6.35
    interest, 6.35.2
      repayments of PRT, 6.35.3
    payment, 6.35.1, 6.37
  assets, *see* Assets
  background, p 1, p 2, 2.1
  blended oil, 6.7.10
  capacity payments, 6.7.9
  charge, 6.2
  chargeable —
    cessation of production, 6.5

Petroleum revenue tax—*cont*
  periods, 6.5
  persons, 6.3
  computation, 6.6
    example, 6.6.1
  critical half year, 6.5
  deduction, as, 2.2, 7.11.8
  delivery point, oil's, 5.5.3
  disposal receipts, *see* Disposal receipts
  double taxation relief, 6.38
  exemptions —
    expenditure relating to, 6.8.1
    gas sales to British Gas Corporation, 6.8.1
    production purposes, oil used for, 6.8.2
    royalty in kind, 6.8.4
    transit, oil in, 6.8.3
  expenditure —
    allowable, 6.1, 6.14.1
    claims, *see* Claims
    contributions to, by others, 6.27
    exploration and appraisal, *see* Exploration and appraisal expenditure
    provisional allowance, 6.24
      reversal, 6.24.1
    relief —
      capital expenditure, 6.14.3
      claim, making, 6,14.1
      exclusion, 6.14.1
      front-end, 6.1, 6.10.1
      generally, 2.2, 6.1, 6.14.1
      incurred expenditure, 6.14.2
      leasing, 6.26
      non-arm's length transactions, 6.26
      oil allowance, interaction of, 6.28.3
      revenue expenditure, 6.14.3
      timing rules, 6.14.1
    research, 6.22
    set-off, grants, 6.27.1
    spreading, election, 6.25
      disregarding, 6.25
    supplement, *see* Supplement
    write-off, 6.25
  extension, 2.1
  field, *see* Field
  gas, *see* Gas
  illustrative agreements, 8.11
  income from production, 6.7
  instalments, 2.1
  licence —
    payments under, 6.12
    share purchase, 8.10, 8.10.1
  licence farm-ins —
    development carry, 8.7
    drilling costs, 8.5
    reimbursement of expenditure, 8.4
    royalties, 8.6
    transfer of interests, 8.3

Petroleum revenue tax—*cont*
  loss relief, 6.29
    unrelievable, 6.29.1, 6.30.2
  market value, *see* Market value
  nature of tax, 6.1
  nomination scheme, *see* Nomination scheme
  overlifting, 6.7.8
  participators —
    associated with, 6.3
    foreign fields, 6.3
    generally, 6.3
    partnerships, 6.3
  payment —
    generally, 6.35.1, 6.37
    instalments, 6.37.1
      withholding right, 6.37.1
    interest, 6.37.3
    obsolete provisions, 6.40
    on account, 6.37.2
      calculation, 6.37.2
    schedule, 6.37.4
  profit, gross, 6.7
  purchase of oil at extraction place, 6.10.4
  rate, 2.2
  relaxation, 2.1
  returns —
    generally, 6.31
    incorrect, 6.31.1, 6.31.2
    participator's, 6.31.2
    responsible person's, 6.31.1
    supplementary, 6.7.2, 6.31.3
  safeguard, *see* Safeguard
  sales at arm's length, 6.7.1
  stocks of oil, 6.7.8
  take or pay contracts, 6.7.9
  tariff receipts, *see* Tariff receipts
  unitisation agreements, 8.12
Propane —
  nomination scheme, exemption, 6.7.3
  valuation, 6.7.2

Regional development grants, 6.27.1, 7.18
Research expenditure, 6.22, 6.30.2, 6.34.2
Royalties —
  abolition, new fields, 5.2
  accountant's report, independent, 5.5.4, 5.5.5
  adjustments —
    cash, 5.5.2
    prior years, 5.5.4
  appeals, 5.4
  apportioning, PRT allowance, 6.13
  assets —
    abandonment, 5.5.3
    depreciation allowance, 5.5.3
    disposal, 5.5.3
    receipts for, 5.5.3

Royalties—*cont*
  background, p 1, p 2
  calculation, 2.1, 5.1, 5.4, 5.5
  corporation tax, 7.11.2, 7.11.6
  costs —
    abandonment, 5.5.3
    allowable, 5.5.3
    apportionment, 5.5.3
    conveying, 5.5.2, 5.5.3
      pre-conveying periods, 5.5.3
    deductions for, 5.5.2
    excess, 5.5.3
    indirect, 5.5.3
    insurance, 5.5.3
    interest on capital, allowance, 5.5.3
    joint, 5.5.3
    licensees' own, 5.5.3
    treating 5.5.2, 5.5.3
  deduction, as, 2.2, 6.13
  Department of Energy, 3.2
  exemption, new fields, 5.2
  farm-ins, 8.6
  gas banking schemes, 6.9
  initial treatment, meaning, 5.5.3
  interest, 5.4, 5.4.1
  kind, payment in, 5.4, 5.5.1, 5.5.2, 6.8.4
    corporation tax, 7.11.6
  liability, 5.1
  licence interests, 8.3
  payment, 5.4
    repayment, 5.4.1, 6.13
  quantity of oil, 5.5.1
  rates, 2.2, 5.3
  relief for payments, 2.2, 6.13
  returns, 5.4, 5.5.
  statement of value, 5.4, 5.5
  stocks of oil, 5.5.1
  unitisation agreements, 8.12
  value of oil, 5.5.1

Safeguard —
  calculation, 6.30.1
  duration, 6.5, 6.30
  generally, 6.1, 6.30
  interaction with other reliefs, 6.30.2
Sales —
  arm's length, 6.7.1
  connected persons, 6.7.1
  consideration, 6.7.1
  market value, at 6.7.1, 6.7.2
  reciprocal acquisition, 6.7.1
  related transactions, Revenue's enquiries, 6.7.1
  seller's interest in subsequent disposal, 6.7.1
State participation, 4.6
Supplement —
  appraisal, 6.19.2

Supplement—*cont*
  background, 2.1
  chartering, 6.19.6
  claims, 6.32
  contractor financing, 6.19.10
  cut-off, 6.19.9
  decisions, 6.32.1
  deferred payment terms contracts, 6.19.10
  disposal of assets, 6.19.7
  generally, 6.1, 6.14.3, 6.19
  hiring, 6.19.6
  initial —
    storage, 6.19.4
    treatment, 6.19.4
  instalment payments contracts, 6.19.10
  interaction with —
    cross-field allowances, 6.23
    safeguard, 6.30.2
  interest relief, substitute for, 6.15.5
  payback, 6.19.9
  pre-production expenditure, 6.19.1
  production rate —
    improving, 6.19.3
    preventing decline, 6.19.3
    reducing decline, 6.19.3
  purposes for expenditure, 6.19.1–6.19.4
  rates, 6.19, 6.19.8
  repairs, 6.19.3
  restriction, 6.19.7
  spreading over periods, 6.25
  stage payment contracts, 6.19.10
  tariff receipts, assets giving rise to, 6.19.5
  test for, 6.15.3
  transporting oil, commencement, 6.19.1
  workovers, 6.19.3
Supplementary petroleum duty —
  charge, 2.1, 6.39
  replacement, 2.1, 6.39

Tariff receipts —
  allowance —
    calculation, 6.10.5
    foreign fields, 6.10.5
    gas banking schemes, 6.10.5
    generally, 6.10.5
    notional, 6.10.5
    periods for receipts, 6.10.5
    qualifying receipts, 6.10.5
  anti-avoidance provisions, 6.10.9
  apportionment, 6.10.3
  charge to PRT, 6.10.3
  corporation tax, 7.8
  cross-tariffing, 6.10.5
  field, attributable, 6.10.3
  generally, 6.10.1
  interaction with —
    loss relief, 6.29.1
    supplement, 6.19.5

Tariff receipts—*cont*
  meaning, 6.10.3
  non-arm's length receipts, 6.10.8
  notional, 6.10.4
  qualifying assets, 6.10.2
Taxation of oil —
  background, p 1
  changes since 1975, 2.1
  havens, 7.22
  House of Commons Report, 2.1
  losses, relief, background, 2.1
  Oil Taxation Office, 3.3
  onshore developments, 2.1
  production levy, 2.1
  residence of company for, 7.2.1
  system —

Taxation of oil—*cont*
  aims, 3.1
  monitoring, 3.1
  tiers, pp 1–2
  see also under names of taxes
Territorial sea —
  boundary, 2.1
  exploration and appraisal expenditure, 6.20
  UK for taxation purposes, 7.2.3
Title to oil, 4.1

United Kingdom Offshore Operators
  Association, 3.1
United Kingdom Oil Industry Taxation
  Committee, 3.1
Unitisation agreements, 8.12